MAN, MYTH, AND MAGIC

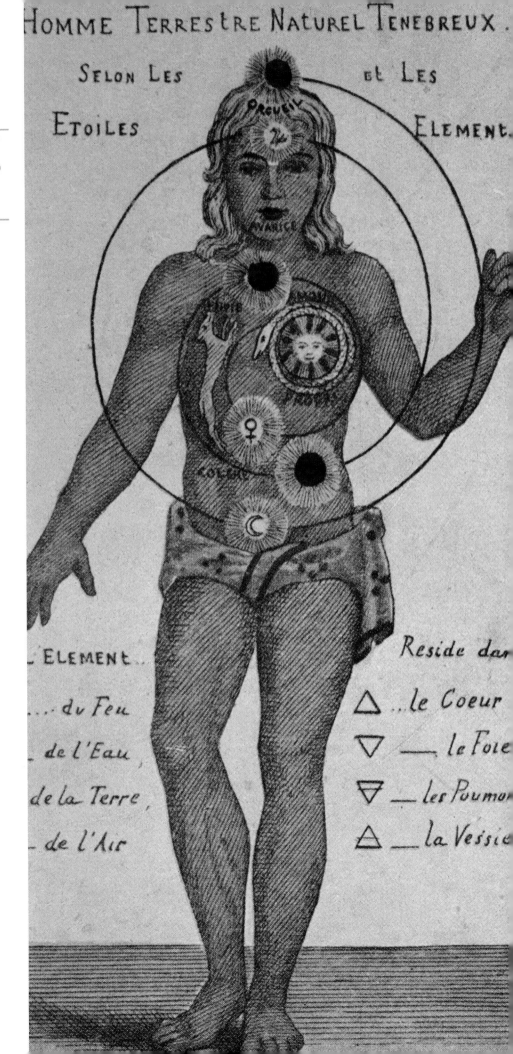

MAN, MYTH,
AND MAGIC

Prophets and Prophesy: Predicting the Future

Cavendish
Square

New York

MAN, MYTH,
AND MAGIC

Published in 2015 by Cavendish Square Publishing, LLC
243 5th Avenue, Suite 136, New York, NY 10016

Library of Congress Cataloging-in-Publication Data

Gleadow, Rupert.
Prophets and prophesy: predicting the future / by Rupert Gleadow, et. al.
p. cm. — (Man, myth, and magic)
Includes index.
ISBN 978-1-62712-675-5 (hardcover) ISBN 978-1-62712-677-9 (ebook)
1. Prophecies — Juvenile literature. 2. Prophets — Juvenile literature. I. Gleadow, Rupert. II. Title.
BF1809.G55 2015
133.3—d23

Editorial Director: Dean Miller
Editor: Amy Hayes
Art Director: Jeffrey Talbot
Designer: Jessica Moon
Photo Researcher: J8 Media
Production Manager: Jennifer Ryder-Talbot
Production Editor: David McNamara

Photo credits: Cover: File: the-crystal-ball-1902/John William Waterhouse/Wikimedia Commons; Illustrations of the Book of Job; Job's Evil Dreams, showing Job's God, who has become Satan with cloven hoof and entwined by a serpent, pointing to the Mosaic Tablets of the Law, 1825 (pen, w/c over pencil), Blake, William (1757-1827)/Pierpont Morgan Library, New York, USA/The Bridgeman Art Library; File: Vitrail Chartres Zodiaque 210209 03/Vassil/Wikimedia Commons; Illustration from "Theosophica Practica", showing the seven Chakras, 19th century/Private Collection/The Bridgeman Art Library, 1; Illustration from a copy of Al-Sufi's "The Book of Fixed Stars"/Werner Forman Archive/The Bridgeman Art Library, 2–3; The British Library/Robana/Getty Images, 5t; FILE: Klytaimnestra Erinyes Louvre Cp710/Bibi Saint-Pol/Campana Collection, 1861/Own work/*, 5m; FILE: Vitrail Chartres Zodiaque 210209 03/Vassil/Own work/*, 5b; FILE: Mayan Zodiac Circle/theilr/Flickr/*, 7; Halley's Comet, Green, Harry (b.1920)/Private Collection/© Look and Learn/The Bridgeman Art Library, 8; NaplesGallery/UmbertoIAcquario/IISistemone/Own work/*, 9; FILE: Zodiaque Amiens 01/Vassil/Own work/*, 11; The British Library/Robana/Getty Images, 12; Dmitri Kessel/Time & Life Pictures/Getty Images, 15; Head of the augur, from the Tomb of the Augurs, c.530-20 BC (wall painting), Etruscan, (6th century BC)/Tarquinia, Lazio, Italy/Giraudon/The Bridgeman Art Library, 20; The British Library/Robana/Getty Images, 22; Illustrations of the Book of Job; Job's Evil Dreams, showing Job's God, who has become Satan with cloven hoof and entwined by a serpent, pointing to the Mosaic Tablets of the Law, 1825 (pen, w/c over pencil), Blake, William (1757-1827)/Pierpont Morgan Library, New York, USA/The Bridgeman Art Library, 25; FILE: NaplesGallery/UmbertoICancro/IISistemone/Own work/*, 26; FILE: Fresko Astrologie Winter 2/Wolfgang Sauber/Own work/*, 27; FILE: Tarocchi-players-borromeo/Unknown/Michael Dummett's The Game of Tarot/*, 28; Universal History Archive/Getty Images, 29; Ben Molyneux/Alamy, 31; Digital N/Shutterstock, 32; Hulton Archive/Getty Images, 35; Feng Yu/Dreamstime, 36; FILE: 20100720 Fukuoka Kushida 3614 M/Jakub Hałun/Own work/*, 37; FILE: KCityParkTiger/HKGpedia/Own work/*, 39; The British Library/Robana via Getty Images, 40; FILE: Themis Aigeus Antikensammlung Berlin F2538 n2/Kodros Painter/*, 42; FILE: Simon Forman - c. 1611/Unknown/hps.cam.ac.uk/*, 43; INTERFOTO/Alamy, 44; Mark Harwood/Alamy, 45; FILE: BedikDiviner/gbaku/Flickr/*, 46; Science and Society/Superstock, 47; Neil Cooper/Alamy, 50; Photos.com/Getty Images, 51; Philip Gatward/Getty Images, 53; Glowimages/Getty Images, 55; FILE: Klytaimnestra Erinyes Louvre Cp710/Bibi Saint-Pol/Campana Collection, 1861/Own work/*, 57; Dennis Hallinan/Alamy, 59; 'Dreams', 1894 (litho), Beardsley, Aubrey (1872-98)/Private Collection/Prismatic Pictures/The Bridgeman Art Library, 61; iukasz Kua'ko/Thinkstock, 62; FILE: Rabbits foot Charm Amulet/Malcolm Lidbury (aka Pinkpasty)/Own work/*, 63; Zodiaque Amiens 03/Vassil/Own work/*, 64; Amar Grover/Getty Images, 65; Keystone-France/Gamma-Keystone via Getty Images, 69; Horace Bristol/Three Lions/Getty Images, 72; Jennifer Borton/Getty Images, 73; Genghis Khan (c.1162-1227) consulting his destiny, illustration from 'Grandeur and Supremacy of Peking', by Alphonse Hubrecht, 1928 (engraving), French School, (20th century)/Private Collection/The Bridgeman Art Library, 75; Illustration from a copy of Al-Sufi's "The Book of Fixed Stars"/Werner Forman Archive/The Bridgeman Art Library, 78; FILE: 9484 - Venezia - Palazzo ducale - Toro, Venere e Bilancia - Foto Giovanni Dall'Orto, 12-Aug-2007/Giovanni Dall'Orto/Own work/*, 79; The Soldiers Casting Lots for Christ's Garments, 1800 (pen, indian ink, grey wash and w/c), Blake, William (1757-1827)/Fitzwilliam Museum, University of Cambridge, UK/The Bridgeman Art Library, 80; Mayan Zodiac Circle/theilr/Flickr/*, 83; FILE: De Occulta Philosophia - Proportionen des Menschen und ihre geheimen Zahlen/Anon/*, 84; artpartner-images/Getty Images, 86; PhotoAlto/Alamy, 87; Mayur Kotlikar/Getty Images, 89; Johnnie Pakington/Getty Images, 90; YAY Media AS/Alamy, 91; FILE: Noah Giving Thanks (3434807981)/A. Davey/Flickr/*, 93; FILE: Coccyzus Americanus by John Gould/John Gould/*, 94; The Eve of St. Agnes, or The Flight of Madelaine and Porphyro during the Drunkenness attending the Revelry, 1848 (oil on canvas), Hunt, William Holman (1827-1910)/© Guildhall Art Gallery, City of London/The Bridgeman Art Library, 96–97; David Muenker/Alamy, 98; Waj/Shutterstock, 100; Popperfoto/Getty Images, 101; FILE: Palmistry Chiromancy Palm Reading/Malcolm Lidbury (aka Pinkpasty)/Own work/*, 103; FILE: Vitrail Chartres Zodiaque 210209 03/Vassil/Own work/*, 107; ASSOCIATED PRESS, 108; FILE: Merthyr Vale Aberfan Aberdare Blog/Darren Wyn Rees/*, 109; FILE: Miriams Tanz/Tarnovo literary and art school/*, 110; FILE: Profeta Osea (Moretto)/Moretto/RobyBS89/Own work/*, 111; Mondadori Portfolio/Getty Images, 103; Mary Evans Picture Library, 116; Mary Evans Picture Library, 118; FILE: Sagittaire naples/Pascal Radigue/Own work/*, 120; FILE: Mishalot P1060588/Deror avi/Own work/*, 121; FILE: the-crystal-ball-1902/John William Waterhouse/*, 123; FILE: John Dee's mirror British Museum 26 07 2013/Vassil/Own work/*, 124; FILE: Wassenberg - Spectaculum 2011 32 ies/Frank Vincentz/Own work/*, 125; FILE: Cassandra1/Evelyn De Morgan/Flickr/*, 127; The Empress, facsimile of a tarot card from the 'Visconti' deck, 1441-47 (colour litho), Bembo, Bonifacio (c.1420-82) (attr.) (after)/Private Collection/The Bridgeman Art Library, 129r; The Fool, facsimile of a tarot card from the 'Visconti' deck, 1441-47 (colour litho), Bembo, Bonifacio (c.1420-82) (attr.) (after)/Private Collection/The Bridgeman Art Library, 129r; The Tower, facsimile of a tarot card from the 'Visconti' deck, 1441-47 (colour litho), Bembo, Bonifacio (c.1420-82) (attr.) (after)/Private Collection/The Bridgeman Art Library, 129d; Petchjira Lueprasert/Thinkstock, 130; Bridger/Thinkstock, 134; FILE: Palazzo schifanoia, salone dei mesi, 04 aprile (f. del cossa), toro 02/Sailko/Own work/*, 138–139; Dregs in the cup, 1838 (oil on canvas), Mount, William Sidney (1807-68)/© Collection of the New-York Historical Society, USA/The Bridgeman Art Library, 140–141; Annunciation, illustration for 'The Life of Christ', c.1886-96 (gouache on paperboard), Tissot, James Jacques Joseph (1836-1902)/Brooklyn Museum of Art, New York, USA/The Bridgeman Art Library, 143; Foto by M/Thinkstock, 144; FILE: Skivholme.5/Erik/*, 146–147; FILE: Palazzo schifanoia, salone dei mesi, 08 agosto (maestro dell'agosto o gherardo da vicenza), vergine 01/Sailko/Own work/*, 149; FILE: Invisible Man/Geoffrey Biggs/Gilberton/*, 150; Photosani/Shutterstock, 152–153.   * Wikimedia Commons.

Cavendish Square would like to acknowledge the outstanding work, research, writing, and professionalism of Man, Myth, and Magic's original Editor-in-Chief Richard Cavendish, Executive Editor Brian Innes, Editorial Advisory Board Members and Consultants C.A. Burland, Glyn Daniel, E.R Dodds, Mircea Eliade, William Sargent, John Symonds, RJ. Zwi Werblowsky, and R.C. Zaechner, as well as the numerous authors, consultants, and contributors that shaped the original Man, Myth, and Magic that served as the basis and model for these new books.

Printed in the United States of America

Contents

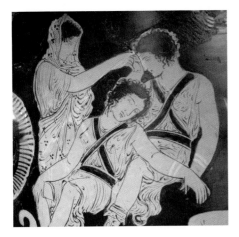

Prophets and Prophecy: Predicting the Future

A Reader's Guide to *Man, Myth, and Magic: Prophets and Prophecy*

Throughout history, every society from every age and every continent has hoped to foretell the future. From looking out to the stars to the patterns on our hands and even the innards of animals, mankind has used a wide variety of methods to ascertain a greater meaning of the past, present, and even the future. Those that claimed the power of second sight were often held in the highest regard, reaping rich rewards for their successes.

Man, Myth, and Magic: Prophets and Prophecy is a volume devoted to the myriad methods people have used to divine the future. The book covers fortune-telling techniques and prophecy from the earliest civilizations throughout the world through modern attempts to predict upcoming events. Both the traditional and Chinese Zodiac are covered, as well as palmistry, tea-leaf reading, dowsing, dream interpretation, haruspicy, pyromancy, and so much more. Religious visions and prophetic traditions are discussed in detail, and prophetic writers such as William Blake are covered as well, highlighting how their work presciently identified trends in politics and technology.

> *The soothsayer . . .burns incense, prostrates himself thrice before the silk-wrapped book and . . . receives in answer to the question in his or her mind one hexagram—or in many cases two of them.*

Objectives of *Man, Myth, and Magic*

Each volume of the *Man, Myth, and Magic* series approaches individual topics from an unbiased position. In *Prophets and Prophecy,* presenting how astrology has evolved and presenting its basic tenets without editorializing commentary allows readers to best comprehend the topic and develop their own position on the sect. The comprehensive coverage of precognition, geomancy, the *I Ching*, as well as numerology, tarot-card reading, and scrying, for example, can aid students researching these controversial topics, and the popularity and growth of these disciplines through the ages.

The Text

An impressive lineup of expert contributors have created articles arranged alphabetically, and the depth of coverage varies from short entries defining a singular subject through multipage contributions providing far-ranging discussion of complex issues. From augury to the zodiac, key movements, figures, concepts, and new-age topics are profiled, with articles focusing on how these fortune-telling methods have evolved over the years and are still practiced to this day.

The work is highly illustrated, with colorful images of symbols and divining tools as well as informative diagrams and charts for the aspiring amateur. Subjects of major interest are provided with individual bibliographies of further reading on the subject at the end of each article, making *Man, Myth, and Magic* an important resource for any avid researcher.

For the past few decades, there's been an explosion in the popularity of mythology and history in the realms of both popular culture and scholarly study. The revival of scholarly interest has shaped the modern study of comparative religion, and modern anthropology with its investigation of so-called indigenous or first peoples and their beliefs and rituals (which have been found far more complex that originally believed). At the same time there has been a flourishing revival of popular interest in ancient civilizations, mythology, magic and alternative paths to truth. This interest has shown no sign of diminishing this century; on the contrary, it has grown stronger and has explored new pathways. Scholarly investigation of these subjects has continued and has thrown much new light on some of our topics. The present edition of *Man, Myth, and Magic: Prophets and Prophecy* takes account of both these developments. Articles have been updated to cover fresh discoveries and new theories since they first appeared.

A Mayan zodiac circle, showing a complete Haab cycle

With all this, *Man, Myth, and Magic: Prophets and Prophecy* is not intended to convert you, to or from any belief or set of beliefs and attitudes. The purpose of the articles is not to persuade or justify, but to describe what people have believed and trace the consequences of those beliefs in action. The editorial attitude is one of sympathetic neutrality. It is for the reader to decide where truth and value may lie. We hope that there is as much interest, pleasure and satisfaction in reading these pages as all those involved took in creating them.

Illustrations

Since much of what we know about myth, folklore and religion has been passed down over the centuries by word of mouth, and recorded only comparatively recently, visual images are often the most powerful and vivid links we have with the past. The wealth of illustration in *Man, Myth, and Magic: Prophets and Prophecy* is invaluable, not only because of the diversity of sources, but also because of the superb quality of color reproduction. Rituals, myths, sacred paintings and modern rites are all recorded here in infinite variety. Examples of artwork from all over the world are represented.

Index

The A-Z index provides immediate access to any specific item sought by the reader. The reference distinguishes the nature of the entry in terms of a main entry, supplementary subject entries, and illustrations.

Halley's Comet by Harry Green (b.1920). Comets were thought to be bad omens, signaling the end of the world.

Skill Development for Students

The books of the *Man, Myth, and Magic* series can be consulted as the basic text for a subject or as a source of enrichment for students. It can act as a reference for a simple reading or writing assignment, or as the inspiration for a major research or term paper. The additional reading at the end of many entries is an invaluable resource for students looking to further their studies on a specific topic. *Man, Myth, and Magic* offers an opportunity for students that is extremely valuable; twenty volumes that are both multi-disciplinary and inter-disciplinary; a wealth of fine illustrations; a research source well-suited to a variety of age levels that will provoke interest and encourage speculation in both teachers and students.

Scope

As well as being a major asset to social studies teaching, the book provides students from a wide range of disciplines with a stimulating, accessible and beautifully illustrated reference work.

The *Man, Myth and Magic* series lends itself very easily to a multi-disciplinary approach to study. In *Prophets and Prophecy*, literature students will be interested in the visionary poetry of Blake and the prophetic dystopias of Robert Erskine Childers, Aldous Huxley, and H.G. Wells. Math students will be fascinated to read about geomancy and numerology, while students of art, sculpture, carving, pottery and other crafts will find the marvelous illustrations and special articles on the symbolism particularly helpful. Readers interested history will gravitate to the discussion of Sibyls and the Oracles of Delphi. Students of physics and astronomy will be fascinated by the explanations of horoscopes and early astrology.

As well as its relevance to study areas already mentioned, the book will provide strong background reference in anthropology, philosophy, and comparative religion.

Conceptual Themes

As students become involved in the work, they will gradually become sensitive to the major concepts emerging from research. Students can begin to understand the role of the modern belief systems and superstitions and how they contribute to current social structure.

Aquarius

The sun enters Aquarius, the eleventh sign of the zodiac, on January 20 or 21, leaving on February 18 or 19. The sign represents a man pouring out water from an urn, symbolizing for Aquarius the traditional character of helpfulness and service to others. It is now often regarded as the ideal sign to be born under. This was not always the case, though the Roman author Manilius, who wrote an astrological poem in the first century AD, did say that:

> 'The Good, the Pious, and the Just are born When first Aquarius pours out his urn.'

In modern astrological opinion Aquarius is preeminently the sign of the scientist, with a touch of the absent-minded professor. Aquarians are quiet, gentle, not forceful, not inclined to insist or demand their own way. They speak moderately and reasonably. They see no point in taking a tough line, for truth will out in the end, and until it does, there is very little to be gained by saying anything at all.

The Amiable Aquarian

Aquarians are frequently shy, perhaps because they are often physically large and rather slow. But, although at times they may appear ponderous, they are not sluggish and have more humour than people think: they just do not consider it worthwhile to snatch at opportunities that will probably recur. Since Aquarius is traditionally 'ruled,' or strongly influenced, by the planet Saturn, patience comes naturally to Aquarians, and less patient people may be irritated by their tolerance. They are said to be sensitive and easily moved to tears, and they dislike being criticized.

Aquarians' characteristic faults are few. The most tiresome is their inability to explain themselves, so that other people, left in uncertainty, will often put the worst construction on their actions and only the passage of time will vindicate them. This is not

> *Two pleasing characteristics of Aquarians are that they are not impressed by pomp and pretentiousness, nor do they attempt to pass themselves off as being better than they are.*

due to laziness, but often appears so. A similar Aquarian fault is the frequent inability to let people know that they are liked or admired. Aquarians assume this is obvious and do not realize that others like to have unmistakable signs of approval. The consequence may be that they will be considered lazy, cold, and unfeeling, a reaction that they will think most unjust.

Two pleasing characteristics of Aquarians are that they are not impressed by pomp and pretentiousness, nor do they attempt to pass themselves off as being better than they are. They know how necessary it is to be patient, and do not expect anything else from others. It is said that they are likely to exaggerate grievances, to think that things will take a long time to improve and are worse than they really are. They have little sympathy for prejudices of race or class, and will try to understand any point of view. They are often great readers: ideas interest them and they are not at all inclined to brush them aside just because they are different from their own.

With this generally pleasing and amiable modern picture of the Aquarian can be contrasted the opinion of Vettius Valens, a Roman writing in the second century AD, who described Aquarians as 'effeminate, inflexible, wicked, unfertile.' Though 'industrious

Mosaic on the floor of the Galleria Umberto I in Naples, Italy, shows the water bearer, Aquarius

and employed in public service,' they were, he said: 'self-willed, misanthropic, atheistic, and grudging.'

The Age of Aquarius

In all astrological matters, it is important to understand that the traditional 'tropical' zodiac, which was first employed by the Greeks more than 2,000 years ago, and has been used for hundreds of years in European astrology, is out of step with the 'sidereal' zodiac, the real constellations. Traditional astrology says that the sun is 'in' Aquarius, but if it were possible to observe the stars in daytime it would be seen that the background to the sun is actually the preceding constellation, Capricorn. Throughout the year this displacement by one sign occurs, right round the zodiac circle. The phenomenon is due to what is known as the precession of the equinoxes.

The equinoxes are the two points in the year, in the spring and fall, when the sun is directly above the equator and the day and the night are of equal length, lasting twelve hours each. At the spring equinox the sun appears to cross over from the southern hemisphere to the northern, bringing longer days and the warmth of spring and summer. At the autumn equinox, it appears to cross back again, leaving the north to the increasing darkness of winter.

The spring equinox occurs on or about March 21, and the autumn equinox on or about September 23. These are also the dates on which the sun is said to enter, respectively, Aries and Libra. Some 2,000 years ago this was true, and the point of the spring equinox has therefore been defined as '0 degrees Aries,' and is still so defined in all celestial navigation calculations.

The apparent movement of the sun toward the north in summer and

toward the south in winter is due, as every schoolboy knows, to the fact that the earth's axis of rotation is inclined at an angle to the plane of its orbit. However, this axis is very slowly wobbling, like a spinning top, and takes some 25,800 years to move round in a small circle. The effect of this 'precession' is to move the position of the equinox, as measured against the background of the fixed constellations, 'backward' by 1.4 degrees every century.

The equinoxes are said to go backward, because they move through the constellations against the direction of the planets. Since the second century BC until now the sun at the spring equinox—'0 degrees Aries'—has actually been in the preceding constellation, Pisces, and from about 2170 it will be in the constellation Aquarius.

Precession of the equinoxes was discovered in the second century BC, but few people concerned themselves about the awkward consequences of the discovery for astrology until recently. Astrologers continued to assert for a long time that the zodiac remained immutable, although it was now clear that the equinox, from which they said that the zodiac had

> *It should be remembered that 'ram' can mean not only the animal but also the battering-ram, a similar instrument of aggression.*

always been measured, was an invisible moving point. That early astronomers, who had no scientific instruments, should have chosen to measure their zodiac from an invisible moving point is not a likely suggestion.

The spring equinox precessed from Aries into the constellation Pisces, the Fishes, in the third century BC. The

fish was a well-known symbol of the early Christians, and so it was thought that this precession foreshadowed the coming Age of Christianity. Similarly the precession of the equinox, fewer than 200 years from now, into the constellation Aquarius, is believed to herald the coming of an Aquarian Age of peace and harmony in a spirit of gentle moderation.

The only Aquarius into which the equinox can precess is the constellation. This must be stressed, because many astrologers are beginning to confuse the two concepts. They attach, for instance, particular importance to the sun being 'in Aquarius' in an Aquarian Age; but the principal significance of the 'Age of Aquarius' is that the sun, between January 20 and February 19, will then actually be in Sagittarius.

RUPERT GLEADOW

Aries

The sun enters Aries on March 20 or 21, and leaves that sign on April 20 or 21. The symbol of Aries is the ram, suggesting energy, initiative, aggression, and push. It should be remembered that 'ram' can mean not only the animal but also the battering-ram, a similar instrument of aggression.

Aries owes its reputation for touchiness and dominance partly to the fact that it is the first of the zodiacal signs and partly to the many political leaders born under it—including Hitler (1889–1945), who was born with the sun on the cusp of Aries and Taurus, Lenin (1870–1924), and Jefferson (1743–1826). The sign also has a great military reputation, though in fact it has not produced as many successful military commanders as the sign of Scorpio.

Carving of Aries appearing on the left portal of the façade of the Cathedral Amiens, France

Most of the famous people born under Aries—with a few exceptions, such as Brahms (1833–97), Chaplin (1889–1977), and Freud (1856–1935)—are men who have made their mark in politics. Although most Arieans are not the single-minded political and military geniuses that the lists of famous Arieans might suggest, they tend to think of themselves as the natural leaders in affairs. This at times results in a certain selfcenterdness, with an assumption that other people are not quite so real or so important.

It was an Ariean, the Florentine Niccolo Machiavelli (1469–1527), who wrote the political textbook, *The Prince,* in which he advocated strong-minded and ruthless leadership of the state in the interests of the people.

The Ariean is said to be bad at early rising, but is very punctual and hates to be kept waiting. As one who inevitably should be considered the leader of any group, he or she does not like people who try to take the credit which, it seems, should naturally be his or hers. In extreme cases the Ariean can degenerate into someone who is always grabbing for credit and honours.

A typical Ariean virtue is the combative one of not taking things lying down. Arieans will assert their own point of view and can be useful leaders, for they are never afraid to make their weight felt. Compromise does not readily occur to them as the easiest way out of a difficulty; they are more likely to think that if their position is stated clearly and emphatically, other people will probably give way.

Arieans usually believe that they attained unaided the position they now hold: no one has ever perceptibly helped them. This often leads to egotism. As Arieans consider themselves number one, and the only person who matters, they attach little importance to the feelings of others. As a result, they are often not ideal partners in marriage.

In the old days Britain, Germany, and Rome—all political great powers—were said to be 'under' Aries. In the days when Britain had an empire, it seemed quite natural to British astrologers that their country should be under Aries, which was thought a noble and imperialistic sign. Now that it is less easy to justify or excuse the habit of telling other people how to run their lives or their countries, it has become more difficult to speak tactfully in praise of Aries, for if oneself is number one this only implies that the rest are insignificant.

Aries is said to be the first of the signs, but this was not always the case. In the first of his *Georgics,* the Roman poet Virgil (70 BC–90 BC) mentions 'the white bull that with his golden horns opens the year,' which suggests that Taurus, the Bull, was once considered the first sign. And the Babylonians did not recognize Aries at all, its place being taken by the constellation called the Hireling, the man who works for wages.

Astrology

Astrology is perhaps the oldest of the sciences. From its early beginnings in Babylonia until the late Middle Ages in Europe, no distinction was made between astrology and what we now call astronomy. On the one hand, astrology was descriptive, naming and charting the constellations and observing the movements of the heavens; on the other hand, it was predictive, as astrologers discovered that they could forecast those movements.

The 'fixed' stars, the vault of heaven, appeared to turn above the earth like a huge bowl; but voyaging through that heaven, sometimes steadily, sometimes erratically, went seven other 'stars,' which the Greeks later called the planets, meaning 'wanderers:' the sun, the moon, and what we now call by the Roman names of Mercury, Venus, Mars, Jupiter, and Saturn (the Babylonians had other names, but with similar implications).

Astrological sphere, *Hemisphae Alis Coeli*, showing a circular chart containing the signs of the Zodiac

For centuries these planets were regarded as the gods themselves. Although some of them sometimes appeared to go back upon their tracks, and all moved at different speeds, they kept within a narrow band of the heavens, marked out by twelve characteristic constellations, which we know as the zodiac, from the Greek meaning 'circle of animals.' To the early astrologers, these constellations represented the houses of the gods, which they visited from time to time, sometimes meeting—two, three or four together—in each other's houses. The sun's house was in Leo, at the height of summer when he was in his greatest strength, and the moon's house next-door, in Cancer. The other five planets each had two houses, one for day and one for night.

The astrologers believed that events in heaven were mirrored by events on Earth. If, then, they could predict the movements of the planets, they believed that it should be equally possible to predict what would happen on Earth. This was certainly true of the cycle of the seasons, and other occurrences such as eclipses, so why should it not be true of all human events?

The Horoscope

The relative positions of each planet at any given moment could be marked upon a schematic map of the heavens. This is what is called a horoscope. It shows the position of each planet in the great circle of the zodiac in relation to the earth at the center. Half of the circle at any one time is invisible below the earth, but the astrologers knew that the circle turned constantly, and their records told them that the circle made a complete cycle each day, and so, although they could not see most of the planets by day, and certainly could not see the stars behind them, they knew which houses they were in.

The most important moment in any person's life was the moment of his or her birth. Since the gods determined all human destiny, the influence of the planets at that moment would affect the whole of that person's life. A horoscope drawn for that moment would therefore form a predictive document of their future. As time passed, and the influences changed, later horoscopes could be drawn, representing changes that the gods had determined, but this natal horoscope remained the most important.

In a modern horoscope, these planetary positions must be calculated in relation to a given moment of time and a specific geographical coordinate, expressed in degrees and minutes of latitude (north or south of the equator) and longitude (east or west of the prime meridian).

Before the invention of radar, all navigation, both terrestrially and in the air, was made by means of observation of such planetary positions. The daily 'shooting the sun' on board ship, by means of a sextant at midday, was the only way of determining longitude for several centuries, and the necessity to know the exact time led to the development of ever more accurate chronometers. If the sun was obscured by cloud, it became even more important to observe the position of other planets visible by night, and yearly 'nautical almanacs,' giving the position of the major planets, are still published for the benefit of yachtsmen. It is perfectly possible to calculate a horoscope from such an almanac, but astrologers use similar publications, known as ephemerides, which give the positions of all the planets, including those that have been discovered by astronomers since the beginning of the nineteenth century, Uranus, Neptune, and Pluto.

Two thousand years ago, the sun was at the beginning of the house of Aries at the spring equinox, round about March 22, and all planetary positions are measured from 0 degrees Aries. However, the earth is not rotating simply about its axis, but is very slowly wobbling, like a spin-

ning top beginning to slow down, and over some 24,000 years the axis describes a small circle. The result of this is that the spring equinox 'precesses' through the circle of the zodiac, moving backward through the constellations. What is called 0 degrees Aries has been moving steadily through the constellation Pisces for the last 2,000 years, and early in the twenty-first century will enter Aquarius. This is what is meant when it is said that we are approaching 'the age of Aquarius,' when the sun at the spring equinox will appear to be in the house of Aquarius; but both navigational almanacs and astrologers still place the equinox at 0 degrees Aries, and say that the sun is in Aries.

Today almost everyone knows his or her zodiacal sign. If a person says that he or she was born 'under Taurus' it means that their birth occurred approximately between April 21 and May 22, when the sun would have been anywhere between 0 degrees to 30 degrees Taurus. If, however, he states that he was born on May 10, 1950, the sun's position was at about 19 degrees Taurus, which is more specific. Finally, in the case of a birth at exactly noon (Greenwich Mean Time) on that day, the sun was at 19° 15' 17' Taurus, which is even more precise. The theories of scientific astrology require the horoscope to be calculated upon the basis of an *accurate* time and, as has already been mentioned, an identifiable geographical location. These are the essential requirements for a strictly *individual* horoscope. The astrological 'information' published in newspapers and magazines does not refer to individual horoscopes.

Truth or Nonsense?
The fact that so many people know their birth sign is a product of the mass circulation newspaper and periodical astrological journalism that began during the early 1930s. Those

who have a detailed knowledge of the principles of astrology almost unanimously condemn this 'popular' astrology as childish nonsense. Nevertheless, the daily forecasts and the feature articles in magazines have persuaded countless thousands that 'the stars' may conceivably influence human destinies and that an individual personality in some way reflects the psychological qualities traditionally ascribed to his or her zodiacal sign.

As for the daily prognostications, it is obvious that by the law of averages a proportion of the readership will suppose that this or that prediction has been fulfilled. All the same, we are confronted with a system that divides humanity into types based on astrological symbolism, and this is perhaps astrology's most interesting feature.

Despite all its unsatisfactory qualities, 'scientific' natal astrology, which means analyzing your personality from your horoscope—as opposed to predicting future events—raises a great many fascinating, although probably insoluble, problems. Logically the 'art' should be dismissed as the obstinate survival of very ancient superstitious beliefs. However, it is possible that fairly accurate, although limited, deductions can, in fact, be made from a natal or birth horoscope.

What is surprising is the survival of a system of divination that eventually reached the West in the twelfth century via Latin translations of Arabic texts (tenth century), and were themselves based upon far earlier Hellenistic Greek texts (c. 150 BC–AD 350).

The Modern Revival
The astrological tradition in the form that is encountered today consists of a huge collection of rules and procedures that have been transmitted through the centuries, although not without substantial alterations and reformulations. In the West the contemporary astrological idiom repre-

sents an up-to-date version of the one current at the time of the Renaissance, when there was a widespread interest in astrology in educated circles. The invention of printing (c. 1440) facilitated the circulation of material that had hitherto existed only in manuscript form, and the publication of ephemerides containing the daily noon positions of the sun, moon, and planets. Astrology still ranked as astronomy's twin sister and enjoyed equal respectability.

Educated men began to lose interest in astrology toward the beginning of the seventeenth century, when the discoveries of the first of the modern astronomers, including Galileo (1564–1642), Copernicus (1473–1543), and Kepler (1571–1630), were beginning to be understood. This increasing scepticism was evident in Europe, but not in England, where there was a noticeably lively interest in astrology during the second half of the seventeenth century. This was reflected by the large domestic output of textbooks and predictive almanacs.

Astrology was already underground in Europe during the eighteenth century and in England the appearance of new textbooks dwindled to a trickle between 1700 and c. l790. While astrology was practically forgotten in Europe until the end of the nineteenth century, there were minor astrological revivals in England during the 1790s and 1820s, and an important one during the 1890s. The French did not rediscover the art until c. l890 and the German revival began only shortly before World War I. Indeed, if the British had not kept astrology alive when it was forgotten elsewhere, it might conceivably have disappeared altogether. The British and French revivals during the 1890s, and the somewhat later German one, were by-products of a new and widespread interest in

occultism, magic, the Cabala and, above all, H. P. Blavatsky's Theosophical teachings. Alan Leo (1860–1917) the first important modern astrological publicist and the author of a long series of popular textbooks, was above all a Theosophical astrologer. This meant, in effect, that for Leo and his followers, astrology had a considerable esoteric or occult component. Even today the ranks of the astrologers contain many who claim to be occultists.

It was the Germans, in particular, who investigated and experimented with astrology with enormous energy

> *The cultural philistines believed until recently that astrology had been disposed of long since and was something that could safely be laughed at.*

and interest during the years between the two world wars. Many of these people were highly educated. During the early 1930s, for instance, at least thirty German medical men practiced astrology and there were undoubtedly many more whose names are unrecorded. While the German astrological movement contained the expected quota of charlatans and mild lunatics, a cultured and intelligent minority worked on the development of a new kind of astrology based, as far as possible, upon current academic psychological and typological concepts.

Jung and Astrology

C. G. Jung (1875–1961), whose renown as a pioneer in the field of analytical psychology almost equals that of Sigmund Freud, had a deep personal interest in astrology. In 1931 he observed that 'the cultural philistines believed until recently that astrology had been disposed of long

since and was something that could safely be laughed at. But today, rising out of the social deeps, it knocks at the doors of the universities, from which it was banished some 300 years ago.'

Elsewhere Jung wrote: 'For those of my readers who are unaware of these things and think that I am exaggerating, I can point to the easily verifiable fact that the heyday of astrology was not in the benighted Middle Ages but is in the middle of the twentieth century, when even the newspapers did not hesitate to publish the week's horoscope. A thin layer of rootless rationalists reads with satisfaction that in the year 1723 Mr. So-and-so had a horoscope cast for his children, and do not know that nowadays the horoscope has almost attained the rank of a visiting card.'

It is evident that Jung himself studied the horoscopes of some of his patients because he believed that a natal horoscope could provide information of a purely psychological nature—for example, why an individual might be latently susceptible to a particular kind of neurosis.

Theoretically, then, if a medically trained psychologist can use astrology successfully for psychodiagnostic purposes, it could also be employed for personnel selection, or to assess whether or not two people who intend to marry are suited to one another. In Germany the present writer has met professional experts on handwriting who are engaged by large firms to sift written applications for jobs, and to identify the most promising applicants. Some of them also take a look at the candidates' horoscopes as an additional check. In Europe copies of birth certificates are frequently required to be submitted in such cases, and on these the birth time is stated, at least within about fifteen minutes. British and US birth certificates do not record the birth time. In the absence of the latter it is impossible to calculate a more or less accurate Ascendant and without the Ascendant the horoscope is incomplete. In the absence of a birth time one can only erect the horoscope on the basis of noon Greenwich Mean Time for the day of birth, and therefore it could equally well apply to everyone else born on that day.

Drawing a Horoscope

Diagramatically a horoscope represents the circle of the zodiac as it surrounds the earth, divided into twelve equal divisions, each given the name of one of the constellations. Into this are inserted the positions of the ten 'planets' at the time for which the horoscope is drawn. Most prominent among these is that of the sun. The second figure below represents the sun ascending at dawn, reaching the Medium Coeli (Mid-heaven) at noon, setting in the evening (Descendant), and below the horizon at midnight (Immum Coeli).

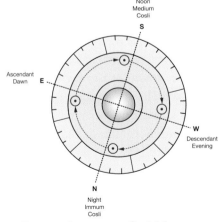

During the course of a 24-hour period every one of the 360 degrees of the zodiac successively 'rises' on the eastern celestial horizon. Roughly speaking, therefore, every two hours a new zodiacal sign is on the Ascendant. In order to discover the position of the Ascendant (expressed for instance as '18° 27' Leo rising') the astrologer must first calculate the MC (Midheaven). This is done with the help of an ephemeris and a few simple arithmetical computations. Once the MC has been identified the degree of the Ascendant can be found in the appropriate tables.

The horoscope of K. E. Krafft, the Swiss who was wrongly supposed to have been Hitler's personal astrologer, will serve as a typical example for an abbreviated account of the procedure for calculating a horoscope.

He was born at Basle on May 10, 1900 at 12.45 p.m. Central European Time. His sun was therefore in Taurus.

Since all the information in an ephemeris is based on noon Greenwich Mean Time (GMT), it is necessary to convert CET to GMT by subtracting one hour, giving a birth time of 11.45 a.m.

Basle is 47° 34' north of the equator and 7° 40' east of Greenwich. First the *sidereal time* ('star-time,' not clock time) must be calculated, because the earth does not make its single revolution in exactly 24 hours. This is determined for 11.45 a.m. GMT, and then the 7° 40' E is converted to minutes and seconds of time (because Basle is east of the meridian of Greenwich, and we require to know the local sidereal time). Following this, a reference to the tables for latitude 47° North shows that Krafft's MC was 24° Taurus and the related Ascendant 1° 43' Virgo.

The next step is to establish the actual zodiacal positions of the planets at 11.45 a.m. on May 10, 1900. The birth time was so close to noon that with the exception of the moon, for which a small adjustment (7' 27') is required, one could take the actual noon positions direct from the ephemeris. If the birth had occurred at, say, 7.45 p.m. some further simple arithmetical calculations

A portrait of the psychologist C. G. Jung at his home, taken in 1949

would be needed. At Kraft's birth, the planetary positions were as shown below.

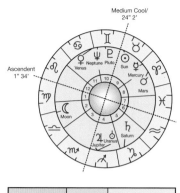

Sun	19.21	Taurus
Moon	2.17	Libra
Mercury	29.08	Aries
Venus	4.20	Cancer
Mars	24.49	Aries
Jupiter	8.08	Sagittarius
Saturn	4.30	Capricorn
Uranus	11.22	Sagittarius
Neptune	25.21	Gemini
Pluto	15.30	Gemini

The division of the horoscope into twelve Houses has no direct connection with the constellations after which they are named because some constellations extend over considerably more than one-twelfth of the zodiac circle, and others are much smaller. In addition, a distinction has to be made between the traditional planetary 'houses,' represented by the twelve divisions of the zodiac circle, and the twelve Houses that are determined by the position of the Ascendant.

The Houses are numbered counterclockwise from the Ascendant. The cusps (boundaries) of the first, fourth, seventh, and tenth Houses are identical with the four angles (Asc, IC, Desc, and MC). The boundaries of the remaining Houses can vary (resulting, as can be seen, in Houses of varying angular size) according to the mathematical system of House division employed. As a consequence, one astrologer will show the sun in, say, the third House, while another, working on an identical chart, will have it

in the second. Since the mathematics of House division requires a knowledge of spherical trigonometry, the majority of astrologers are content to use published Tables of Houses.

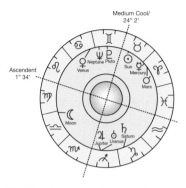

Finally there are the so-called 'aspects,' which are certain angular distances, expressed in degrees, between any two or more planets. The aspects mainly considered are:

Conjunction	0°
Square	90°
Trine	120°
Sesqui-quadrate	145°
Opposition	180°
Semi-square	45°
Sextile	60°

The Key to the Code

To sum up: a horoscope erected upon the basis of a known birth time and geographical coordinate contains the following factors: twelve 30 degree zodiacal sectors; ten planets in their respective zodiacal positions; twelve Houses, the boundary of the first being the Ascendant; four 'angles' Asc, Desc, MC, and IC; and the planetary aspects.

We have, then, a diagram that purports to record an 'astral' moment of time, but expressed in a symbolical code which must now be deciphered. This is the most difficult task of all. The astrologer begins his or her analysis on the basis of a number of assumptions:

1. Each planet works or operates in a different and characteristic manner, hence the occurrence in

everyday speech of adjectives such as *martial* (Mars), *mercurial* (Mercury), *saturnine* (Saturn), and *jovial* (Jupiter). It is supposed that a planet's 'influence' will be particularly strong if it is close to an angle and, in particular, to the Ascendant or MC. In Krafft's case Neptune, Pluto, and sun are all 'dominant' because they are near to the MC. His moon is possibly sufficiently near to the Ascendant also to be assessed as dominant.

2. A planet reflects the particular qualities of the zodiacal sign in which it is placed: so Mars in Gemini will not have the same significance as Mars in Sagittarius, and its presence in Aries (its night house) or Scorpio (its day house) will be of importance.

3. A planet will operate according to its House position. Thus Venus in the tenth can suggest one thing and Venus in the fifth another.

4. Their angular relationships, or aspects, will modify the influences of the planets concerned.

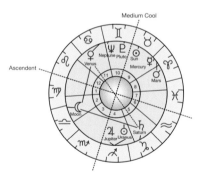

The art of interpretation involves the combination of all the available evidence and, as we have mentioned, this is where the difficulties begin. There are countless astrological manuals or 'cook books,' which provide guidance of a kind for every conceivable factor. For instance, the novice may make a note: 'sun in Taurus in the ninth House; Mars in Aquarius in the sixth House; sun square to Mars.' According to the manual he uses he will now have to consider anything from a bald and very brief statement to a detailed essay. So he jots down his interpretative material and is then uncertain how to combine it together. If he happens to be acquainted with the person whose chart he is studying, he will believe that this or that 'appears to fit' but will be left with a good deal of apparent nonsense. Most astrologers never get much beyond this 'cook book' method of interpretation.

Expert Deductions

The few who seem to excel at horoscope interpretation, including the people who can often make quite impressive deductions on the basis of a 'blind diagnosis'—meaning that they have no personal knowledge of the native (subject)—do not have to depend on such 'cook book' techniques. Nor do they necessarily try to find an interpretation for every factor in the chart. They appear to have an almost instinctive knowledge of astrological symbolism and at the same time a highly developed intuition. The writer's own experience is that they can often deduce a few extremely salient facts of a purely psychological nature.

The quality of such experts' work is apt to become diluted when they attempt to wring the last shred of 'evidence' from a horoscope, for it is a fallacy to expect that the chart itself will 'reveal all.' Nevertheless, when correctly interpreted, a horoscope will sometimes yield information of a surprisingly accurate nature.

There are, of course, a great many logical objections to astrological analysis of this kind. For example, suppose that two children have been born at the same time in the same hospital, and that one becomes a manual worker and the second a surgeon. The astrologer will be confronted with two identical horoscopes, but the subjects' respective social and educational backgrounds will necessarily be different. Then how can one talk in terms of identical 'fates?' We are not so much concerned with fate, however, as with

the hypothesis that each will react to life's psychological situations according to a common pattern, although always in specific relation to his social milieu and understanding—there will, for example, be a large element of free will. To identify the common denominator is in any case extremely difficult. Thus in astrological interpretation very little is absolutely cut and dried.

It would be tempting to write astrology off as a waste of time were it not for case histories such as the one recorded by the Institute for Border Areas of Psychology, at the University of Freiburg in Germany. A team of qualified psychologists spent time interviewing a young juvenile delinquent who had been sent to them by the local police, and their extensive written reports were then locked away in the Institute's safe. In the meantime Herr Walter Boer, a schoolmaster who was an expert astrologer with psychological training, was invited to study the boy's horoscope.

Herr Boer did not know the identities of either the young man or of the psychologists who had examined him. Nor had he any access to their reports. Yet Herr Boer's findings were very much in line with those of the psychologists, so that he was able successfully to identify a disturbed and erratic personality. It is not that Herr Boer possessed some unknown astrological secret. One can only point to an unusually sound grasp of the principles of astrological interpretation, allied to what were evidently highly developed intuitive powers.

Here it is only possible to provide a brief summary of some of the basic interpretative material established by tradition: it is by no means definitive and gives only a fragmentary idea of astrological concepts.

The Planets

Sun: the living being, the physical body, psychic energy, male principle.

Moon: the soul or psyche; fantasy and feeling, change and fluctuation (tides and months).

Mercury: intelligence, reason, movement, associative or connective function, communication (Mercury as the messenger of the Gods).

Venus: love, art, physical attraction, sentiment, sentimentality, sex.

Mars: action, energy, impulsion, aggressive function, libido (Mars as the god of war).

Jupiter: expansion, richness (material or metaphysical), health, humour, developing function.

Saturn: limitation, contraction, concentration, inhibition, separation, maturity, loss, parting (and death), saturnine temperament, restrictive function.

Uranus: suddenness, revolution, violence, transmutation (magic, alchemy, the occult arts), creative function.

Neptune: susceptibility, fantasy, romanticism, mysticism, deception and self-deception, psychic powers.

Pluto (dwarf planet): power, demagoguery, dictators, the masses.

The Signs of the Zodiac

Aries: courage, impetuosity, energy.

Taurus: patience, persistence, obstinacy.

Gemini: progressiveness, cleverness, instability.

Cancer: inspiration, sensitivity, evasiveness.

Leo: dignity, breadth of mind, power

Virgo: reason, logic, exactitude, pedantry.

Libra: harmony, evaluation, trivialities.

Scorpio: profundity, insistence, roughness.

Sagittarius: justice, propriety, sophistry.

Capricorn: independence, abstraction, stubbornness.

Aquarius: spirituality, conviction, illusion.

Pisces: compassion, tolerance, indolence.

The Twelve Houses

1. (Ascendant) development of personality, environment, childhood, physical body and constitution.
2. Material possessions and money.
3. Family relationships, communication.
4. Parental home, hereditary characteristics.
5. Procreation, sexuality, pleasure, risks, speculation.
6. Servants, health.
7. The community, partnership, marriage, open enemies.
8. Accidents, death, inheritances, the wife's or husband's money.
9. Spiritual life, philosophy, religion, travel.
10. Vocation, profession, public life.
11. Wishes and hopes, friendships.
12. Secret enemies, seclusion (hospitals, prisons), obscure difficulties.

The Aspects

Traditionally there are 'good' and 'bad' aspects (angular relationships between two or more planets). The conjunction (0 degrees) and opposition (180 degrees) can be either good or bad, according to the planets concerned. A conjunction would increase the mutual influence of the planets in question. Some examples are:

sun conj. Saturn: difficulties in connection with the development of the personality.
moon conj. Venus: intense emotional life, artistic leanings, self-love.
Mercury conj. Mars: quick mental reactions, aggressive instincts.
Venus conj. Uranus: strong emotional tensions, unusual preoccupations.

The square (90 degrees) and semi-square (45 degrees) are supposed to be 'malefic,' unfortunate, or difficult aspects. The trine (120 degrees) and sextile (60 degrees) are said to be beneficent or fortunate aspects.

An Analysis

With hindsight, what can one make of Krafft's horoscope? Here there is only room for an abbreviated analysis of a few of the factors.

One might begin by examining the sun, which is in Taurus and in the Ninth House, in relation to his Virgo Ascendant. At the same time, one would look for the 'dominant' planets, those close to the Midheaven and Ascendant. It is true that Krafft was a Taurean and his sun, high in the Midheaven, is dominant. The same also applies to Neptune and Pluto. One must ask how his Virgo Ascendant affected his personality.

Sun (Krafft's living being, essence) in Taurus reflects patience, persistence and obstinacy. He had the patience to embark upon vast, though fruitless, astrostatistical projects, and as a young man persisted in this work in spite of his father's sometimes violent objections. He was, to put it bluntly, a pig-headed person. He obstinately believed that he was destined to create a new kind of scientific astrology (which he named Cosmobiology) and, after 1937, that he could successfully exercise his strange gifts in Hitler's Germany.

Ascendant in Virgo: exactitude and pedantry. His temperament enabled him to attempt tasks that required these qualities. The dominant Neptune in Gemini in the tenth House (vocation, profession, public life) could reflect his markedly unstable character, as a result of Neptune's influence—fantasy, romanticism, mysticism, and self-deception. Pluto (power) is in a strong position. Krafft hoped for both power and influence. In a strictly limited sense he achieved both for a brief time, but he died in a German concentration camp after a lengthy imprisonment. Krafft, who for years had studied his own horoscope so closely, obviously had no inkling of his fate.

Moon in Libra square to Venus in Cancer, and also square to Saturn in Capricorn, and Venus in opposition to Saturn: all may reflect Krafft's sexual complexes and unfulfillment, also his inhibitions regarding sexuality and pleasure.

Sun in the Ninth House: his preoccupation with a spiritual life. Neptune in the Tenth House suggests Neptunian interests, which could include astrology and the prophecies of Nostradamus (1503–66), as a vocation or profession. During 1940 Krafft worked on the Nostradamus texts for Goebbels's Propaganda Ministry. Moon in the Second House: his fluctuating attitude to money and material possessions.

From these snippets one can begin to understand how a full-scale interpretation must consist of an adequate synthesis of a great many fragmentary and hypothetical propositions. In the case of Krafft one can now see how this or that would probably apply to him. An accurate blind diagnosis is far more difficult to achieve. Experience suggests that some sixty percent of any interpretation will appear to be correct, but the validity of the remainder can seldom be easily evaluated.

New Systems of Astrology

During the last century two completely nontraditional astrological systems were developed in Germany. The first was Alfred Witte's 'Hamburg School' of astrology with its eight hypothetical 'Trans-Neptunian' planets, for which equally hypothetical ephemerides have been published. This system still has a number of devoted supporters. Latterly some of its textbooks have been available in English in the United States.

An interesting by-product of the Hamburg School is the Ebertin system, developed by Reinhold Ebertin (1901–88), who did not use the hypothetical planets. Herr Ebertin jettisoned most of the medieval astrological tradition and his system can be operated without bothering about the Houses or, for that matter, the so-called zodiacal influences. A dial apparatus is used in conjunction with the horoscope chart to identify planets and their 'midpoints' on a common 90° axis. The only aspects considered are the conjunction, opposition, square, semi-square, and sesqui-quadrate. The trines and sextiles are ignored. A fair amount of simple arithmetical work is required to establish a sequence of 'planetary equations' from which a synthesis can be made with the help of Herr Ebertin's excellent manual *Combinations of Stellar Influences*. It would appear that this heretical system works just as well as any traditional one, and at least a lot of old-fashioned and suspect ballast has been ruthlessly thrown overboard.

Modern Scientific Research

The French statistician Michel Gauquelin (1928–1991) decided to investigate some of the claims of astrology in 1950. Until then, there had been no really thorough attempt to apply scientific methodology to astrological data. Gauquelin analyzed the horoscopes of around 25,000 French people (it is a legal requirement in France to register the time of birth, and so he was able to construct accurate natal charts). From a sample of 576 eminent medical professionals he found that a surprising proportion were born just after Mars or Saturn had risen, or had passed the mid-heaven. He then examined another group of 508, and achieved the same correlation. He estimated that the odds against this occurring were around one million to one.

Research into the influence of the planets on 'professional types' revealed

yet another intriguing factor. He found that the position of the planets was only very significant in the charts of those people who were *positively* distinguished and successful in their field. In a group of 1,458 scientists that he analyzed, whose careers could be described as no more than mundane, the position of Mars and Saturn at the time of birth did not seem to be of great significance statistically. Gauquelin and his wife Françoise continued to develop their work in this area for more than thirty years.

Extroverts tended to belong to the odd-numbered sun signs—Aries, Gemini, Leo, Libra, Sagittarius, and Aquarius.

In the United States and Great Britain, similar work was initiated. Since times of birth are not registered in these countries, researchers could only look for general trends. Even so, the results proved interesting. Edmund van Deuson (b. 1923) in the United States processed 163,953 dates while, in Britain, Joe Cooper and Alan Smithers from Bradford University processed another 35,000.

Their statistics appeared to be in accord with the indications of astrological tradition that an individual's birth date will be reflected in the choice of a career. For example, the figures showed that a significant proportion of bankers are Virgos. As the sign is traditionally seen as meticulous, orderly, and precise, this is in keeping with an appropriate career choice. Virgos are also said to be drawn to writing, and, again, a significant number are writers.

Other scientific studies of astrological 'leanings' have been carried out in

a variety of different areas. A group of British doctors analyzed the birth signs of those patients who had been in psychiatric care over a long period of years. They were able to find correlations of certain kinds of mental illness with birth signs. Significant percentages of schizophrenics and manic-depressives were born early in the year.

The emotional 'profiles' attributed to subject's sun signs would be an obvious spinoff for this kind of research. In 1977, Hans Eysenck (1916–97), an eminent psychologist, teamed up with Jeff Mayo (1921–98), a professional astrologer. Working with Eysenck's standard personality test for extroversion and introversion, they found high correlations in the sun-sign 'types.' Extroverts tended to belong to the odd-numbered sun signs—Aries, Gemini, Leo, Libra, Sagittarius, and Aquarius. Introverts predominated in even-numbered signs—Taurus, Cancer, Virgo, Scorpio, Capricorn, and Pisces.

ELLIC HOWE

FURTHER READING: F. King. The Cosmic Influence. (Menlo Park, CA: Aldus Books, 1976); K. Merlin. Character and Fate: The Psychology of the Birth Chart. (New York, NY: Arkana, 1989); D. and J. Parker. The New Compleat Astrologer. (New York, NY: Harmony Books, 1984); J. Anthony West. The Case for Astrology. (New York, NY: Viking, 1991); J. Dickey. Zodiac. (New York, NY: Doubleday, 1976); R. Gleadow. The Origin of the Zodiac. (New York, NY: Atheneum, 1969); J. Mayo. How to Read the Ephemeris. (St. Paul, MN: Llewellyn Publications, 1977); E. Howe. Astrology: The Story of Its Role in World War II. (New York, NY: Walker & Co., 1968).

Augury

The Romans attached considerable importance to the taking of omens, called *auguria* or *auspicia*. The object was not so much to see into the future as to find out whether the gods approved or disapproved of some proposed course of action.

Domestic augury, in which the omens were taken by the master of the house, gradually dropped out of use, except on the occasion of a marriage. However public augury remained important in official and military matters until at least c. 30 BC. The public practice of augury was restricted to the members of the college of augurs, whose function was to advise those state officials who had the legal right to take omens. The official could reject the augur's advice but Roman history told of many disasters that had followed defiance of the omens.

The augurs distinguished two kinds of omen: those that were deliberately waited and watched for, and those that occurred casually. Omens of the first kind were taken more seriously and alone had legal validity. They included thunder, lightning, and comets; the flight and cries of birds; and the behaviour of certain sacred chickens. Casual omens consisted of the unexpected appearances of animals, and certain minor happenings (which were known as *dirae*), such as the spilling of salt or wine, stumbling, sneezing, or unintentional noises such as the creaking of chairs. With the passage of time, the number of dirae grew so large that the augurs were obliged to close the list. It is recorded that the Roman general, Marcus Marcellus (42 BC–23 BC), used to travel in a closed litter, in order to shut such untoward omens out of sight and hearing.

Omens from Birds

The official who took the omens sat in a special tent, which shielded him against troublesome omens and had only one opening, facing south. The pitching of this tent in the right place at the right time, and with the correct alignment, was a closely guarded professional secret of the augurs. The tent was set up on the eve of taking the omens and the official had to sleep in it, rise early, and sit on a stone or a solid seat, so as to avoid the risk of a creaking chair. A rumbling stomach or an object inadvertently dropped at this moment were interpreted as unfavourable signs. If everything was in order, however, the augur declared a silence, and pronounced an invocation. The official then fixed his gaze on the space in front of him.

If the omens were to be taken from wild birds, the augur stood on high ground or on a tower. Facing east, he marked out an area for observation (the *templum*) in the sky with his staff. He then covered his head and sacrificed to the gods.

Not all birds counted for the purposes of augury. Those that did were divided into those whose flight was significant (including the eagle, buzzard, and vulture), and those whose cries were regarded as ominous (the crow, raven, and owl). The woodpecker and the osprey belonged to both categories. The augur had to mark the direction of flight in relation to the four sections into which the templum was divided, the height of the birds above ground, the rapidity and sound of wing-beats, the frequency, pitch and strength of cries, and the general behaviour of the birds.

The rules were very complicated and in time a whole technical literature grew up on the subject, which had a jargon of its own. The college of augurs kept archives recording actual cases, and these were used as the basis of handbooks, which explained, for example, that the cry of the crow was a favourable omen if it was heard on the augur's left; that of the raven, if it was heard on the right. They set out the precise meaning of a bird seen shedding its feathers or letting droppings fall. If there were many contradictory signs, an attempt was made to see where the predominant tendency lay. Some birds carried more weight as omens than others—the eagle more than the rook, for instance.

The Sacred Chickens

Divination from the behaviour of the sacred chickens had its origin in the significance attributed to a bird flying

Head of the Augur, **from the Tomb of the Augurs. Wall painting (c. 530-20 BC)**

with something in its beak. The most favourable sign was when the birds ate gluttonously, letting food drop from their beaks as they did so. But Cicero (106 BC–43 BC), whose work, *On Divination,* is the chief ancient source for our knowledge of augury, complains that the chickens were kept in cages and deliberately starved, so that their greediness was no true sign from Jupiter. Taking the auspices from chickens was a favourite method with Roman generals.

Although augury seems to have been held in high esteem by the Roman public at large as 'foreknowledge of the truth that is to be,' some maintained that it was merely a tool in the hands of public officials.

Originally there were only three augurs and until the year 300 BC, only members of Rome's aristocracy were eligible for this office, which carried with it a salary and certain privileges not granted to other priests. The number of augurs was gradually increased, until in the first century BC Julius Caesar (100 BC–44 BC) finally raised it to sixteen, including himself in the capacity of chief priest.

The augurs wore a mantle with a purple border, and their distinctive emblem was the *lituus,* a curved rod with which they marked out the limits of the templum. In imperial times the art of augury fell gradually into neglect, partly because the rules of divination had become so complicated, and the conditions required for favourable omens so numerous, that it became almost impossible to conduct an augury that led to a favourable result.

William Blake

William Blake (1757–1827) has been called by some a mystic, by others a gnostic. Swinburne (1837–1909) praised him as a champion of evil;

W. B. Yeats (1865–1939) believed him to have been a Rosicrucian initiate; Marxists have claimed him as an early prophet of revolution. He has been acclaimed as a surrealist; as an expressionist; as a forerunner of Freud (1856–1939) or Jung (1875–1961), in advance of his time. Yet his disciples called themselves 'the Shoreham Ancients,' indicating in this appeal to antiquity their intention of returning to a tradition stemming mainly from Plato (427 BC–347 BC).

What is in no doubt is Blake's stature. He has been called 'the Greatest Englishman.' Yet to call him the greatest English poet would be absurd. Many find his turbulent Michelangelesque forms repellent; his long 'Prophetic Books' contain magnificent fragments but are incoherent, lacking the formal structure that epic poetry demands. His lyrics are often beautiful, but less so for their artistry than for the resonances they set in motion in the reader's mind.

Blake's genius was principally that of a creator of myths. When we think of Blake, we think of a living world of gods and demons in the continuous activity of their uninhibited energy. His pantheon of spiritual beings, or energies, whose names he himself invented, seems to exist in its own right no less than the pantheons of Greece or of Egypt, independently of those works in which the gods are depicted. Blake is an outstanding example of a polytheist, a believer in many gods, who was also a Christian.

The Spirit of Prophecy

Blake's gods, the 'Zoas,' their 'sons,' 'daughters,' and 'emanations' are what Jung called archetypes, those 'self-portraits of the instinct' or basic mental patterns or images; and these images he discerned within that order of the mind that he called the collective unconscious, since it is common to all humankind. Blake believed that

'all Deities reside in the human breast,' that 'all religions are one,' and that 'the Religions of all Nations are derived from each Nation's different reception of the Poetic Genius, which is everywhere call'd the Spirit of Prophecy.'

There is no orderly formulation of Blake's mythological system, though commentators from Yeats in the 1880s to the present time have attempted to discover or impose such an order. Blake seems to have been at all times possessed of a kind and degree of consciousness which comes to those mortals who are less gifted only in flashes. His 'visions' seem to have been of two kinds: an acute perception of the content of the collective unconscious; and an illuminated vision of Nature.

He saw himself as a prophet in the Hebrew tradition; and his 'visions' as relating to the national mind of England, 'the Giant Albion.' He wrote: 'Prophets, in the modern sense of the word, have never existed. A Prophet is a Seer, not an Arbitrary Dictator.' Inspired poets are no less prophets than Moses or Ezekiel: 'Milton's *Paradise Lost* is as true as Genesis or Exodus,' for the truth of inspired art is not that of historians, but the abiding realities of the mind itself.

There are two extreme views about the nature and source of Blake's knowledge. We must take him at his word when he says that his visions came to him spontaneously, and evidently with a speed and energy that outran his powers of recording his impressions. He said that much of his poetry was 'dictated' and, on completing his *Milton,* he wrote in a letter: 'I may praise it, since I dare not pretend to be any other than the Secretary; the Authors are in Eternity.'

On the other hand, throughout his work there is evidence, not only of a powerful intellect, but also of an extensive knowledge of English poetry and history, of contemporary political events and writings, and of that body

ΟΤΙ ΟΥΚ ΕΣΤΙΝ ΗΜΙΝ Η ΠΑΛΗ ΠΡΟΣ ΑΙΜΑ ΚΑΙ ΣΑΡΚΑ, ΑΛΛΑ ΠΡΟΣ ΤΑΣ ΑΡΧΑΣ,
ΠΡΟΣ ΤΑΣ ΕΞΕΣΙΑΣ, ΠΡΟΣ ΤΕΣ ΚΟΣΜΟΚΡΑΤΟΡΑΣ ΤΕ ΣΚΟΤΕΣ ΤΕ ΑΙΩΝΟΣ ΤΕΤΕ, ΠΡΟΣ
ΤΑ ΠΝΕΥΜΑΤΙΚΑ ΤΗΣ ΠΟΝΗΡΙΑΣ ΕΝ ΤΟΙΣ ΕΠΟΥΡΑΝΙΟΙΣ.

ΕΦΕΣ: 5 Κεφ. 12

2

VALA

Night the First

1   The Song of the Aged Mother which shook the heavens with wrath
2   Hearing the march of long resounding strong heroic Verse
3   Marshalld in order for the day of Intellectual Battle
6   The heavens quake the earth was moved & shudderd & the mountains
7   With all their woods, the streams & valleys: waild in dismal fear
2   4
3   5

4   Four Mighty Ones are in every Man; a Perfect Unity
Cannot Exist. but from the Universal Brotherhood of Eden
The Universal Man. To Whom be Glory Evermore Amen

John XVII c. 21 n 22

John Tc. 14 v
ΚΑΙ ΕΣΚΗΝΩΣΕΝ
ΕΝ ΗΜΙΝ

Los was the fourth immortal starry one, & in the Earth
Of a bright Universe Empery attended day & night
Days & nights of revolving joy, Urthona was his name

In

of esoteric or occult knowledge that led Yeats to conclude that Blake had access to the secret oral tradition of the legendary Rosicrucians.

Perhaps on the strength of this supposition, paraphrases of Blake were incorporated into the rituals of the Order of the Golden Dawn, to which Yeats himself belonged.

It is not necessary to assume that Blake was an initiate in any other sense than the only real initiation—insight into spiritual reality and an imaginative understanding of whatever works he read or studied. There is nothing in his writings that he could not have learned from his wide and deep reading in the Hermetic alchemical and Neoplatonic texts available to him in English.

As a young man, he was a member of the Swedenborgian New Church; he almost certainly knew Thomas Taylor (1758–1835), the Platonist philosopher; he deeply venerated the mystic Jacob Böhme (1575–1624) and Paracelsus (1493–1541). He seems to have read Agrippa (c. 64/63 BC–12 BC), Fludd (1574–1637), and other alchemists. As an apprentice, he worked on the engravings of Jacob Bryant's *New System of Mythology*, which gave him an introduction to comparative mythology to which he continued to add, throughout his life, whatever knowledge was available. Blake also knew something of Indian religion, and of Welsh and British antiquities, and he was well-read in Latin and Greek authors.

Single Vision and Newton's Sleep

Blake consistently and cogently condemned the materialist philosophy of Bacon (1561–1626),

Opposite page:
Autograph manuscript with corrections of *The Four Zoas* (1797). Below is a drawing of the reclining figure of the goddess Vala. Originally published/produced in England.

Newton (1642–1727), and Locke (1632–1704), whom he countered with arguments derived from Plato, Plotinus (204–270), and Berkeley, delivered with an energy all his own. He followed the Cabalistic tradition of four worlds, each representing a state of consciousness. His terms for these worlds or states are Eden, Beulah, Generation, and Ulro.

> *Now I a fourfold vision see,*
> *And a fourfold vision is given to me;*
> *'Tis fourfold in my supreme delight,*
> *And threefold in soft Beulah's night*
> *And twofold Always. Nay God*
> *us keep*
> *From Single vision and*
> *Newton's sleep.*

'Newton's sleep' is the materialist view that takes the quantitative aspect of the world for its total reality. Blake regarded the creation as a system of appearances rather than of material objects external to the mind.

> *The Sky is an immortal Tent built by*
> *the Sons of Los*
> *And every Space that a Man views*
> *around his dwelling place*
> *Standing on his own roof or in his*
> *garden on a mount*
> *Of twenty-five cubits in height, such*
> *space is his Universe.*

Every man inhabits his own Eden, his 'garden on a mount,' and in this sense, his own universe, a somewhat similar view has since been put forward by the philosopher Whitehead (1861–1947).

> *As to that false appearance which*
> *appears to be reason*
> *As of a Globe rolling through*
> *Voidness, it is a delusion of Ulro.*
> *The microscope knows not of this nor*
> *the Telescope: they alter*
> *The ratio of the Spectator's Organs,*
> *but leave Objects untouched.*

Blake considered Wordsworth's vision of Nature to be distorted by the Lockean philosophy, which regards man as the passive recipient of impressions from an external world.

Blake held that we are able to perceive the world according to our kind and degree of consciousness: 'As a man is, so he Sees. As the Eye is formed, such are its Powers. You certainly mistake, when you say that the Visions of Fancy are not to be found in This World. To Me This World is all One continued Vision of Fancy or Imagination,' he wrote. In his conception of mind as the reality and Nature as a system of appearances, Blake was conceivably almost as much indebted to the Indian as to the western occult tradition.

The Four Zoas

Blake was a lifelong Christian, whose theology was based upon the Swedenborgian belief that a 'new Church' (which began in 'the heavens,' or inner world, in 1757, the year of Blake's birth) was to be the religion of 'God as man;' a Christian humanism.

Blake's Poems

Tyger, Tyger, burning bright
In the forests of the night,
What immortal hand or eye
Dare frame thy fearful symmetry? . . .

When the stars threw down their spears
And water'd heaven with their tears
Dare he laugh his mark to see?
Dare he who made the lamb make
  thee?
The Tyger

To see a World in a Grain of Sand
And a Heaven in a Wild Flower,
Hold Infinity in the palm of your hand
And Eternity in an hour.
Auguries of Innocence

The sword sung on the barren heath,
The sickle in the fruitful field:
The sword he sung a song of death,
But could not make the sickle yield.
From Blake's poems

Blake took the term 'Divine Humanity' from Swedenborg (1688–1772) and his affirmation of 'Jesus the Imagination,' present in and to every individual being, certainly derives its peculiar emphasis from Swedenborg. Swedenborgian also is Blake's conception of spiritual communities, the collective identity of those in the same spiritual 'state.' Swedenborg's 'Grand Man,' who contains in his one life all human souls, gave Blake one of his finest conceptions:

We live as One Man; for
  contracting our infinite senses
We behold multitude, or
  expanding we behold as one,
As One Man all the Universal
  Family, and that One Man
We call Jesus the Christ, and he in
  us, and we in him
Live in perfect harmony in Eden,
  the land of life.

The principal enactors of the interior drama of man's 'Fall into Division and his Resurrection to Unity' are the Four Zoas, the 'living creatures' of Ezekiel's vision of the Chariot (Ezekiel, chapter 1) and the Beasts of the Apocalypse. These 'four mighty ones,' whom Blake has so powerfully characterized both in his poetry and in his designs, are named Urizen, Luvah, Urthona, and Tharmas. They are identical with Jung's four functions of reason, feeling, intuition, and sense. The 'fall' of man results from the separation of these functions from 'Jesus the Imagination,' the God within, and from one another. Each in turn attempts to dominate man; but especially (since Blake's myth relates specifically to 'the giant Albion,' the collective being of the English nation) Urizen, the rational power.

From this usurpation by reason of 'the throne of God' that is in every man, all our national ills have followed. Each of the Zoas has an eternal and a temporal aspect; thus Luvah (love) becomes, when thwarted, Orc, the destructive spirit of war and revolution, and also the cunning serpent of sexual lust. The senses (Tharmas) become mere formless energy proliferating in a blind 'polypus' of vegetation. Los, the temporal vehicle of Urthona, is relatively unfallen, in Blake's picture of the national psyche, and is said to have 'kept the Divine Vision in time of trouble'—a comment, perhaps, upon the prophetic role of the arts in England.

Each of the Zoas has, besides 'sons' and 'daughters,' a feminine counterpart or vehicle or 'emanation.' The emanation of Los is Enitharmon, or space, who brings to birth the conception of time. Luvah's emanation is Vala, the 'veil' of Nature. When Vala, who is in reality a 'shadow' of the soul (Jerusalem, in Blake's mythology), lays claim to substantial and independent reality, she becomes a cruel and destructive principle. The 'sickness of Albion' Blake diagnosed as a tyranny of Vala made possible by the usurpation of abstract reason, Urizen. The Redemption of man is perpetually enacted as 'the Saviour'—the God within—reintegrates the separated faculties into the Imagination.

Satan of the Self

As Blake's 'saviour' is 'Jesus the Imagination,' so his Satan is 'the Selfhood,' or separated ego; whose freedom is delusive, and whose kingdom is the world cut off from God, the Hades of the spiritually dead, whom Blake calls the Specters. The separated Specters functioning independently and without orientation are, in modern psychological terms, complexes; and Jung has called the ego a special instance of the complex. Like Blake, Jung saw the cure as a return of the parts to the whole to which they belong. Blake called Satan's Kingdom 'a kingdom of nothing;' for there is no being called Satan, only a 'state.'

For Blake there is no irredeemably evil being; evil he assigns to 'states' of mind and not to individuals. 'These States Exist now. Man Passes on, but States remain for Ever; he passes thro' them like a traveler who may as well suppose that the places he has passed thro' exist no more, as a Man may suppose that the States he has pass'd thro' Exist no more.' Blake's account of the Fall shows affinities with various formulations of the western occult tradition, and especially with Boehme (1575–1624). The Fall comes about through the usurpation of a 'second creator' who in Blake's mythology is Urizen. The Creation (which for Blake is the same as the Fall) comes about through the 'binding' of Urizen within the 'cave' of the five senses, an event described in a passage several times repeated in the Prophetic Books: 'For man has closed himself up, till he sees all things thro' narrow climbs of his cavern.'

The Visions of Eternity

The remaining Zoas and the four Emanations are drawn down with this Demiurge into his fallen world of 'error, or Creation.' Boehme describes the same event as the corruption of the Seven Fountain Spirits, whom he names from the gods of the seven planets known in antiquity. Blake in this context often calls the fallen beings the 'starry ones,' in this same astrological sense. They return to their beauty and perfection when the repentant Urizen acknowledges the supremacy of 'Jesus the Imagination' over reason.

Blake's most famous designs—the twenty-two illustrations of the *Book of Job*—are a pictorial narrative of the fall of Satan from the unity of the 'God within.' Job is tormented by the reasonings of his own selfhood until he acknowledges the divine mystery, which reason cannot fathom. The same rejection of reason appears in a fine passage in Milton (1608–74):

> *To cleanse the Face of My Spirit by*
> *Self-annihilation,*
> *To bathe in the Waters of Life, to*
> *wash off the Not Human*

> *I come in Self-annihilation and the*
> *grandeur of Inspiration*
> *To cast off Rational Demonstration*
> *by Faith in the Saviour.*

A central theme in Blake's mythology is the Last Judgment, the subject of one of his most ambitious compositions, and of his magnificent prose account of this work. The Judgment is not, for Blake, the arbitrary punitive intervention of a tyrant god, but the manifestation of 'that which eternally exists, really and unchangeably.' It is the supreme human revelation of things as they are, in their full being; an awakening from sleep, a resurrection from spiritual death. 'The world

Job's Evil Dreams, **from** ***Book of Job***. **Blake's illustration, showing God who has become Satan**

of Imagination is the world of Eternity; it is the divine bosom into which we shall all go after the death of the Vegetated body. This world of Imagination is Infinite and Eternal, whereas the world of Generation or Vegetation, is Finite and Temporal. There Exist in that Eternal world the Permanent Realities of Everything which we see reflected in this Vegetable Glass of Nature. All things are comprehended in their Eternal Forms in the divine body of the Saviour, the True Vine of Eternity, the Human Imagination . . .' Blake's 'eternal forms' are not abstract ideals but the total being of those things that we normally perceive only dimly and partially. Natural forms, trees and mountains, the heavenly constellations, and the smallest maze of dancing flies are, seen with the supreme vision, not less themselves but more:

> *. . . These are the Sons of Los: these*
> *the Visions of Eternity,*
> *But we see only as it were the hem of*
> *their garments*
> *When with our vegetable eyes we*
> *view these wondrous Visions.*

In the light of the supreme vision all illusions, self-deceptions and misconceptions cease to exist. 'Error is Created. Truth is Eternal. Error, or Creation, will be Burned up, and then, and not till then, Truth of Eternity will appear. It is Burned up the Moment Men cease to behold it.'

KATHLEEN RAINE

FURTHER READING: D. Bindman. William Blake: His Art and Times. (London, UK: Thames & Hudson, 1982); M. Davis. William Blake: A New Kind of Man. (Berkeley, CA: University of California Press, 1977); M. Eaves. William Blake's Theory of Art. (Princeton, NJ: Princeton University Press, 1982); R. Grimes. The Divine Imagination: William Blake's Major Prophetic Visions. (Lanham, MD: Scarecrow, 1972); N. Hilton. Literal Imagination: Blake's Vision of Words. (Berkeley, CA: University of California Press, 1983); B. Blackstone. English Blake. (New York, NY: Shoe String Press, 1966).

Cancer

Depending upon the precise time of the summer solstice, the sun enters Cancer, the fourth sign of the zodiac, on June 21 or 22, and leaves this sign on July 22 or 23. Cancer is the crab, traditionally held to be ruled by the moon, which also controls the tides, and these two watery influences are reflected in the Cancerian's emotional make-up.

On the other hand, the obstinate, thick-skinned characteristics of the crab have long been attributed to the Cancer native. The outcome of these two opposing tendencies is revealed in the Cancerian's love of theatricality; although it is not the stage itself that appeals, so much as the excitement of the spectacle, the ebb and flow of passion and action. For the Cancer native is a spectator rather than a protagonist; he or she may be deeply moved by the fortunes of the leading actor, but they are experiencing them vicariously.

When Cancerians do decide to participate in politics, for example, they are still more likely to be the anonymous supporter than the party leader on the platform. Nevertheless, when the moon is in Sagittarius or Virgo, they can show great ability as public speakers.

So, although those born with the sun in this sign are fundamentally conservative and home loving, they can frequently be carried away by the exciting prospect of shaping their lives in imitation of some romantic example. Usually they are successful in this, for they are inventive, with an original streak, and good business organizers with an eye for a bargain. A result of this is that their homes are likely to be dark and mysterious, filled with antiques and curios.

Good memory and a sharp ear characterize Cancer natives, and many journalists were born under this sign,

Mosaic on the floor of the Galleria Umberto I in Naples, Italy, shows Cancer

as well as writers such as George Bernard Shaw (1856–1950), Aldous Huxley (1894–1963), and Ernest Hemingway (1899–1961). They are good mimics, but the ease with which a Cancerian can identify with a situation, coupled with this inherent tendency to copy others, means that great care should be exercised in their choice of friends. Although affectionate and sociable, they can be shy and possessive, although showing great sensitivity to those they love.

Traditionally, Cancer as the ascendant sign determines stature that is often below average, with a rather fleshy body and legs that are short in proportion to the rest of the build, and sometimes a noticeably ungainly gait. The face may be rounded, with a prominent forehead, relatively light complexion, and small eyes; the nose is likely to be shorter than average and may possibly even be upturned.

When the moon is in this sign, its influence is deeply emotional, sometimes manifested in an over-dependence on the mother. Domestic security and happy marriage play a prominent part in the Cancer native's dreams, and in time this ideal may be transferred to the children, who can find themselves overwhelmed by parental love and interference.

Those with moon in Cancer show an awareness of the feelings of others that is almost telepathic. Among Cancerian mystics have been the philosopher Henri Bergson (1859–1941), Helena Blavatsky (1831–91, and Mary Baker Eddy (1821–1910).

Capricorn

The sun is in Capricorn, the tenth sign of the zodiac, between either December 21 or 22 and January 20 or 21 depending upon the precise time of the winter solstice. Capricorn is *kusarikku*, the fish-ram, or *suhurmashu*, the skate goat: two of the names given to the great Babylonian god Ea, ruler of the region described in the Bible as 'the waters under the earth.' But Ea the friend of mankind, and the personification of knowledge and intelligence was a very different character from Saturn, who has been regarded as the astrological ruler of Capricorn for the past 2,000 years.

The dual nature of this relationship is reflected in the astrological attributes of those born with the sun in Capricorn, for the word 'capricious' may well describe them. Saturn traditionally represents restriction, limitation and control, and the Capricornian is often represented as a hard-working, humble, rather dreary person who never ventures to take a risk and constantly expects things to go wrong. It is true that Capricorn natives show a tendency to be over-serious, pessimistic, and emotionally inhibited; but, just at the moment when they need to be shrewd and cautious, they may be seized by the urge to ruin everything by an outburst of irresponsible flippancy, and only the strongest self-control will prevent them from giving way to temptation.

Economy and Precision

Chief among the qualities derived from Saturn that the Capricornian often turns to good account is economy. This does not necessarily reveal itself in the form of meanness, although Capricornians often feel that the gods keep them a little short, so that there is not much that they can willingly afford to give away. Among artists, typical Capricornian musicians include Mozart (1756–91) and Schubert (1797–1828). When Mozart showed one of his orchestral scores to the emperor of Austria, the emperor remarked: 'What a terrible lot of notes, Mr. Mozart;' to which the composer replied, 'No more than is necessary, your Majesty.' To this day we admire the clean, economical style of Mozart, who never wrote a superfluous note of music.

As writers, Capricorn natives display the same economy, and their brevity often results in wit. They say what they have to say in the fewest possible words, and are far more likely to provide too little explanation of their meaning than too much. Some may say that it is from laziness that they write so concisely, but the elegant precision of Francis Bacon's *Essays* was not due to laziness. Nor was the work of two of the most condensed and (to some) difficult modern writers Gertrude Stein (1874–1946) and James Joyce (1882–1941), both of whom were born 'under Capricorn.'

The same qualities, of maximum effect with minimum effort, make Capricornians notable public speakers, shrewd and to the point. The concern with economy and precision would also be vital in a good general: Robert E. Lee (1807–70), Stonewall Jackson (1824–63), and Douglas MacArthur (1880–1964) were all Capricornians.

Fresco showing Saturn, flanked by Aquarius and Capricorn in the Hall of Justice, Angera Castle, Italy

The average Capricorn native is confident and rather self-centered, suspicious, and capable of waiting a long time to reach a goal. They tend to be ambitious and frequently succeed in becoming wealthy; but their lives are not always altogether happy, and they may attract considerable enmity from people who do not understand or trust them. When their ambitions remain unfulfilled they tend to become surly and melancholy, avaricious, and given to complaining. Capricornians are good managers, and are never happy until they can exercise authority; but they expect their subordinates to perform exactly what they have undertaken, no more and no less, and they are fair but strict judges. They reveal a clever and subtle intellect, and delight in winning arguments; they make good friends within a relatively small circle, but bitter, revengeful enemies.

Not a Creator

Herbert T. Waite, the English occultist who first formulated much of modern astrology, made a very perceptive comment: 'If all the world consisted of Capricornians it would be a hive of industry and order; but we should be offering up human sacrifices to wooden gods as of old and doing much as we did thousands of years ago; for Capricorn does not create, at most it improves, organizes, and sacrifices.'

Traditionally, Capricorn as the ascendant sign determines a stature slightly below average, with a dry and rather bony body; a long and angular face, with thin neck, and sparse hair; narrow chest and weak knees, resulting in a slightly odd carriage. Although the constitution is quite strong, those with Capricorn as the ascendant sign frequently complain of ill health, and are subject to melancholia and depression. The moon in this sign is said to be 'in detriment,' signifying a cautious disposition. There is ambition still, but

The Tarocchi Players from the Casa Borromeo, in Milan, Italy, and painted in the 1440s

it is directed to material self-interest and the pursuit of status, without any consideration of spiritual matters.

Cards

Reading the past, present, and future by means of a pack of ordinary playing cards or by the more elaborate and larger pack known as the Tarot, is one of the most popular methods of divination. The use of symbolically decorated cards for fortune telling probably preceded their use in games of chance, and later replaced the more primitive forms of divination, such as the throwing down of a bundle of

arrows or sticks, or the inspection of entrails. Often the clairvoyant resorts to additional methods, gazing into a crystal ball or into a bowl of water, to confirm the reading already taken from the cards.

Cards have been made of bark, bamboo, ivory, skin, or linen as well as of pasteboard and plastic. The designs have been painted by hand, hand-printed from blocks, engraved, or lithographed. Among the fine examples of cards to be seen in the national museums and private collections there are many variations in design. German packs, for instance, use different emblems for the 'pips' from those common in France and England.

The origin of our modern packs is still a matter of dispute and there are almost as many theories propounded by occultists and historians to choose from as there are addicts of the cards. Cards were known as early as 969 AD in China and according to a Hindu legend they were invented in India by a Maharajah's wife to cure her husband of the nervous habit of pulling his beard, by keeping his hands occupied. Others claim that the ancestors of our modern cards were imported into Europe by the Roma, who had originally brought them from Egypt. References to the Tarot cards are found as early as 1299 in Italy. A fourteenth century manuscript shows a king and two courtiers playing cards, and the pips are arranged in the same way as they are today.

The Devil's Pack Book

The decorative and colorful Tarot cards, from which our more simplified standard packs are thought to be descended, are still used in Mediterranean countries in a game called *tarocchi*. A complete Tarot pack consists of seventy-eight cards, divided into four suits: Cups, Wands, Coins, and Swords. Each suit has fourteen cards, comprising the numerals one to ten, and four trumps or court cards —King, Queen, Knight or Chevalier, and Valet or Jack, named after the picture of a blazoned or coated figure of a court personage. Sometimes the court cards represent ancient and contemporary heroes, and they have even been known to commemorate political events.

In addition to the four suits of the Tarot there are twenty major trumps, which are called the Major Arcana, because they are believed to contain hidden occult mysteries. These picture cards with their unusual design and such bizarre titles as the 'Hanged Man' and 'Death,' are of great significance when used for fortune telling.

The standard pack of today, though bearing some resemblance to the ancient Tarot, consists of only fifty-two cards, divided into four suits, two red and two black: Hearts, Clubs, Diamonds, and Spades. The Knight of the Tarot is omitted from the standard pack, leaving only three court cards in each suit. Some packs, those of Spain for example, did not include the Queen as it was thought unseemly to represent a woman in the Devil's Pack Book, as cards were often called. In France, the Queens sometimes exposed their voluptuous breasts, and there were sets of naked ladies to satisfy the tastes of licentious gamblers.

How to Tell Your Fortune

Every card reader has his or her favourite method for laying out the cards. Often two methods are used one after another, if greater clarification is needed or if there are additional questions that require more precise answers. When using the standard pack, it is necessary to start with a simple interpretation of each of the fifty-two cards and later to gain an understanding of all they mean, by themselves and in different combinations with other cards.

There are variations in the interpretation of each card but a general consistency is apparent if different authorities are consulted. In addition, every card is given a qualified or extended meaning and a 'dark' or 'light' significance when modified by other cards in close proximity. The following, is known as the Wheel of Fortune.

The fortune teller chooses from the standard pack the court card that most resembles the client. In the case of a married woman, the Queen of Hearts would be taken and placed face upward in the center of the table, between the reader and the client. Having shuffled the rest of the pack so that no 'influences' remain attached to the cards from any previous contact, the fortune teller hands them to the client, instructing her to shuffle them and to put her thoughts concerning her hopes and fears, her wishes, and questions, into them. She is then asked to cut the cards into three packs with her left hand—said to be that of the Devil—and to place these face downward on the table. A good reader may say: 'this is a naughty superstition and you must not believe a word of it,' a phrase that in no way deters the client from drinking in every word, but it is to be hoped that it salves the reader's conscience.

> *A good reader may say: 'this is a naughty superstition and you must not believe a word of it,' a phrase that in no way deters the client from drinking in every word . . .*

The Tarot card of Death, the Grim Reaper

The fortune teller then turns each pack face upward and gains a general indication from the three top cards that are now exposed. Suppose the cards revealed are the King of Clubs, the Seven of Hearts, and the Ten of Spades. A brief interpretation might read thus: 'A man, well placed, powerful and possibly in the Consular Service, is bringing you good luck; I think he has a gift for you. He tells you that you must make your home anew in some faraway place. I think it must be your husband, Madame.' If the fortune teller receives a positive response from the client, she gathers the three packs together again, reshuffles them and deals nine packs of three cards each, face downward, while saying: 'three above you (one), three below you (two), three behind you (three), three before you (four), three for your house and home (five), three for your hopes and fears (six), three for what you don't expect (seven), three for what you do expect (eight), and three for what is sure to come to pass (nine).' Under each heading the following indications might be expected as pack by pack is turned face upward by the reader and each card has its significance revealed:

1. *Above you:* this pack represents both the blessings and the evils that are being experienced at the present time, 'hanging over one's head.' They will be material, psychological, and spiritual.

2. *Below you:* both the good and the bad things that one is responsible for oneself. All that is under control.

3. *Behind you:* joyful and sad times in the past.

4. *Before you:* a description of coming events in the near future.

5. *Your house and home:* a description of how these are now and how they will be in the future

6. *Your hopes and fears:* These will be described, confirmed, or refuted.

7. *What you don't expect:* good or bad news and the turn of events to come.

8. *What you do expect:* a clarification of the client's own often vague thoughts and wishes or fears about the future.

9. *What is sure to come to pass:* a final and, it is to be hoped, rousing prediction for both the near and the distant future of the client.

To conclude, the fortune teller makes a summary of the whole Wheel of Fortune so that events and the people appearing as these come about are impressed on the client's mind. To clarify or to answer any questions arising out of the reading, the client may draw three cards out of the discard pack which, when placed face upward, will give the divinatory answer.

Many people are alarmed when the Ace of Spades, known as the Death Card, appears and the fortune teller should take care to interpret this in a way that will dispel the fears of the client and bring reassurance and hope.

> *Every true adept of the cards should acquire a pack of Tarots, of which there are many different versions, although basically their symbolism is the same.*

The Greater Trumps

The curiously decorated collection of seventy-eight cards that form the Tarot pack are *the* cards for fortune telling and are said to reveal the hidden mysteries of the universe. Every true adept of the cards should acquire a pack of Tarots, of which there are many different versions, although basically their symbolism is the same. There are several variations in establishing the sequence of the twenty-two major trumps or Major Arcana and many different symbols have been used. The French Tarot of Marseilles is per-

haps the most faithful to the originals, while those depicted by the occultists Oswald Wirth (1860–1943) and A. E. Waite (1857–1942) stress the Rosicrucian, cabalistic, Grail, and Cathar aspects.

Adaptations of the Tarot in the last century presented the symbolism in naturalistically engraved pictures, often with a text added to facilitate their reading by the uninitiated. Eliphas Levi (1810–75) and other occultists link the Major Arcana with the Hebrew alphabet and Arnold Usshar links them with runic letters.

For the collector, nothing can be more fascinating than to go in search of ancient and modern packs with local variations in shape and design. Those of Naples, Russia, and Mexico are enchanting, while those from Germany are hard in design and mechanically crude in printing.

The Tree of Cards

A simple reading, using the Tarot cards, can be made by applying the same interpretation of the numerals and court cards as outlined for the standard pack. The addition of the Chevalier or Knight gives an extra court card for clarifying a prediction.

For a more detailed analysis the fortune teller lays out the cards according to a pattern based on the Tree of Life of the Cabala. This reading is performed only once for a general indication, but more comprehensive results are obtained if the process is repeated three times, first for the past, second for the present, and third for the future.

Opposite page:
The twenty-two major arcana cards in a traditional pack of tarot cards

THE FOOL. THE MAGICIAN. THE HIGH PRIESTESS THE EMPRESS. THE EMPEROR.

THE HIEROPHANT THE LOVERS. THE CHARIOT. STRENGTH. THE HERMIT.

WHEEL of FORTUNE JUSTICE. THE HANGED MAN. DEATH. TEMPERANCE.

THE DEVIL. THE TOWER. THE STAR. THE MOON. THE SUN.

JUDGEMENT. THE WORLD.

The fortune teller shuffles the full pack, and after the client has also shuffled, the reader makes ten packs of seven cards each and lays them face downward in the order shown in the diagram. Proceeding from pack to pack, the cards are turned face upward and each card read separately, then in conjunction with the other packs, and finally the whole revealed Tree of cards is read as an unfolding 'story' woven into an integrated whole. Each individual pack can be interpreted in the following way: pack one relates to that which is divine; pack two to fatherhood; pack three to motherhood; pack four to compassion; pack five to strength or conquest; pack six to sacrifice; pack seven to love; pack eight to the arts and crafts; pack nine to health; pack ten to worldly matters.

It will be seen that the packs have the pattern of a tree with a central trunk and two supporting branches. Seen from the reader's viewpoint, the central pillar represents Harmony, the left hand branch Discipline, and the right hand Love. The packs form three triangles on the Tree: at the top, an upright one, below this two downward pointing ones. The first triangle is that of the Spirit, the second that of Reason, and the third that of Intuition. The lowest pack (ten) at the foot of the Tree symbolizes the earth. The discard pack may be used for clarification or for qualifying if necessary. Some study of the Cabala is essential for this method of divination.

Besides the indication obtained from the numerals and court cards of the Minor Arcana, the twenty-two trumps of the Major Arcana enable the fortune teller to elaborate on the reading. With the Hanged Man, for example, number twelve of the major trumps, the image is of a youth hanging upside down by one leg from a gibbet. The positive prediction is of self-sacrifice; the negative of treachery.

Among some Roma communties, the Master subjects his disciple to a trance-initiation in which the disciple experiences for himself the symbolism of each trump card. In the case of the Hanged Man the experience is of being offered as a human sacrifice, of being tortured and dismembered, of a separation between the astral and the physical body. The 'shade' of the disciple seems to wander, hopelessly lost, in the underworld where he faces the negation 'God is not.' Only if his love for, and faith in, the Master is so strong that he can still, in the darkness, feel identity with him, will he be reborn to live more fully on the earth above him. In identifying himself with the Master he comes to understand and experience the yearly and continuous death and rebirth of the sacrificed God. In this resurrection, 'God is.'

A Tale of the Tarot

A delightful though improbable story is told about the origin of the Tarot cards. When the civilization of Egypt with its temple libraries of occult lore

The tarot card showing the hanged man, an individual hanging upside down from a tree, has two possible meanings: the positive is that the card symbolizes self-sacrifice, the negative interpretation is one of betrayal and treachery.

was about to be destroyed by invading barbarians, the priest-initiates gathered to discuss how best to preserve their ancient wisdom for posterity. In spite of much head-scratching, no idea was forthcoming until one initiate proposed that it should be memorized by the most virtuous and learned among them, and that he should be smuggled out of the land in the hope that he could found a new College of the Mysteries in some more propitious place.

An excellent suggestion but not one initiate present was found worthy of the task. Not one possessed the required memory capacity, nor dared to submit himself to the test of utter virtue. All had been contaminated by the flesh one way or another. The conference was at a standstill, the enemy all but thundering at the gates. 'I have it,' an aged priest cried out at last. 'Virtue is all but nonexistent in this evil world of ours and certainly is not appreciated by barbarian hordes. Let us appeal to vice, which is forever triumphant among mortal men. Let us hastily inscribe under glyph and symbol upon a pack of easily concealed papyrus cards, our stored wisdom of the ages. We will then confide these cards to any passing rogue or vagabond, explaining that they are to be used for games of chance or hazard, in fact for gambling. Then we will speed him on his way, knowing that he will cheat all he meets by this cunning method and thus, unknowingly, save the wisdom for a more enlightened day.'

A passerby, hoping for a little loot, gleefully pocketed the cards. Down the ages the wisdom traveled, passed from hand to hand, copied from one pack to another, an instrument for gain or loss, to be seen in every tavern of the world to this day. So the wisdom has remained for us to unveil, sheltered by the chicanery of tricksters.

The Seed of the Future

Telling fortunes with the cards can be an amusing pastime. It can also be a deeply serious method of divination and spiritual awakening when practiced by one with the gift of far-seeing as well as a profound knowledge of occult symbolism. The daily practice of taking a single card and meditating

If both the past and the present are made known to the conscious or waking mind, the future will almost inevitably unfold itself.

on it, thus bringing its meaning to life, is one which is highly recommended.

All this inevitably leads us to question the validity of card-reading, to wonder whether there is really 'anything in' the cards, whether messages conveyed by the random fall of shuffled cards can be rationally explained. The devotee of the art naturally has no doubts about this. However, it necessitates a belief that there is no random element in anything we do; that the seemingly chance arrangement of cards is, in reality, 'designed' by the unconscious mind of the subject.

Belief in clairvoyant powers is also a requirement. Some would attempt to explain these powers as a form of telepathic communication that spans or is outside time and space. The subject's mental processes are transferred to the symbols on the cards, which the reader is able to retranslate or interpret. The stored memories in the subject's unconscious uncover the past, immediate preoccupations give the present. If both the past and the present are made known to the conscious or waking mind, the future will almost inevitably unfold itself.

In other words, the future lies hidden like a seed in the earth, ready to

sprout, grow, and flower. To the seer, the flower may be known from its seed, the future is the child of the past. The symbols on the cards correspond to the archetypal images, the basic factors that lie deep in the collective unconscious of every man. When these living archetypes 'click' with their counterparts on the cards, they make themselves known by means of the intuition and speak through the lips of the seer. Destiny is in the hands of the archetypes.

BASIL IVAN RAKOCZI

FURTHER READING:
N. Dee. Fortune-telling by Playing Cards. *(New York, NY: Sterling, 1982); Papus.* The Tarot of the Bohemians. *(Chatsworth, CA: Wilshire Book Co.); M. Jones.* It's in the Cards. *(York Beach, ME: Weiser, 1984).*

Channeling

Almost entirely replacing the nineteenth-century term 'mental mediumship,' 'channeling' is a word applied to an activity that is probably as old as humanity itself, the attainment of an altered state of human consciousness in which information is transmitted from supposedly supernatural sources to the material world. In other words, the channeler of today is believed to be performing the same function that is still that of the shaman in certain societies and was carried out by the Delphic and other oracles in classical times.

The term derives from the concept that the human agent acts as a channel through which messages from a disembodied entity variously identified as the Higher Self, the God Energy, the collective unconscious, or 'spirit guides' are transmitted.

There are only two substantial differences between contemporary channelers on the one hand, and the shaman, the oracle, and the medium on the other. The first of these is that the latter have almost invariably delivered their messages in what was, or purported to be, a state of full trance, avowedly unaware of the words they uttered. In contrast, many modern channelers remain fully conscious of what they say, receiving the messages from the entities with which they are in touch by a process akin to telepathy, as a 'still, small voice within.'

The second difference is that a minority of contemporary channelers believe themselves to be transmitters of messages and teachings from sources even stranger than those with which we are familiar from the literature of modern spiritualism; from, for example, Neanderthal men, the spirits believed to be incarnate in large stones—even from something as apparently inanimate as a Barbie doll.

The majority, nevertheless, channel in a style that has long been familiar to habitués of spiritualist seances: the messages they transmit originate frequently from Indian chiefs, Egyptian priests, or Chinese sages. Among these 'guides' are numbered Silver Birch, who spoke through the British journalist Maurice Barbanell (1902–81), and White Eagle, spiritual teacher of Grace Cooke; Ramtha, an allegedly 35,000-year-old who claims to have once lived in Atlantis and is channeled by J. Z. Knight, a former housewife from Washington; the obscure Lazaris, who speaks through Los Angeles art dealer Jach Pursel; and, perhaps most notorious of all, Seth, who began dictating a series of books to Jane Roberts and her husband in 1963 and continued for many years.

Although many channelers can, indeed, receive in a fully conscious condition, or in no more than a relaxed, meditative state, the more dramatic communications have come when the channeler is in deep trance. Of this kind was the manuscript dictated by Seth, between January 1970 and August 1971, through 'Ruburt,' the male aspect of Jane Roberts's trance personality. With little editing, the manuscript was published as a book, with the title *Seth Speaks: the Eternal Validity of the Soul*, in 1972.

The text provides Seth's explanation of how Jane Roberts (1929–1984) communicates in trance:

'There is an expansion of her consciousness and a projection of energy that is directed away from three-dimensional reality. This concentration away from the physical may make it appear as if her consciousness is blotted out. Instead, more is added to it. Now from my own field of reality I focus my attention toward the woman, but the words that she speaks these words upon the pages are not initially verbal at all . . . In these communications, Ruburt's consciousness expands, and yet focuses in a different dimension between his reality and mine, a field relatively free from distraction. Here I impress certain concepts upon him, with his permission and assent. They are not the personality who holds it or passes it on. Ruburt makes his verbal knowledge available for our use, and quite automatically the two of us together cause various words that will be spoken.'

Channeling has attracted the attention of the rich and famous. The film actress Shirley MacLaine (b. 1934) has written extensively of her experiences, and appeared in a television feature, *Out on a Limb*, in which scenes of trance channeling were shown.

Channeling Barbie

Most Americans and Western Europeans are familiar with the form of the Barbie doll and its associates, such as Barbie's boyfriend Ken, and some of them, through their own or other people's children, probably feel that they have a certain reluctant acquaintanceship with Barbie and her eternally youthful companions. The following advertisement appeared in the Winter 1992 issue of the small US magazine *Common Ground*:

'I channel Barbie, archetypal feminine plastic essence who embodies the stereotypical wisdom of the '60s and '70s. Since childhood I have been gifted with an intensely personal growth-oriented relationship with Barbie, the polyethylene essence who is 700 million teaching entities . . . I'm happy to answer your questions, and my enlightening newsletter shares my experiences as guided by Skipper, Ken, Poindexter, and my own Higher Inner Child. Send questions with $3 to Barbara . . . San Anselmo, CA 94960.'

Artificial Elementals

Compared with such intensely human entities as Ramtha or Seth, the idea of a plastic doll even one of which there are several hundred million identical images—endowed with the power of answering questions and the advertised 'stereotypical wisdom of the 60s and 70s' tends to strike even those inclined to a belief in the marvelous as somewhat ludicrous. In reality, however, the concept is perfectly acceptable, both to those present-day esotericists who believe that it is possible to create 'artificial elementals,' and to those who accept the existence of the Collective Unconscious of Jungian depth psychology.

According to Dion Fortune (1890–1946) the twentieth century occult writer and practitioner of ritual magic who bore a large share of the responsibility for the popularization of the concept of the artificial elemental, one of these created entities begins to come into existence whenever a sufficiently large number of people start to believe in its reality. If their faith in it is of such intensity that they try to communicate with it by prayer, invocation, or even the holding of imaginary conversations, the artificially created entity begins to accumulate power from the group-mind of those who pray or talk to it. And this power may eventually increase to such an extent that it can be, as it were, tapped by those who choose to tune into it.

If, for example, a sufficiently large number of men and women come to believe in the existence of a spirit or god concerned solely with radio communication and choose to implore its assistance, then that originally imaginary entity will not only come into existence but also be able to communicate with its worshippers.

Dion Fortune was deeply influenced by Jungian theories, so much so that some esotericists have accused her of having 'psychologized the magical tradition;' that is to say adopted a reductionist approach in which all mystical experience was interpreted as essentially subjective.

Whether or not this was the case, there is a marked resemblance between her concept of how artificial elementals are created and Jungian ideas concerning the appearance of new forms of ancient archetypes in the Collective Unconscious.

From a Jungian point of view there is no reason why feminine or masculine archetypes should not manifest as Barbie and Ken, who could also be considered as artificial elementals. If one or both of these is the case, those who enter the depths of the unconscious should indeed be able to channel Barbie or any other entity, real or imaginary, which with which large numbers of people have concerned themselves.

FURTHER READING: J. Roberts. Seth Speaks. *(Upper Saddle River, NJ: Prentice-Hall, 1972); S. Roman and D. Packer.* Opening to Channel. *(Tiburon, CA: H. J. Kramer Inc, 1987).*

Robert Erskine Childers

Robert Erskine Childers is remembered principally as the author of an important work of spy fiction, *The Riddle of the Sands*, published in 1903, a book that prefigured Germany's expansionist plans before World War I. The specifics of this particular prediction make him worthy of even supernatural note, but by any measure, his was an extraordinary life. Writer, committee clerk in the House of Commons, volunteer army driver in the South African War, lieutenant commander in the Royal Naval Volunteer Reserve during World War I, one of the first members of the Royal Air Force, and an Irish nationalist, he was executed by firing squad in 1922 for the possession of a revolver by the authorities of the fledgling Irish Free State. At his last meeting with his fifteen-year-old-son in the condemned cell, he asked the boy, who was later to be fourth president of the Irish Republic, to forgive those responsible for his father's death, and, should he decide to enter politics, never to speak publicly of his execution.

Robert Erskine Childers was born in London, England in 1870, the second of five children. His father had been a civil servant in Ceylon, now Sri Lanka, and his mother was from an Irish Protestant family. He experienced grievous loss at the age of six, when his father died from tuberculosis, and his mother, who had contracted the same disease probably while nursing her husband, was removed to a sanitorium, where she died seven years later without ever seeing her children again. Erskine and his siblings were taken to his mother's childhood home in County Wicklow to be raised by an uncle and aunt. His time at Cambridge University brought him into contact with the intellectual elite of his day including the young Bertrand Russell (1872–1970). It was at this time that he first became interested in small boat sailing.

With typical thoroughness, Erskine applied himself to learning seamanship as well as the art of navigation. In 1897, he bought the vessel that was to become famous as the *Dulcibella* in *The Riddle of the Sands* and in the autumn of that year made his first journey to the Frisian Islands, the setting for his novel.

At the end of the nineteenth century, Britain was undisputed master of the seas, at the zenith of her powers economically and industrially, having enjoyed the long years of relative peace, the so-called 'Pax Britannica' that lasted for almost a century from the end of the Napoleonic Wars. Meanwhile, one of Queen Victoria's grandchildren, the German Kaiser,

Erskine Childers in the British Army in 1895

Wilhelm II (1859–1941), was determined to build a navy to rival that of Britain, an ambition that he began to realize with Admiral Von Tirpitz (1849–1930). Tirpitz's theory was that German seapower concentrated in the North Sea would be able to thwart British attempts to curtail Germany's economic or imperial ambitions. England's eastern seaboard had always been vulnerable to attack, the main point for incursions by Germanic or Norse invaders 1,000 years previously, a point not lost on hostile strategists, who knew that as an offshore island, with a far-distant Empire Britain was dependent on its navy for survival.

The Riddle of the Sands is the account of two young men on a sailing trip who uncover and foil a plot by Germany to invade Britain across the North Sea. Beautifully and compellingly written, the book set a stan-dard for adventure and spy fiction to which later authors aspired. It was an immediate success, *The Glasgow Herald* noting that 'Every minute detail is set down with a realism that compels belief in its accuracy.' It was also timely: although unknown at the time, Germany had formulated a plan in 1896 for the invasion of England by its eastern coast. In response to the perceived threat from Germany, eventually the British government started construction of a naval base at Rosyth in Scotland to meet any threat from across the North Sea. The warnings had been heeded.

ELIZABETH LOVING

FURTHER READING: L. Piper. Dangerous Waters: The Life and Death of Erskine Childers. (London, UK: Hambledon and London, 2003).

Children's Fortune-Telling Games

In 1923 the United States' Children's Bureau published '*A Brief Manual of Games for Organized Play*' detailing activities that would enhance specific aspects of child development, such as concentration, alertness, or self-control. Organized play for children represents only one part of play. Most play, the play that takes place in school playgrounds or on the streets, or wherever children congregate together and play spontaneously, represents their rich culture of games and beliefs, part of their way of interpreting and quantifying the world as they experience it, by which they unconsciously develop a range of skills.

Paper fortune-telling device used by children is called a Cootie Catcher

One aspect of this play is games and rituals to do with divination or fortune telling, in particular ascertaining the names of possible boy- or girlfriends or future marriage partners. One of the commonest is a rhyming game beginning 'Tinker, tailor . . .' generally known as Cherry Stones. Often played by girls with fruit stones or beads, the stones or beads are numbered by each name of the rhyme. Thus four stones are counted—*Tinker, tailor, soldier, sailor*—indicating that the player will marry a sailor. The rhyme continues with a range of possibilities including different types of fabric indicating what the player will wear at the wedding, different types of conveyance indicating how the player will get to the wedding, where the couple will live, and how many children the couple will have. In New Zealand a skipping version with the rhyme used as a chant has a contemporary twist as it includes a provision as to whether or not the couple will split up.

Bus tickets, specifically their serial numbers, were also used in Britain as a fortune-telling device: for example, if the numbers on the ticket added up to 21, this was considered particularly lucky. Games using knucklebones are known in Turkey where attempts are made to find out the personality of the players by seeing on which side the knucklebones fall, each side of the knucklebone being allocated a particular characteristic.

One game that has remained popular in the years following World War II is Cootie Catcher (a cootie is a body louse), known as Salt Cellar in England from the shape of the device. It is essentially a form of origami or paper folding. The game involves folding a square piece of paper twice to form a smaller square shape with four points into which the fingers can be inserted. The device can then be manipulated to

The carvings with Chinese Zodiac on the ceiling of the gate to Kushida Shrine in Fukuoka, Japan

reveal different faces and provide 'answers' to specific questions. Numbers, colours, or names are written on different folds of the Cootie Catcher and are revealed as part of the fortune-telling process, the device being opened and closed rapidly to give an impression of magic.

A manufactured version of Cootie Catcher using the same principal of providing replies to specific questions is Magic 8-Ball, the name taken from the pool game. (The object looks like a larger version of a pool ball.) The ball has a range of twenty answers, each written on a different face of a dice suspended in liquid contained within the ball. One face floats to the top within the ball when it is turned so that the 'answer' to the question is revealed.

ELIZABETH LOVING

FURTHER READING: *Iona and Peter Opie.* The Lore and Language of Schoolchildren. *(New York, NY: Oxford University Press, 1959); Iona and Peter Opie.* Children's Games with Things. *(New York, NY: Oxford University Press, 1997).*

Chinese Astrology

So-called Chinese astrology is, properly speaking, not astrology at all in the Western, Arabic, and Indian sense of the term. For it is based neither on the movement of the sun, moon, and planets through the zodiac, nor on their spatial relationships (aspects) to one another.

Instead it is concerned with the supposed nature of particular years and the characters of individuals born in those same years, on the basis of a sixty-year calendrical cycle which permutates twelve animal (real or mythical) forms with the positive (+) and negative (-) aspects of the five 'elements' (metal, water, wood, fire, and earth) of Taoist cosmology.

These elements must not be regarded as, or confused with,

elements in the physical sense. Rather they are particular qualities that are partially displayed by their material analogues. Thus the 'water element' is the quintessence of such qualities as changeability, flux, fluidity, the ability to reflect, and so on, which we normally associate with water in the daily sense of that word.

Moveable Feasts

The years as shown in the table below are only approximations to the year period covered in Chinese astrology. For example, in the table the year of the Positive Metal Rat is shown as 1960, but it actually began on January

28, 1960 and ended on February 14, 1961: the 'year' of the Positive Metal Rat was eighteen days longer than the year of the standard western calendar, in terms of which the Chinese New Year can fall on no less than thirty-one different dates.

This is sometimes found confusing by Westerners who are used to the date of the New Year being a fixed one. New Year's Day is always January 1, and has been so for centuries.

In the Chinese system of chronology the situation has been, and is, very different. The year is measured in two different ways. One is lunar, that is, calculated by reference to the moon and its phases. The other is solar, computed by reference to the tilting of the earth's axis. Both the lunar and solar calendars have their own New Year's Days, which rarely coincide with one another.

Even more strange to an occidental is the fact that the New Year of both calendars is a moveable feast, its date altering from one New Year to another. The exact date of the solar New Year falls somewhere between February 4 and 20. The lunar New Year, however, falls on the day of the second new moon after the winter solstice. This means that the Chinese lunar New Year can fall on any date between January 21 and February 20, and that the two Chinese New Year's Days can only coincide when there is a new moon between February 4 and 20 and even then they will in practice coincide only rarely.

Positive and Negative

From the table it is apparent that six of the animal forms Rat, Tiger, Dragon, Horse, Monkey, and Dog are always positive, no matter to what element they are attributed, and the other six are always negative. This does not mean that practitioners of Chinese astrology believe or teach that any person born in a year pertaining to one

of the six negative forms is innately inferior to one born in a positive year.

What is believed is that those born in a positive year will be happier in life and more successful in their chosen careers if they pursue an active, thrusting attitude toward both the public and the private sides of life. In other words, such people are well advised to try to make their own destinies to influence the outside world more than they are influenced by it.

On the other hand, it is believed that those born in a negative year should avoid approaching external reality, whether things, people, institutions, or even ideas, in a combative spirit they will be happier and more prosperous if they are prepared to be influenced by outside forces, to go, so to speak, with the tide.

Animals and Elements

The general characteristics of those born in the various years associated with the twelve animal forms are as follows:

Those born in years of the Rat are likeable, gregarious, hard working, ambitious, and thrifty.

Those born in years of the Ox are loyal, patient, conventional, courageous, and tend toward stolidity.

Those born in years of the Tiger are lucky, dynamic, prepared to take risks, unpredictable, tending to enjoy life to the full.

Those born in years of the Rabbit are sensitive, artistic, quietly intellectual, fortunate, and generous.

Those born in years of the Dragon are energetic, strong, passionate, bold and tending to become prosperous.

Those born in years of the Snake are mysterious, wise, strongly sexed, self-reliant, and extremely tenacious.

Those born in years of the Horse are popular with almost everybody, adventurous, cheerful, sociable, and tending to changeability.

Those born in years of the Sheep

The Twelve Animal Forms

The animal forms are the Rat, Ox, Tiger, Rabbit, Dragon, Snake, Horse, Sheep, Monkey, Cockerel (or Rooster), Dog, and Pig.

How these animal forms are permuted with the elements is exemplified in the following table for the years 1960—1979:

1960	Metal	Rat
1961	Metal	Ox
1962	Water	Tiger
1963	Water	Rabbit
1964	Wood	Dragon
1965	Wood	Snake
1966	Fire	Horse
1967	Fire	Sheep
1968	Earth	Monkey
1969	Earth	Cockerel
1970	Metal	Dog
1971	Metal	Pig
1972	Water	Rat
1973	Water	Ox
1974	Wood	Tiger
1975	Wood	Rabbit
1976	Fire	Dragon
1977	Fire	Snake
1978	Earth	Horse
1979	Earth	Sheep

The sequence continues, so that it is not difficult to calculate that 1980 was the year of the Positive Metal Monkey and 1981 the year of the Negative Metal Cockerel. And so it goes on until 2020, when a new sixty-year calendar cycle begins and it is once again the year of the Positive Metal Rat, just as it was in 1960.

One of the twelve Chinese zodiac in Kowloon Walled City Park in Kowloon, Hong Kong

and each year is divided into twelve sections attributed to one or other of the animal forms.

As an example of the consequences arising from this, consider a woman born at 10 p.m. on August 12, 1970, the year of the Metal Dog. Her basic Metal Dog characteristics would supposedly be greatly modified by the fact that she was born in a month ruled by the Monkey and at a time attributed to the Pig, and as a result her character would be expected to display a blend of Dog, Monkey, and Pig influences.

FRANCIS KING

Clairvoyance

The term clairvoyance is used by parapsychologists to refer to a supposed variety of extra-sensory perception (ESP) in which the information concerned is related to physical objects or events. It is generally contrasted with 'telepathy,' in which the information acquired relates to events in or states of a mind other than that of the person who perceives it.

If it is also admitted that precognitive clairvoyance and precognitive telepathy may take place, it becomes extremely difficult to design an experiment that would in theory distinguish clairvoyance from telepathy, because sooner or later the 'targets' (such as cards in a card-guessing experiment) will become known to the experimenter who checks the guesses, and hence accessible to precognitive telepathy by the guesser. For these and kindred reasons modern parapsychologists tend to be cautious in their use of the words 'clairvoyance' and 'telepathy.'

The term 'clairvoyance,' however, has commonly been, and still is, used in an older, wider, and linguistically more correct way, according to which any apparent instance of ESP in which the information presents itself in the form of a visual image or

are kind, sensitive, artistic, very emotional, and subject to gloom.

Those born in years of the Monkey are charming, clever, resourceful, flexible, and have a tendency to be deceptive.

Those born in years of the Cockerel (Rooster) are critical both of institutions and of other people, amusing, tactless, and efficient, and sometimes have a tendency to eccentricity.

Those born in years of the Dog are intelligent, open minded with a love for fairness and justice, capable of unusual objectivity, and sometimes tending to be suspicious of the motives of others.

Those born in years of the Pig are pleasure-seeking, gifted with the ability to make themselves popular, honest, considerate toward others, and physically passionate.

Complexities of Interaction

Such a brief delineation of animal form characteristics would be looked upon by students of Chinese astrology as useful to a degree, but easily capable

of misinterpretation by the unwary.

This is because the character of almost no individual is adequately summed up in the qualities of only one animal form. This view is analogous to that held by serious students of Western astrology in relation to the 'sun sign astrology' featured in popular newspaper and magazine columns that it is not to be taken as being of any real value because only very rarely is any one person a 'pure Capricornian' or a 'pure Piscean.' The horoscope of an individual normally displays a complexity of planetary aspects and zodiacal influences that requires skilled interpretation.

Similar complexities are to be found in Chinese astrology. The animal form nature of the birth year is modified by the elemental attribution; whether, for instance, a year is that of the Fire or the Water Pig.

The supposed characteristics of the elemental animal of the year of birth are thought to be modified by the animal forms attributed to the time and month of birth, for each day,

Alexis Didier, whom by the middle of the nineteenth century had become the most famous traveling clairvoyant of his time.

visual hallucination may be ascribed to clairvoyance meaning as it does 'clear-sightedness.' Comparable auditory cases are ascribed to 'clairaudience.'

Hence all sorts of fortune-tellers, crystal-gazers, 'psychic consultants,' and so forth, are apt to be styled clairvoyants. In 'clairvoyant mediumship,' the medium concerned, usually without passing into trance, claims to see and hear the deceased friends and relatives of persons present, and to relay messages from them. A demonstration of this 'platform' clairvoyance forms the centerpiece of most Spiritualist church services.

The deliverances of platform clairvoyants are sometimes remarkably accurate, but are very difficult to assess, and have not been seriously investigated often, because it is impossible to be sure what prior opportunities the medium may have of acquiring information about the audience.

There have, however, been a few extended studies (notably those published by E. Osty (1887–1991), G. Pagenstecher, and W. F. Prince in the 1920s) of the ability of certain gifted sensitives to give clairvoyant 'readings' for individuals brought to them by the experimenter; or (very often) to give such readings when simply handed objects which had belonged to the target individuals.

The readings might embrace the past, present, and future of the individuals concerned, and their personal characteristics, emotional states, homes, belongings, etc. It is impossible here to convey an adequate impression of the strengths and weaknesses of this material; but there is no doubt that certain of the cases were very remarkable. For instance, Pagenstecher's subject was once handed (without further information) a carefully sealed piece of paper. She described a man who (amongst other features) had a prominent scar above his right eyebrow. She also described the sinking of a large liner, and the man writing on the paper, corking it in a bottle and throwing it into the sea. The scrap of paper had in fact been found in a bottle, washed up on the Azores. On it a man had written a farewell message to his wife in Havana, stating that his ship (apparently the *Lusitania*) was going down. The wife in Havana was found, recognized her husband's handwriting, and concurred with the clairvoyant's description of him.

Perhaps the best-known phenomena that have passed under the name of clairvoyance are the cases of 'traveling clairvoyance' that achieved prominence in the wake of the animal magnetic (or mesmeric) movement of the mid-nineteenth century. Certain 'mesmerized' subjects developed the apparent ability to 'travel' while in trance to distant locations not known to them (frequently the homes of persons present), and report on the scenes to be found there (there is some similarity to out-of-the-body experiences).

One of the most remarkable of these 'traveling clairvoyants' was the French professional magnetic subject, Alexis Didier (1826–86). To take just one example of his performances: in 1851 Alexis was visited without warning in Paris by the Rev. G. H. Townshend, a well-known English poet and writer. Townshend had not previously met Alexis, he did not reveal his name, and he magnetized Alexis himself.

At his request Alexis 'visited' both Townshend's town house (in London) and his house near Lausanne, Switzerland. He described both houses with accuracy and provided many details of the pictures with which they were both furnished.

There is no doubt that the career and feats of Alexis, like those of certain other traveling clairvoyants from the nineteenth century, present considerable puzzles. It is of course highly unlikely that these puzzles can be retrospectively solved; and traveling clairvoyance, for whatever reason, markedly subsided with the decline of the mesmeric movement. However, in recent years, somewhat analogous phenomena have been revived and experimentally investigated by modern parapsychologists under the name of 'remote viewing.'

In these experiments, the standard procedure has been to isolate the subject, while a target site is randomly chosen from a list of possible sites within a given, moderately extended, area. Usually members of the team then proceed to the designated site, and the subject (not hypnotized, but possibly in a state of relaxation) visualizes and describes the location.

Subsequently the subject's description is compared to each listed site by independent assessors, who are unaware which was the site actually selected. Highly significant levels of correct matching have been achieved. It may be that such experiments will eventually throw light on the old phenomenon of traveling clairvoyance.

ALAN GAULD

FURTHER READING: E. Osty. Supernormal Faculties in Man: an Experimental Study. (London, UK: Methuen, 1923); R. G. Jahn and B. J. Dunne. Margins of Reality: The Role of Consciousness in the Physical World. (San Diego, CA: Harcourt Brace Jovanovich, 1987); R. Broughton. Parapsychology: the Controversial Science. (New York, NY: Ballantine Books, 1991).

Crystal-Gazing

Also known as scrying, crystal-gazing is divination by looking into a ball of

> *By the seventeenth century it had become the accepted thing for an occultist to have a crystal ball, and perhaps a sizeable clientele paying for predictions through it.*

rock-crystal, a mirror, a pool of ink or other liquid: events at a distance or in the future may show themselves in the crystal as pictures or symbolic images.

Mirrors and water remained in common use for divination during the Middle Ages. Roger Bacon (1214–94), Cornelius Agrippa (1486–1535), and Nostradamus (1503–56) all had their names linked with the use of mirrors. But the crystal ball was becoming a serious rival, and received the seal of approval of Dr. John Dee (1527–1609), astrologer to the court of Elizabeth I (1533–1603). Dee and his associate Kelley (1555–97) peered into a crystal globe about the size of an egg, which the doctor called his 'shew-stone' or 'angelical stone,' the latter name indicating its supposed origin. Dee's stone has been the object of much scholarly dispute. Different accounts give it different sizes or shapes, for example, asserting that it was solid black.

By the seventeenth century it had become the accepted thing for an occultist to have a crystal ball, and perhaps a sizeable clientele paying for

predictions through it. The ball tended to be called a 'speculum'—but the gazing was rarely termed speculation, though this would have well described the use of the crystal by such famous charlatans as William Lilly, the seventeenth century astrologer.

By the nineteenth century, crystallomancy had become firmly established as one of the most popular forms of fortune telling, ranking with astrology and palmistry, cards, and tea-leaves. The British astrologer and, fortune teller who called himself Zadkiel (R. E. Morrison) also published almanacs, as did many after him who used the same pseudonym; the publication for 1851 purported to offer 'Wonderful Revelations from the World of Spirits, which have been given through a Magic Crystal.'

ELIZABETH LOVING

Divination

The enduring popularity of the sun-sign horoscopes in newspapers, magazines, and books demonstrates the continuing demand for divination to help people make decisions in the multi-opportunity, multi-choice world of the modern West. At a more sophisticated level, in the 1980s it was revealed that in President and Mrs. Reagan's time the White House regularly consulted an astrologer, while the CIA admitted that for years it had been palming off fake astrological forecasts on the leaders of Asian and African governments, with the aim of influencing their policies in directions favourable to US interests.

'To divine' something means to know it without having been told it, without having deduced it on rational grounds and without being aware of how the knowledge has come into one's mind. Far from considering knowledge of this kind inferior and unreliable, we generally value it more highly than knowledge gained in more readily explicable ways. 'Divine' is derived from the Latin word for a god, and the underlying assumption is that knowledge that is gained by intuition or inspiration, which has come into the mind from some unknown source, has been put there by a supernatural agency. 'Something tells me' we say, or 'I feel in my bones,' that such is the case.

In the past, this confidence in intuition was justified by the belief that it was divinely inspired. However, it was also a common conclusion of human experience that the gods sometimes speak 'with forked tongue.' The famous oracle at Delphi, for instance, which was consulted by individuals and governments from all over the Greek world, was renowned for couching its responses in enigmatic language that could, and sometimes did, imply something altogether different in its significance from what the words might appear on the surface to mean.

All the same, people always and everywhere have relied on divination to bring them reliable information not obtainable by other means. On the whole, allowing for numerous exceptions, it has done this to general satisfaction. People do not go on and on consulting diviners and relying on divining systems unless they are broadly content with the results.

Some diviners have a greater capacity for seeing to the heart of things than is given to most people, and some have a shrewd grasp of what it is that those consulting them want to be told. Many diviners certainly couch their predictions in language so vague and all embracing that they can hardly fail to come true. Beyond all this, the tendency nowadays is to explain successful examples of divination in terms of extra-sensory perception (ESP), as examples of precognition, clairvoyance, or telepathy.

Word from the Spirit World

Today's professional diviners, from the astrologers and clairvoyants in their consulting rooms down to their humbler colleagues in palmists' booths or astrologers' stalls, are the successors of generations of specialist practitioners —priests and priestesses, shamans, magicians, oracles, prophets, seers, soothsayers, weather wiseacres, cunning men and wise women, conjure doctors, and medicine men.

Some of them have operated by first going into trance. At Delphi, for example, at the most sacred sanctuary in all Greece, a young priestess, called the *Pythia*, was put into a trance, induced or assisted by chewing bay leaves, in which the god Apollo took possession of her and spoke through her mouth. She did not reply directly to the enquirer. The god's words might be jumbled and unintelligible, and had to be translated by the male priests of the shrine, who made it their business to be exceptionally well-informed and combined a shrewd grasp of contemporary realities with a gift for using phrases that could be interpreted in more than one way.

In the *Aeneid* Virgil (70 BC–90 BC) gives an account of a trance oracle of Apollo, in the episode in which Aeneas and the Trojans go to consult the famous Sibyl of Cumae: 'Suddenly her countenance and her colour changed and her hair fell in disarray. Her breast heaved and her bursting heart was wild and mad; she appeared taller and spoke in no mortal tones, for the God was nearer and the breath of his power was upon her.'

Later, 'she ran furious riot in her cave, as if in hope of casting the God's power from her brain. Yet all the more did he torment her frantic countenance, overmastering her wild thoughts, and crushed her and shaped her to his will.' It is hardly surprising that those who witnessed these dramatic spectacles came away impressed.

Aegean, the mythical king of Athens, consults the goddess Themis. Attic red-figure, kylix, from Vulci (c. 440 BC–430 BC)

In the story in the Old Testament (1 Samuel, chapter 28) of Saul consulting the witch of Endor to discover what the future held for him, the witch was apparently what would now be called a medium, able in a trance or altered state of consciousness to open up a channel with a spirit guide from beyond the veil of death. Saul was reduced to consulting her because he could not get an answer from more orthodox methods of divination—dreams, casting lots, or consulting a professional prophet.

Thousands of miles from Delphi, Cumae, or Endor, meanwhile, at the other side of the world among the Navaho people of the southwest of the United States, sick patients were diagnosed by a 'hand trembler,' who in a state of trance divined the cause of the symptoms and recommended a cure, which was then carried out by another practitioner, called a 'curer.' The Navaho's experience of the results inclines them to prefer these methods to those of conventional Western doctors.

The Cunning Man

As in the case of diagnosing disease, much divination is concerned with the present and the past, rather than the future. Diviners are called in to find lost property, to sniff out witchcraft and malevolent magic, to discern the meaning of some unusual, worrisome portent that has occurred. Their scope can range from advising a king on high matters of state to finding a lost trinket. The cunning men and wise women to whom ordinary people resorted in the past—and still do in much of the world—functioned as a combination of diviner, magician, and psychiatrist. They not only diagnosed a disease or witchcraft or a threatening conjunction of events, but also provided a remedy, a recommended course of action and a sympathetic ear.

A good example is Simon Forman (1552–1611), a busy and successful

Portrait of Simon Forman (c. 1611)

self-taught cunning man, astrologer, and doctor in London, whose records have survived. His clients, who came from every social level, consulted him for cures of their ailments, for astrological advice in questions of love and marriage, to find out if anyone was scheming against them and who it might be, and to trace things that were missing, including stolen money and lost pets. Businessmen then and now, including the City merchant who wanted know if he should risk his goods in a projected voyage to open up the Northwest Passage, paid for astrological guidance.

An important consideration in relation to customer satisfaction in this field is that the client is not neces-

sarily expecting a prescription that cannot fail. He or she is frequently looking for advice from an authoritative source, which it consequently makes sense to act upon, whatever the outcome may afterward prove to be. What is more, other people in the client's sphere—other businessmen, for example—will regard the advice as authoritative, so that the client is relieved of the responsibility for failure, should things not turn out as hoped. The client has acted sensibly, it will be felt, and things often do not turn out as planned.

Forman made his own herbal remedies, as well as talismans and charms to induce love. He was consulted by aristocratic ladies who needed help in erotic matters, and his notebooks show what a demand there was at every level of society for advice over matters ranging from locating a lost canary to serious medical, marital, and financial problems. The work undertaken today by social workers, counselors, and psychiatrists was then carried out by magicians, astrologers, and diviners; and possibly with greater success, because their clients had more confidence in their skills.

Engraving from *La physique occulte* (1693) showing the way to hold a divining rod

The Dowser's Rod

One currently flourishing form of divining the present is dowsing, sometimes called 'water witching.' This way of discovering concealed water, oil, or natural gas underground enjoys general respect because over and over again it works—though no one yet understands how. Its origins seem to lie in the Middle Ages, in the mining areas of Central Europe, where it was found that some people could discover new seams in this way. By the fifteenth century a dowsing rod was standard equipment for prospectors in the Harz Mountains in Germany. More recent developments are the use of pendulums to 'dowse' maps and to diagnose disease.

Divining the past is flourishing, too, under the name of object reading or psychometry. Here an object is given to a medium or a 'sensitive' who, simply by handling it and with no other clues, can sometimes give a surprising amount of accurate information about a person who owned the object or was intimately linked with it in the past, or about events in which the object played a part. Far back at the turn of the fifth and fourth centuries BC the Greek philosopher Democritus believed that objects become charged with the mental activities and emotions of those who own or use them, and in our own century sensitive's claim to have helped police to solve crimes or trace missing persons through object reading.

The Patterns of Life

Writing in the first century AD, the Roman author Cicero drew a distinction between divination,

Coins used in *I Ching*

which depends on intuition and is an art that cannot be taught, and inductive divination, which can be taught because it interprets events according to established rules. Diviners who operate in trance rely on knowledge obtained directly from gods or spirits, who can see farther than mere mortals. Inductive methods of divination, by contrast, rely on what appear to be chance indications, like the fall of lots or the pattern of tealeaves in a cup. Underlying them, however, is a rooted disbelief in chance.

Everything that happens, in this view, is part of a gigantic and immensely complicated pattern in which all the phenomena and events of the world have their place, and so anything that happens, properly interpreted, is a clue to the rest of the pattern and the course of events.

The most prestigious oracles of this kind in the West at present are probably the *I Ching*, or *Book of Change*, and the Tarot pack. The *I Ching* has been held in high esteem by intellectuals, from Confucius (551 BC–479 BC) in China to C. G. Jung in the twentieth century in the West. It is both a philosophical system and a sophisticated form of divination by lots, with the advantage that anyone can consult it. It involves the random casting down of fifty yarrow stalks and their selection in groups (or for simplicity and speed three coins can be used). This leads to the construction of hexagrams, whose meanings the *I Ching* supplies, and enquirers apply the meanings as best they can to their own situation or problem.

Like the Delphic oracle, the *I Ching* may not give a clear-cut answer, and the true application of its wisdom may only become apparent after the event. Cicero's distinction between intuitive and inductive divination is not nearly as clear-cut as it might seem, in fact, because inductive methods in practice depend heavily on the diviner's intuition in interpreting the indicators.

By comparison with the *I Ching*, the Tarot pack is a mere infant, whose obscure history has not been traced back much farther than the later Middle Ages. Early Tarot decks had different numbers of cards and varying names for the suits, but today's standard pack consists of seventy-eight cards, of which fifty-six are organized in four suits of fourteen cards each, from the ace up to the ten, Page, Knight, Queen, and King. The suits are Swords, Cups, Coins (or Pentacles), and Wands (or Staffs). It is the other twenty-two cards (the trumps), however, which mainly distinguish the Tarot from conventional playing cards. Each has its own name and picture—the Fool, the Lovers, the Hanged Man, the Falling Tower, and so on—and these richly evocative cards have an enticing air of ancient mystery and wisdom. This is basically another method of divining by lots, as the cards are shuffled and so ostensibly randomized, before being dealt out in whatever pattern the diviner favours to get the best results.

Here again, books on reading the Tarot can only give very broad meanings for each card, and interpretation involves applying the broad general meaning, in relation to those of other cards in the spread, to the enquirer's circumstances, problems, and interests. With experience, professional readers develop a sympathetic eye and ear for what the client's situation is and what the client wants to hear or will accept. There is frequently, again, a strong need on the enquirer's side to consult the *I Ching* or the Tarot for authoritative guidance that is a source of strength in a worrying situation—while recognizing that the ultimate outcome may be too complex to forecast.

Out of the Mouths . . .

The *I Ching*, the Tarot cards, palmistry, astrology, and many other methods of divination combine a basic principle of order with a large enough number of factors—sticks, cards, lines on the hand, or whatever—to supply numerous possible permutations. This is felt to do justice to both the assumed underlying orderliness of the universe and its perceived complexity.

Far simpler methods have been tried, however. Pausanias, a Greek travel writer of the second century AD, told a story about a man who was uncertain which of two women to marry, the one who was younger or the one who was richer. While he was anxiously turning the matter over in his mind, some children were playing nearby and he heard one of them shout, 'Take care of yourself.' He took this to be a sign that he should choose the richer woman.

Pausanias also described the custom at the town of Pharai in Greece, where there was a statue of the god Hermes in the marketplace. An enquirer with a question would go to the statue in the evening, burn incense, and leave a coin on the altar and whisper his question into the statue's ear. He would then go away, keeping his hands pressed firmly over his ears to prevent his hearing anything until he was clear of the marketplace. Then he would uncover his ears and take the first words he heard as the answer to his question.

Signs and Portents

The belief that every event—even a stray remark—holds a clue to the underlying pattern of the universe and the direction in which events are moving lies behind the universal tendency to see omens and portents everywhere. Particularly striking and rare events, such as an eclipse of the sun or moon or the appearance of a comet, can arouse considerable alarm, but all sorts of lesser events may convey information to the wise. Traditional weather lore was built up over centuries, from the simple—and meteorologically justified—chant of 'red sky at night, shepherds' delight, red sky at morning, shepherds' warning' to the belief in some places that a black snail crossing one's path was a sign of rain on the way, or the widespread conviction that if the oak trees put out their

Bedik from Senegal, West Africa, divines outcomes by examining the colour of sacrificed chicken's organs.

new leaves in the spring before the ash trees, it was a certain sign of a dry summer ahead.

In 217 BC, which proved to be the disastrous year in which Hannibal invaded Italy, public anxiety was aroused in Rome by a whole parade of portents. Soldiers were struck by lightning, the spears of other soldiers mysteriously caught fire, a shower of fiery stones dropped from the sky, a statue of the god Mars was seen to sweat, two shields began sweating blood, and so on.

These alarming prodigies were reported to the Senate, which decided to hold a large-scale sacrifice of offerings to the gods and make costly gifts of gold and silver to the temples of Jupiter, Juno, and Minerva. When these measures proved inadequate and Hannibal smashed the Roman army at Cannae in 216 BC, the Senate took the rare and grave step of resorting to human sacrifice. A Gaul and a Greek man and woman were buried alive, walled in with stone in the cattle market, in a desperate effort to restore the right relationship between the Romans and their gods.

All manner of odd minor happenings were treated as omens in Rome,

from somebody stumbling or sneezing or an owl hooting at midday to the unexpected appearance of an animal or the creaking of a chair. Official augury, which took omens from the appearance and behaviour of birds, was not directed toward predicting the future, but to determining whether the gods were or were not favourable to a suggested course of action. Prophecy and politics are old bedfellows and the augurs were not infrequently suspected of biased interpretation of the omens. It was not from academic interest that Julius Caesar (100 BC–44 BC), when he had achieved his dominant position in Roman politics, appointed himself head of the augurs.

Once a year in the Roman countryside, on each farm, the farmer and his family and the labourers put on clean clothes and wreathed the heads of the oxen with garlands. Then they led a male lamb three times round the boundary of the farm—drawing a magic circle round it, in effect. The lamb was sacrificed as an offering to the gods of corn and wine, who were asked to protect the farm, to make sure it was fertile and to keep wolves away. The liver and entrails of the slaughtered lamb were inspected and, if they were normal, it signified that the gods had accepted the offering and everyone could sit down happily to a good feast. The lamb's liver and entrails would be normal far more often than not, so that everyone on the farm could feel cheerful and confident for the coming year. This is a good example of the useful social role of divination in promoting the optimism needed for effective work.

In India, too, the interpretation of omens, including weather phenomena and the flight and cries of birds, goes back to the beginning of recorded history. The direction of smoke rising from a sacrifice was considered significant, as was the behaviour of the domestic house-lizard. At human sacrifices, omens were read from the victim's cries and from the way in which his severed head fell.

Dreams were also considered meaningful in India, and they still are in many corners of the world. The strange plane of existence, with its own curious logic, into which they transport the dreamer, can readily be identified as the supernatural realm of gods and spirits, and people everywhere have felt that a particularly striking dream is trying to tell them something important. The oldest manual of dream interpretation which has survived, the Chester Beatty papyrus of about 1350 BC comes from ancient Egypt, and it employs much the same plays on words and associations of ideas that have been relied on by Freud (1856–1935) and other recent psychoanalysts.

The Stars in Their Courses

The queen of the divinatory arts, however, is astrology, which has recruited more believers around the world than any religion has ever been able to command. The magnificent panoply of the stars at night and the orderliness and predictability of their motions has suggested to awed human beings

everywhere that here, in the sky, is to be found the divine key to the pattern of events on Earth.

The Western and Indian astrological traditions both go back to the astronomer-priests of Mesopotamia, who identified the sun, the moon, and the planets with deities, which gave each of the heavenly bodies an individual character and sphere of influence. They also identified the circle of the zodiac and divided it into twelve equal sections, or 'houses.' Events in the sky, including the movements of the planets, eclipses, comets, and the behaviour of clouds, were carefully noted, recorded, and

compared with subsequent events on Earth so that they could be used to predict future events affecting the royal government.

The invention of natal astrology, the drawing up of horoscopes for individual men and women based on the positions of the planets in the zodiac at the time of birth or conception, apparently came later. It seems to have been practiced in Egypt as early as the fifth century BC and was definitely reported from Babylonia in the fourth century BC.

There were direct connections between Mesopotamia and Greece, through which astrology began to

A carving of the Buddhist horoscope from the eighteenth or nineteenth century

Methods of Divination

The following are the technical terms for some of the many methods of divination

Aeromancy	by atmospheric phenomena; weather predicting	**Horoscopy**	by planets and stars
		Hydromancy	by water
		Ichthyomancy	by fishes
Alectromancy	by a cock picking up grain	**Lampadomancy**	from the flame of a candle or torch
Amniomancy	by a caul	**Leconomancy**	from the shape taken by oil poured on water
Anthroposcopy	by facial features		
Arithmancy	by numbers	**Lithomancy**	by stones
Astrology	by planets and stars	**Margaritomancy**	by pearls
Augury	from the behaviour of birds	**Moleosophy**	by moles on the body
		Myomancy	from the movements of mice
Austromancy	by the winds		
Axinomancy	by a balanced axe, or by a stone on a red-hot axe	**Necromancy**	through communication with the spirits of the dead
Belomancy	by arrows		
Bibliomancy	by random passages in books	**Numerology**	by numbers and names
		Oenomancy	from the appearance of wine poured in libation
Bletonism	by currents of water		
Botanomancy	by herbs	**Oneiromancy**	by dreams
Capnomancy	by smoke	**Onomancy**	by the letters of a name
Cartomancy	by cards	**Onychomancy**	by the fingernails
Catoptromancy	by mirrors	**Ophiomancy**	from the behaviour of snakes
Ceromancy	by molten wax dropped in water		
		Ornithomancy	by the flight of birds
Cheiromancy	by the hands	**Palmistry**	by the hands
Clairaudience	by hearing things inaudible to normal hearing	**Pegomancy**	by fountains
		Pessomancy	by pebbles
		Physiognomy	by the face
Clairvoyance	by seeing things invisible to normal sight; second sight	**Phrenology**	by the head
		Psychometry	by handling an object
		Pyromancy	by looking into a fire
Cledonomancy	from chance remarks or events	**Rhabdomancy**	by a wand or divining-rod
Cleromancy	by dice or lots	**Scapulomancy**	by the shoulder-blades of animals
Coscinomancy	by sieve and shears		
Crystallomancy	by a crystal	**Scatoscopy**	by inspection of excrement
Dactyliomancy	by a finger-ring		
Dowsing	by means of a divining-rod	**Sciomancy**	by shadows, or ghosts
		Scrying	by a crystal
Geloscopy	by a person's way of laughing	**Sideromancy**	by the movements of straws on red-hot iron
Genethlialogy	from the stars at birth	**Sortilege**	by drawing lots
Geomancy	by dots on paper, marks on the earth, or particles of Earth	**Spodomancy**	from ashes
		Stichomancy	from random passages in books
Gyromancy	by whirling round until dizziness causes a fall	**Tephromancy**	from sacrificial ashes
		Theomancy	by oracles, and by persons inspired by a god
Halomancy	by salt		
Haruspicy	from the entrails of animals		
		Uromancy	by urine
Hepatoscopy	from the liver of animals	**Xylomancy**	by dry sticks
Hieromancy	by observation of sacrificed things	**Zoomancy**	from the behaviour of animals

spread into the classical world, but the main stream that bore astrology westward flowed by way of Egypt. The father of Western astrology, the astronomer and geographer Claudius Ptolemy, lived at Alexandria in the second century AD. He wrote in Greek and his books circulated all over the Roman world. Several of the Roman emperors consulted astrologers and one of them, Domitian (81–96), had the horoscopes of leading citizens checked for subversive tendencies.

From Mesopotamia and Greece astrology spread to India, along with the signs of the zodiac, the week of seven days and the 24 hour day. Astrology has been generally accepted there ever since and the heavens are consulted, as a matter of course, to find an auspicious time for a wedding, concluding a business deal, digging a well or laying the foundations of a house or a bridge, setting off on a long journey, or any other undertaking of importance.

On a Rising Tide

Astrology was accepted at the popular level in the West from Roman times onward, all through the Middle Ages and during the Renaissance, but it went out of intellectual fashion during the Age of Reason of the eighteenth century. In Britain it was actually made illegal by the Vagrancy Act of 1824, which prohibited the casting of horoscopes along with other types of fortune telling.

However, it was that very same year, ironically enough, which saw the emergence of the founder of modern newspaper astrology, Robert Cross Smith (1795–1832), who wrote under the pseudonym Raphael. In 1824 he was made editor of a weekly magazine entitled *The Straggling Astrologer*. Published in London, it purported to have the approval of the famous Parisian card-reader and clairvoyant, Madamoiselle Lenormand (1772–1843), who counted the Empress Josephine (1763–1814) among her fashionable clientele, and it included articles, among others, by 'Princess' Olive of Cumberland, an eccentric lady who claimed to be the daughter of one of George Ill's brothers.

The magazine survived for only a few issues, but it made history by being the first to run regular astrological predictions about love and marriage, business, travel, and so on, like the familiar newspaper and magazine astrology columns of today. It even boldly ran an article on how to tell if the lady whom you planned to marry was really a virgin.

Smith later produced an almanac with astrological predictions for every day of the year, which became *Raphael's Almanac* and was kept going for many long years after his death by a succession of 'Raphaels.'

Meanwhile a more heavyweight figure had appeared on the scene in the shape of Richard James Morrison (1795–1874), a retired naval officer and a better-educated man than his friend Smith. He turned professional astrologer in 1830, wrote under the name Zadkiel and published *Zadkiel's Almanac*, which lived on until 1931, long after his death. He also practiced scrying with a crystal ball, through which he believed he made contact with the spirits of the dead and other supernatural beings. Morrison flatly rejected Copernican astronomy and stoutly maintained that the sun revolved round the Earth, and he published several textbooks of astrology.

Smith and Morrison laid the foundations of a new popular astrology, accessible to the masses, concerned with ordinary people's everyday lives, hopes, fears, and problems, and giving much space to the astrological prospects of the royal family and other people in the public eye. Zadkiel's 1861 almanac made gloomy prognostications about the health of the Prince Consort, who did in fact die of typhoid that same year.

Victorian universal education provided a much larger literate working-class public for astrological publications. Building on the pioneers' work came William Frederick Allen (1860–1917), who wrote as Alan Leo. A commercial traveler for a sewing-machine company, brought up among the Plymouth Brethren in London, he studied astrology in his spare time, married a professional palmist, and in

> *On another occasion, he . . . asked if he could add to his article because there was going to be an earthquake . . . eleven hours later southern England was duly rocked by an earthquake.*

1890 joined the Theosophical Society, which encouraged him to see astrology in high-flown terms as an ancient symbolic system of profound insight.

He was a thoroughly practical and efficient businessman, however, and in 1898 he set up as a professional astrologer in London and pioneered the modern mass-produced horoscope. So successful was he that by 1903 he was employing nine assistants, owned the magazine *Modern Astrology,* and turned out popular textbooks under the general title *Astrology For All*.

By this time the new popular astrology had spread to the European continent, but it was not until 1930 that it was taken up by the mass circulation newspapers in Britain, when R. H. Naylor (1889–1952) started to write a regular astrology column in the *Sunday Express*. Naylor claimed to have predicted the R101 airship disaster of that year. On another occasion, he walked into the editor's office and asked if he could add to his article because there was going to be an earthquake. The editor said it was too late to add anything—and eleven hours later southern England was duly rocked by an earthquake.

Readers liked the column and it was soon copied by *The People*, the *Sunday Express's* main rival, with a regular column by Edward Lyndoe. Other popular papers followed suit, as did the French and US press, and by the 1940s there were no less than seven mass-circulation astrological monthly magazines in the United States. The day of the media astrologer had arrived and the professional diviner could now enjoy a popular audience of previously undreamed-of proportions.

RICHARD CAVENDISH

FURTHER READING: R. Cavendish. A History of Magic. *(New York, NY: Penguin Arkana, 1990); E. Howe.* Urania's Children. *(London, UK: Kimber, 1967).*

Dowsing

The popular view of a dowser is a man with a forked stick in his hands, striding across a field, and waiting for some mysterious force to drag the stick's end downward indicating the presence of water underground.

The picture may be inaccurate but it persists in spite of the facts. The popular idea of dowsing appears to have a degree of the supernatural about it. Tradition says, for instance, that the stick should be hazel—but an even older tradition places hazel near the top of the list of 'magical' woods, a vital ingredient in many charms, amulets and folk cures. Folklore offers rowan and ash substitutes for hazel in the dowsing rod, and these are also magical woods. The forked stick, too, has its witchcraft associations.

It is the central premise of dowsing, however, that arouses skepticism: that some unseen power or force exerts itself on the stick, in the presence of unseen water (or other materials); and that this unexplained effect takes place only when the stick is held by someone with the dowsing talent, who acts as a kind of transformer or perhaps amplifier of the unseen force.

Not 'Water Diviners'

Many dowsers and a few other interested parties have been anxious in recent years to reject imputations of the supernatural, and have borrowed (from J. B. Rhine (1895–1980) and other experimenters in telepathy) the less loaded and more modern term 'paranormal' to describe the dowsing ability. They also reject the familiar term 'water divining'—claiming with considerable justification, first that many more things than water can be sought, and second that the seeking has little or nothing to do with divination. So 'dowsing,' an elderly term with obscure origins, has become their favourite name for their art. There are many organized societies of dowsers in Britain and Europe, and none of water diviners.

What happens in dowsing is relatively straightforward. A person uses some implement to find, by a nonphysical means, the whereabouts of some material that would otherwise be hidden to his senses. Subterranean water in all its forms (streams, artesian wells, pools, and so on) is the most common object of the search. But almost as often the goal is some mineral, such as coal, iron, or other metal. Dowsing was also used for centuries in searches for treasure, because of its metal-finding efficacy, until modern technology supplanted dowsing rods.

In archeology, too, dowsers have played a part in determining the position and extent of ancient remains. Yet another use for dowsing is to search for lost objects, but it is sometimes employed in more important matters. Dowsers were in demand during the California gold rush and in other mining areas, and others claim that they have frequently been requested, often by the police, to help in searches for corpses of the drowned. Medical dowsing has been used to locate the whereabouts and nature of an illness within a patient's body.

A Variety of Implements

Just as the object need not always be water, the implement need not be a forked stick, or indeed any kind of stick. One well-known Oregon dowser used a copper rod and radio tube as his personalized equipment—another Oregonian, the even more famous Clyde C. Hammerley, used a forked bronze bar. But then the implement could also be a pendulum or similar weight on a silk or nylon thread. Often the pendulum is used together with a ruler or a protractor-like disc, especially in medical dowsing, when the pendulum's movement along the gradations of rule or disc provides information toward the diagnosis. Many dowsers have their own highly individualized implements,

Water diviner in Zimbabwe searching for the best place to dig a well

Rendering depicting methods of gold prospecting

which work for them, if for nobody else. In the case of rods or sticks, they may be held in several ways, lightly with the fingertips, or gripped tightly in front of the chest with the heels of the hands outward and palms down.

An Unconscious Ability

The dowser chooses his favourite implement and searches for whatever is wanted. At that point we leave the area of hard facts and confront mystery. For when the rods tremble and dip above a perfectly unremarkable spot of ground, or when the pendulum alters the direction of its swing, something has caused the phenomenon. Dowsers know that the implement cannot do the work itself: the manipulator must have the dowsing ability. Somehow, in the presence of water or whatever, that ability responds and, most dowsers believe, causes unconscious muscular contractions that affect the rod.

It must be emphasized that the dowser believes himself (or herself) largely unable (on a conscious level) to detect the object of the search without using the implement. Certainly he or she would agree that they could not pinpoint its location. Nor do dowsers believe that their talent can work unless they have first concentrated the mind on the material for which they are searching. As he sets out across a field with his dowsing rods, the dowser is clearing his mind and thinking only (for instance) about water; this concentration gives his talent space to operate, while the rods reinforce and focus it, as a means of bringing into conscious awareness the dowser's unconscious perception of water.

Dowsing at a Distance

Frequently the effect can be achieved without the dowser's physical presence on the scene. Many searchers after

water or minerals do their dowsing in the comfort of their own homes by moving their rods or pendulums above maps of the area in question. Henry Gross of Maine, perhaps the best known dowser in the United States, claimed many successes by map work; Uri Geller (b. 1946), although more famous for his metal-bending activities, subsequently turned his attentions profitably to prospecting at a distance. The dowser may visit the sites later, to confirm his findings and to pinpoint them more accurately. But such dowsers believe that distance has no effect on their perceptions.

It seems there is nothing difficult about dowsing. Anyone can try it with a bit of bent wire in the garden, or over a good big map with a home-made pendulum to see if they have the talent. It is all the more odd, then, that such a simple process with such great potential value should be comparatively young.

It may be true that the charmed sticks of primitive peoples that trembled and vibrated when a ghost had been conjured up (as in old Melanesian lore) or in the presence of a thief or his hidden loot (as in old African lore), are in fact early forerunners of the dowsing rod. Dowsing as we know it, with its more practical uses, was born later. Even classical times seem to have been without it: ancient Greek and Roman water finders had an armoury of spells and incantations but were not dowsers.

Not until the Middle Ages do references unmistakably concerned with dowsing begin to occur in learned works. It is known that dowsing was used by prospectors for minerals in the Harz mountains in the fifteenth century, and German miners later brought the practice to England during the reign of Elizabeth I (1533–1603). By the mid-sixteenth century it had become well established, enough to cause Martin Luther (1483–1546) to abjure it, and Georgius Agricola (1494–1555) to include, in a treatise on mining, the first (though hardly extensive) investigation of it.

Scoffers and Skeptics

By the seventeenth and eighteenth centuries the dowsing rod stood prominently in lists of essential 'scientific' instruments, and had gathered a considerable documentary background. That background included a sturdy array of scoffers, including Sir Thomas Browne (1605–82) and Jonathan Swift (1667–1745). In spite of rationalist attacks on dowsing as a superstition, and religious attacks on it as devil's contrivance, it went on gaining in popularity. Hordes of men in Europe and Britain, by the nineteenth century, were engaged in the practice.

Modern scientists on the whole remain skeptical. They are not impressed with the documented successes from past dowsers: the quantity of the evidence does not necessarily prove (they say) each individual case. Geologists, as would be expected, hold particularly strong views on the subject. They tend to feel, first, that dowsers are too often wrong, and therefore too unreliable, to be taken seriously; and that when the dowsers are right it is probable that their experience has made them subconsciously aware of land configurations and other physical signs pointing to the presence of water. Certainly not all geologists dismiss the dowsers' claims: some eminent geologists have themselves been dowsers, using it in their work and a great many others maintain commendably open minds on the subject.

A few scientists have set up experiments to test dowsing. A number of accounts of experiments can be found in Sir William Barrett's book *The Divining Rod* (1926), including a well-documented account of a test in the 1890s, involving the great British dowser John Mullins, who found abundant water on an estate in Sussex where hydraulic engineers had failed.

D. J. West (b. 1924), an authority on psychical research and allied matters, acknowledges the number of cases in which dowsers apparently achieved spectacular successes 'in the field.' But he adds that in systematic laboratory tests 'the level of success has always been inferior to the reports of outstandingly accurate performances in natural surroundings.'

A Controlled Experiment

In 1968 the British author and broadcaster Brian Inglis (1916–93) made an investigation of dowsing in a television program, in which his representative skeptic, a university professor and psychologist named John Cohen (b. 1911), asserted that dowsing's reality 'has not been demonstrated yet—not scientifically.' Accordingly, a controlled demonstration was arranged at which a part-time dowser named Robert Leftwich scored considerable success.

Professor Cohen claimed, however, that the experiment was not really scientific and at Mr. Inglis's request set up a second experiment entirely under his own control. A patch of ground was chosen and five cans of water, a knife and some dummy containers were buried by the Professor and his assistants at spots unknown to anyone else. The dowser picked up three out of five cans of water but failed to find the knife. Although Leftwich himself considered the result disappointing, Professor Cohen was impressed—particularly because there was no possibility of visual clues having been picked up from the topography—and handsomely admitted his amazement and his agreement that there seemed something more to dowsing than he had thought.

All this can be seen to reinforce the dowsers' standard response to accusations that they usually do badly under test conditions: they reply that being surrounded by scientists and other observers, few of whom are sympathetic and many of whom are openly critical, tends to throw off their finely tuned faculty. In the experiment there was the added pressure from the presence of television cameras and crew, causing natural nervousness that would interfere with Mr. Leftwich's concentration.

No one should dismiss the dowsers' excuse too swiftly. The ability, if it exists at all, is not a controlled function of the body or the intellect, like running or reading, both of which can be easily tested in laboratories. It is a nonrational, unconscious, or subliminal phenomenon; and science has never been favourably enough disposed toward such matters to develop special laboratory techniques for them. There are indications that considerably more individuals may have the ability, in latent form, than we might think—about one in twenty, according to one British dowser's estimate.

A Paranormal Awareness

Obviously dowsing involves some form of ESP—a 'sensing' of the presence of water and the rest, but one that does not operate through the normal five senses, setting aside the possibility that some normal, physical explanation can yet be found. Some dowsers, but far from all, actually claim to 'see' the object of their search underground when contact is made. Also, it has been suggested that the ability is more like the operation of a radar screen: a mental 'probe' is sent out that bounces back to register on the rods.

Most often, however, the dowsers turn to another technological area for their explanations. They claim that the water or the metal itself gives off 'radiations,' and the dowsing talent picks them up. From this widely held idea has come dowsing's quasi-technical name, radiesthesia—often restricted to mean only the medical form of dowsing, but equally often used to cover the whole field.

Certainly dowsing ought to provide a valuable road to an understanding of ESP in general—perhaps more valuable than the telepathy experiments with cards, or the telekinesis experiments with dice, if only because it has in the rod an outward manifestation, and because it is focused on material objects. In telepathy tests the results must always be accessed through statistical probability, which critics seem ready to question. In dowsing the results are ascertained merely by digging. So perhaps scientists will look more closely at dowsing, and that eventually they will evolve some new techniques for their experiments.

DOUGLAS HILL

The Dowser's Tools

Dowsing is a skill that can be learnt, and the tools required are of the simplest nature. They are simply mechanical accessories that act as 'amplifiers' of three possible influences. They may react to small neuromuscular reflexes in the hands; or possibly they act as interpreters of subconscious senses of which we are not normally aware; or they react objectively to some kind of otherwise undetectable 'radiation' given off by the target material. No one really knows which.

Dowsers have used a variety of simple tools, of which the following are typical:

The traditional dowser's rod is a Y- or V-shaped twig cut from a hazel or similar tree such as hawthorn or cherry, which should be fairly springy. This is held in the hands so that the V points forward or toward the dowser, and parallel to the ground. Upon reaching a critical point the V-point should dip sharply downward or upward, often with considerable force.

Similar to this is the whalebone 'spring rod.' This rod should be held by the hands in a way that induces an unstable tension.

A pair of angle rods may also be used, consisting of two L-shaped pieces of wire, often cut from coat hangers, each with the short end inserted into a handle so that the long end can swing freely from right to left. The dowser walks forward with the long arm of each piece of wire held horizontally; relaxed balance is crucial.

Fortune-telling paraphernalia, including pendulums, dowsing rod, and a divination tapper

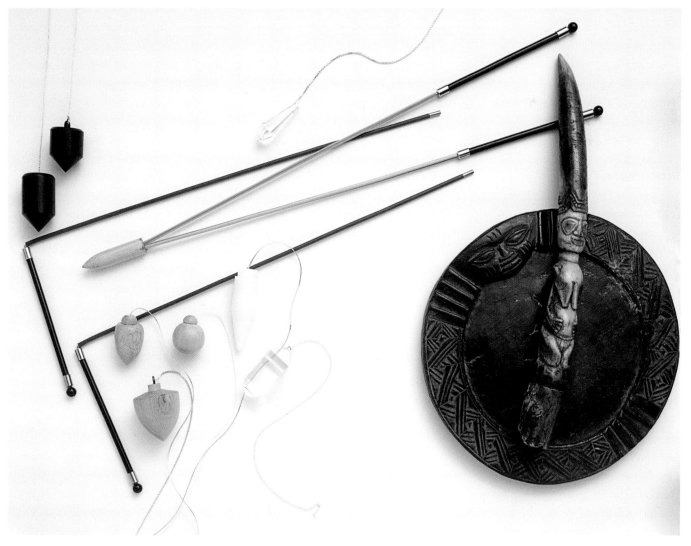

Once he has become accustomed to the 'feel' of these rods, the dowser finds that the wires will tend to cross as he passes over his target.

Pendulums can be made from any small weight suspended on a thread, a fishing line, or something similar. The weight or 'bob' can be made from all sorts of material, but it is better if it is made in a symmetrical shape, so that the pattern of its swing is not distorted. Specialized pendulums are often made of, or contain a small quantity of, the substance being sought, but for ordinary use a builder's plumb bob is perfectly acceptable.

When a pendulum is used for dowsing, the equivalent of the rod dipping is for the motion of the bob to change from a backward and forward movement to a circular movement, or for the bob to change the direction of its swing, as the target is crossed. The adjustment of the thread's length is said to be important, but the theory put forward to justify this, and the calculation that has to be made, is somewhat complicated.

Procedures

The standard technique of dowsing consists of crossing and recrossing the area of exploration, marking any points where the rod or wand reacts. Joining up these reaction points in a line will often show the path or flow of the target, whether it is an underground stream, a pipe, a mineral seam, or an archeological feature.

Once a pattern has been built up so that the feature being searched for can be mapped, then other questions such as 'how deep down is the target?' can be dealt with. There are several dowsing 'rules' to answer this question. One of the most popular is 'Bishops' rule,' which solves the problem easily.

First the dowser stands directly over the line or feature that has been detected, and relaxes. Then he or she raises the rods or wand again and walks slowly away from the chosen point in any direction, while concentrating upon the concept of the target's depth. The point is marked where the rods or wand react. This procedure is carried out several times, starting each time from the same point but moving outward in a different direction, until a rough circle can be drawn round the central point. The radius of this circle, says Bishop's rule, should be equal to the depth of the target: 'the distance out is the distance down.'

The use of a pendulum to determine a location on a map of the area . . . has no satisfactory explanation, but it appears to work almost as well as field dowsing.

The use of a pendulum to determine a location on a map of the area, rather than physically walking over the ground, has no satisfactory explanation, but it appears to work almost as well as field dowsing.

One such map-dowsing experiment was carried out with, as the target, the finding of gold deposits. As the map chosen covered an area in which it was geologically highly improbable that gold would be found, it was assumed that the experiment had proved a failure when several strong indications were registered in densely urban areas. Upon further research, however, it was discovered that these points coincided with the location of several major bank branches with safety deposit vaults, apparently vindicating the result of the experiment.

STEPHEN SKINNER

FURTHER READING: E. Z. Vogt and R. Hyman. Water Witching USA. *(Chicago, IL: University of Chicago Press, 1979); T. Graves.* Dowsing: Techniques and Applications. *(Winnipeg, Canada: Turnstone Press, 1976); P. Screeton.* Quicksilver Heritage. *(Hammersmith, UK: Thorsons, 1974).*

Dreams

The experience of dreaming is one that can still profoundly disturb and puzzle the modern educated person, even though he is disposed to seek a scientific rather than a supernatural explanation of it. Moreover, the theories of Freud (1856–1935) and Jung (1875–1961), as well as the practice of psychiatry, attest to the importance of dreams as evidence of the deeper levels of personal existence. It is understandable, therefore, that in earlier ages dreams assumed a far greater significance and played a very important role in human affairs. Dreams gave every person, each night, apparent contact with another world or form of existence, mysteriously different from that experienced when awake. Sir Edward Tylor (1832–1917) rightly emphasized the importance of dreams in causing primitive man to conceive of himself as possessing a soul, a nonmaterial self that moved and acted in the dream world.

The variety of dream experience, which can be both pleasant and horrifying, naturally stimulated speculation. Beings of all kinds were encountered in dreams: some were recognized as the dead; some seemed superhuman in appearance and power; some had monstrous forms. Then there was experience of events that had never happened in the waking world, and sometimes the sense of supernormal insight or knowledge. Inevitably the dream acquired an aura of supernatural. It was regarded as a source of information about future events in

The Great Sphinx in Giza, Egypt, where one of the most well known dreams was set

this world, by way of divine warning or encouragement. Through dreams, the gods might reveal their will, and demons tempt to ill. Dream experience made men aware that they were constantly in contact with a mysterious supernatural world, from which much might be learned about their destiny in this world and the next.

Egyptian texts record a number of the dreams of kings, in which gods were concerned; their preservation doubtless owed something to the political and religious issues involved. The most notable example has also the most dramatic setting: it is recorded on a stele of pink granite placed between the paws of the great Sphinx of Giza. The inscription tells how the future Pharaoh Thothmes IV (1425 BC–1408 BC) once rested, during a hunting expedition, in the shade of the colossal image that represented the sun god Re in his form of Harmakhis,

'Horus of the Horizon.' He fell asleep and dreamed that the god appeared and spoke to him. Harmakhis told the sleeping prince that he would confer the kingdom of Egypt upon him and give him a long and prosperous reign. Then he told Thothmes to observe the sorry situation of his image, the Sphinx, which lay half buried in the drifting desert sand, and charged him to preserve it. When he became king, Thothmes remembered the dream and cleared the Sphinx of the encroaching sand, recording his deed on the stele.

The meanings of this and of other royal dreams, in their recorded forms, are clear; they generally attest to the divine providence enjoyed by the kings. But this was not so with most of the dreams which other Egyptians had, and they were evidently much concerned about their interpretation. A science of dream-divination (oneiromancy) was established to meet their

need, and something of its technique may be learned from the fragmentary remains of 'keys' to dream-interpretation that have been found.

The following extracts come from the *Papyrus Chester-Beatty III*, which possibly preserves a tradition dating from the Middle Kingdom period (2000 BC–1785 BC). They occur in a long list of dream experiences, presented in a set formula: 'If a man sees himself in a dream looking at a snake—Good, it signifies (abundance of) provisions.' 'If a man sees himself in a dream looking at a dead ox—Good, it signifies (the death) of his enemies.' 'If a man sees in a dream his bed on fire—Bad, it signifies the rape of his wife.' These written 'keys' were for specialist use.

The practice known as incubation, meaning sleeping in a temple to obtain divine advice through a dream, or a cure by dream-contact with a healing god, is attested in Egypt during the Graeco-Roman period; it is not certain whether it had existed there in the earlier period.

The records of Mesopotamia provide ample evidence of a widespread concern about dreams among the Sumerians, Babylonians, and Assyrians. The types of dream and the manner of their interpretation are generally akin to the Egyptian tradition, thereby indicating that human reaction to dreams, like the experience of them, follows a common pattern. On the whole, however, the Mesopotamian evaluation reflects the morose spirit that characterizes Mesopotamian culture. Thus, the Sumerians called dreams Ma-Mou, which meant 'creation of the night.' A dream god, An-Za-Qar, was also recognized, who ranked among the nocturnal demons, suggesting that dreams issued forth from the underworld, the grisly place that the Babylonians called the 'Great Land.'

Mesopotamian literature reveals that warnings of impending doom often came in dreams. For example, in a Sumerian version of the flood legend, the hero Ziusudra learns of the coming catastrophe in a dream 'such as had not been (before).' The famous *Epic of Gilgamesh* describes the ominous dream that Enkidu reported to his friend Gilgamesh: 'My friend this night I saw a dream. The heavens (groaned) and the earth answered. I found myself alone.' Then he tells how the death god appeared and dragged him off to the underworld. Oneiromancy was an established practice in Mesopotamia.

The cuneiform texts of Ugarit (Ras Shamra), which document the culture of the ancient inhabitants of Canaan before the settlement of the Israelite tribes, show the importance attached to dreams by these people also.

Of particular interest is the curious fact that they imagined that gods also dreamed: the great god El learns of an important event through a dream.

Biblical Dreamers

Ancient Hebrew literature abounds with accounts of dreams through which Yahweh communicated his will and purpose to his devotees.

In ancient Greek and Roman society dreams were regarded as one of the chief means whereby the gods communicated with men, and men might learn the future.

To cite a graphic example, the patriarch Jacob, when fleeing from the wrath of his brother Esau, learns of his destiny in a marvelous dream at Bethel, which was probably an ancient Canaanite sanctuary. 'And he dreamed that there was a ladder set up on the earth, and the top of it reached to heaven; and behold, the angels of God were ascending and descending on it! And behold, the Lord stood above it and said, "I am the Lord, the God of Abraham your father, and the God of Isaac; the land on which you lie I will give to you and to your descendants; and your descendants shall be like the dust of the earth …"' (Genesis, chapter 28). The sequel is also significant: 'Then Jacob awoke from his sleep and said, "Surely the Lord is in this place; and I did not know it" And he was afraid, and said, "How awesome is this place. This is none other than the house of God, and this is the gate of heaven."'

What is probably the best known account in the Old Testament of dreams and their interpretation is the episode of which Joseph is the hero, and which is significantly located in Egypt (Genesis, chapters 40 and 41).

The Hebrew writer presents his Israelite hero as a highly skilled interpreter of dreams; yet he is careful to represent Joseph as attributing the power to interpret dreams to God: 'Do not interpretations belong to God?' he asks, and he says of Pharaoh's dream: 'The dream of Pharaoh is one; God has revealed to Pharaoh what he is about to do.' However, although the dreams are represented as divine warnings to those who receive them, the recipients cannot themselves understand the meaning of them. Joseph shows his superiority, and his god's favour to him, in being able to interpret Pharaoh's dream that the Egyptian sages have failed to do. The three dreams concerned in the story, those of the butler, the baker, and the Pharaoh, all involve a number-factor (three vine-branches, three baskets, seven cows, and seven ears of corn). The first two contain warnings of personal fate to be accomplished in three days, the third concerned the fate of Egypt in seven years of plenty and seven of famine.

Oneiromancy appears as an established practice in ancient Israel. It is related of Saul that when 'he enquired of the Lord, the Lord did not answer him, either by dreams, or by lots (Urim) or by prophets' (I Samuel, 28.6). There seems to be a reference to the custom of necromantic incubation in Isaiah, chapter 65.4: 'who sit in tombs and spend nights in secret places.' In Hebrew apocalyptic literature, dreams have a major role. The book of Daniel is the classic example of this, with Daniel presented as one who had been divinely endowed with 'understanding of all visions and dreams.'

The Shadowy Gates

In ancient Greek and Roman society dreams were regarded as one of the chief means whereby the gods communicated with men, and men might learn the future. The dramatist Aeschylus, writing early in the fifth century BC, reckoned the science of oneiromancy among the chief benefits which the 'culture hero' Prometheus had conferred on mankind. Both Greek and Latin literature abound with stories of notable dreams. The poems of Homer provide the earliest and some of the most vividly recounted examples. Zeus is the sender of dreams, and sometimes he deceives men thereby as in the case of Agamemnon (*Iliad*, book 2). Dreams usually take the form of a visit to a sleeping person made by a dream figure *(oneiros)*, which could be a god, a ghost, or specially created *eidolon* (image) that had the shape of some

person known to the sleeper; the oneiros that visited Agamemnon, for example, took the form of the venerable Nestor. The oneiros stood at the head of the sleeper's bed. He saw it and heard its message: the Greeks always spoke of dreaming as 'seeing a dream.' A dramatic example of such a visitation occurs in the *Iliad* (book 23) where the appearance of the ghost of Patroclus to the sleeping Achilles is graphically described.

Dreams were very highly regarded by some philosophers. For instance, Plato (427 BC– 347 BC) in the *Republic*, represents Socrates as maintaining that the dreams of a good man are pure and prophetic, since when he is sleeping his soul is free and is not fettered by bodily concerns.

The problem of interpreting dreams was recognized in a curious distinction that is drawn in the *Odyssey* (book 29). Penelope says to the disguised Odysseus: 'Stranger, verily dreams are hard, and hard to be discerned; nor are all things therein fulfilled for men. Twain are the gates of shadowy dreams, the one is fashioned of horn and one of ivory. Such dreams as pass through the portals of sawn ivory are deceitful, and bear tidings that are unfulfilled. But the dreams that come forth through the gates of polished horn bring a true issue, whosoever of mortals behold them.' The problem naturally produced a class of professional interpreters *(oneirokritai)*, who evolved their own esoteric methods of solution. Dream books were written in the Graeco-Roman world, as elsewhere; one of the most notable, the *Oneirokritika* of Artemidorus (second century AD) has survived.

Dreams of divine origin were frequently sought by the Greeks and Romans. A favourite means of obtaining them was incubation, a practice already noticed in describing Egyptian oneiromancy. Delphi, the famous shrine of Apollo, was probably once the location of a dream oracle. More notable was the practice of medical incubation, particularly in connection with Asclepius, the god of healing. Patients would sleep in his celebrated temple at Epidauros, in the hope that the god would visit them in a dream and ordain their cure. The many votive-inscriptions found in shrines of Asclepius witness to the faith of those who believed that they had thus been cured.

Dreams figure prominently in the records of early Christianity. Indeed, in the New Testament they are the usual means by which God communicates his will. Joseph is instructed in a dream to marry the pregnant Mary, who was to bear Jesus (Matthew, chapter 1.20). The Wise Men

Clytemnestra tries to wake Erinyes. Orestes, here unseen, is being purified by Apollo on the right. Detail from an Apulian red-figure bell-krater (380 BC–370 BC)

and Joseph are advised about the evil Herod in dreams, and in a dream Joseph is told to flee with the infant Christ and his mother (Matthew, chapter 2). Pilate's wife is prompted by a dream to warn her husband at the trial of Jesus (Matthew, chapter 27.19). Peter is prepared by a dream to accept the gentile Cornelius as a convert (Acts, chapter 10.9) and Paul is directed in a dream to preach the Gospel in Macedonia (Acts, chapter 26.9).

S. G. F. BRANDON

Dreams in the Modern West

The art of interpreting dreams and, more especially, of using them for divination, was likened to witchcraft by the Christian Church, but dreams played an important role in mediaeval life. They were, on the one hand, the inspiration of great vocations—as in the case of St. Francis of Assisi (c. 1181–1226) or St. Dominic (1170–1221)—and on the other they probably formed the basis of many accounts of witches' sabbaths. During the Renaissance the publication of the first interpretative keys to dreams, inspired by Arab writings, did at least free the subject from the illicit aura that surrounded it during the Middle Ages, although the interest did not go beyond the level of parlor games.

It was not until the nineteenth century and the Romantic Revival that dreams became acceptable in the West, although they had never lost their significance in ancient societies, in which they were regarded as a cultural phenomenon deserving the attention of the greatest intellects. The subject attracted the attention of scholars, mystics, and poets, whose approach to dreams was more poetic and metaphysical than experimental and scientific. Several of the Romantics kept dream diaries: the German writer Jean-Paul (1763–1825), for example,

did not limit himself to the observation of dreams but also experimented, trying to retain consciousness and to impose his will, to control them.

The publication of *Dreams and the Means of Controlling Them* (1867) by Hervey de Saint Denis (1822–92),

> . . . even people who deny dreaming do in fact have dreams, and the connection between dream images and external sensory stimuli.

a professor of Chinese at the College de France, marked an epoch in the scientific study of dreams. It echoed the work of Alfred Maury (1817–92), whose book *Sleep and Dreams* (1861) was the culmination of a series of researches into the analogies between dreams and mental illness, and between the images that occur during the intermediate states between waking and sleep (known as hypnagogic images), and the hallucinations of the mentally sick.

From all sides valuable observations were being made concerning the association of ideas by which the dream thread was woven, the discovery that even people who deny dreaming do in fact have dreams, and the connection between dream images and external sensory stimuli. Without doubt the chief importance of the work of these two scholars was that through them, the dream emerged from the mediaeval secrecy and popular superstition in which it had been held since the Renaissance.

The first approaches to the dream in the nineteenth century were based on an essentially physiological theory, and Alfred Maury was among those who tried to establish that the fundamental cause of dreams lay in external stimuli. He made many experiments attempting to prove this. On one oc-

casion, he asked somebody to tickle his lips and the tip of his nose while he slept—this made him dream that his face was being tortured. When a bottle of eau de cologne was placed under his nostrils, it made him dream that he was in a bazaar in Cairo.

Maury's most celebrated dream occurred when part of his bed fell on the nape of his neck, and made him dream that he was being tried by a French Revolutionary tribunal; he was put to the guillotine. One wonders whether the same incident would produce a similar dream sequence in dreamers who had different backgrounds and different memories. Maury seemed to doubt this and his doubts were confirmed by Hildebrandt, another scientist working on the theory that dreams were caused by external stimuli, and author of an important study, *The Dream and Its Value to Life* (1875).

Hildebrandt's experiments showed that the same external stimulus produces different dreams even in the same dreamer, and even more so in different dreamers. Although he was woken up from sleep in the same way three days running, three different dream scenes resulted. The experiments showed without doubt that the external stimulus is never the cause of the dream sequence but, at most, its pretext.

It remained to be demonstrated that the same was true of internal stimuli. The way was opened to Freud who was to describe dreaming as an autonomous psychic process. Jean-Paul and Hervey de Saint Denis, as a result of their attempts to control dreaming, came to recognize the

Opposite page:
Dream painting by Joan Miro (1893–1983). The Catalan Spanish painter, sculptor, and ceramicist was born in Barcelona, Spain.

autonomous character of this process; concentration and will could introduce images and themes of their choice into dreams but they were unable to create the dream sequence in which those images and themes would appear: this sequence remained unexpected and unpredictable. The field of physiological experiments with dreaming is still being explored today.

In 1900 that Freud published *The Interpretation of Dreams*. Of all his works this was the one he valued most and that he considered would earn him the gratitude of posterity. Freud reinstated the 'science' of dreams and presented in clear analytical terms observations often scattered among numerous ancient treatises, as well as those of more recent authors.

Complexes and Repressions

The use of dreams for therapeutic purposes and the sexual interpretation of them were two characteristics of psychoanalysis in 1900. They had been used for healing in the ancient world but Freud made use of dreams for therapy, not for the purpose of tracking down organic illnesses undetected by ordinary examination, nor to cure by healing images, but to reveal through the association of ideas and analysis the conflicting complexes and repressions which hinder the development of the personality. In Freud's time, and especially amongst the rich women who formed the majority of his patients, repression was of a sexual type. This is why at the conclusion of his dream analyses, Freud so often discovered sexual meanings, though he protested very strongly against the accusations of being obsessed with sex that were leveled against him. He was always aware that dreams can have nonsexual causes, such as hunger or thirst.

The Freudian technique of interpreting dreams is not very different from that of the ancients: the difference is that instead of appealing to the interpreter's association of ideas, it appeals to those of the dreamer himself. It has above all the merit of being expressed in a new language, which made sense to modern man. In deciphering dreams Freud talked of a 'manifest content' and a 'latent content.' The manifest content is the memory the consciousness retains of a dream on waking. The latent content is something that is disguised but can be uncovered by means of analysis. This becomes possible when you put yourself into a receptive state. You have to isolate each dream scene and every detail of the dream, to unleash everything that each suggests, even if it is utterly repugnant, grotesque, or immoral. The rule of the game, as for the whole process of analysis, is 'the truth and nothing but the truth.' According to Freud, only the latent content can reveal the meaning of dreams.

Why, one may well ask, should there be a latent content and a manifest content? How does the latent content become the manifest content? It is possible, of course, to adopt the attitude that 'it's only a dream:' dreams would therefore be absurd and insignificant. Freud took the opposite attitude to this sterile viewpoint. He took the view that all dreams have meaning, even though he was unable to find any meaning in some of them. To explain the existence of a hidden content and a manifest one, he elaborated a theory of resistance and censorship. These ideas were born not so much from the study of dreams, as from that of neurotic phenomena, particularly hysteria. In the course of treating neuroses, Freud was able to establish that hysterics know the 'whole truth' at an unconscious level but refuse, or are unable, to admit it. He likened the dream to a neurotic phenomenon. The manifest content he attributed to a resistance that prevents the latent content from revealing

itself. This is where the 'censor' exerts itself, imposing from that time onward a 'dream work' by which the latent disguises itself in the manifest.

The dream work operates by means of processes more or less known to the ancients. Firstly, there is a process termed identification, often linked to a play on words, a pun, or verbal assonance. Freud himself recounted a patient's dream that he called 'a pretty instance of the verbal bridges crossed by the paths leading to the subconscious,' *(The Interpretation of Dreams)*. A young woman, apprehensive about her approaching marriage, dreamt of arranging a bunch of flowers, amongst which were violets, as a centerpiece for the table. Freud detected a significant play on words between 'flowers' and 'defloration,' between 'violets' and 'violate.'

Displacement is the name for another process in which the emphasis is shifted from one symbol or figure to another more 'neutral' one in the dream. Say you have an illness that you prefer not to think about; your dream may present this in the form of a woman with cancer of the throat. Yet another process has been termed projection; you have done something dishonest and in your dream this action is attributed not to yourself but to someone whom you dislike.

If the Freudian description of the working of dreams seems satisfactory, indeed obvious in many cases, the interpretative technique lends itself to as much discussion as the theory itself. On the one hand, Freud maintained that all dreaming is the expression of a desire, even if a masochistic one, and on the other, that its primary function is to be the guardian of sleep. The dream was a hallucinatory realization of a desire that reality or prejudiced morality prevented from being satisfied, and this hallucinatory realization allowed it to unfold in sleep without any barriers.

Jung's 'Voice of the Other'

C. G. Jung, taking a different viewpoint, showed that dreams upset sleep as often as they protect it. Other authorities have held that a dream is less the realization of a desire than its expression, so that drinking in a dream does not quench your thirst; you have to drink when you wake.

If dreaming has other functions than those attributed to it by Freud what are they? What purpose do they serve? Jung, instead of enquiring into the causes of dreaming, preferred to look into its purpose. He detected a surprising gap in the Freudian approach: the latter escaped from the need to examine the manifest structure of the dream under the pretext that it was only a 'facade.' But what would a house be without a facade?

For Jung, dreams were a kind of impartial photography of unconscious life, the compensation of our rational vision of things, the voice of the 'other' in us. But this voice uses a language that is strange or lost to us. It is a language that it is important to decipher not because it deliberately hides something but rather because it is archaic, symbolic. Since the unconscious life is not static, dreams also express a search motive, a delving into the future.

Jung believed that dreams opened up to the individual the paths of the future, hidden to his conscious mind. This is why he attached less importance to the study of a single dream than to a series. These series of dreams revealed the lines of force of the unconscious and, through what he called the 'individuation process' urged the individual to integrate the unknown parts of his personality and thereby achieve the Self, or wholeness. This is why he contrasts the 'reductive' analysis and causal analysis of dreams that he attributes to Freud with an 'amplifying' one, appealing to the creative imagination.

The Universal Dimension

Jung attaches more importance than Freud to what the latter had called fixed or universal symbols, and what Jung termed 'archetypes,' belonging less to the stratum of the individual's unconscious than to those of the collective unconscious. Freud had already noted that dreams contained fixed elements, not to be detached from the technique of analysis by association of ideas, just as there also exist certain types of dream, such as those of earthquakes, the end of the world, journeys by night across the sea, death, or (more simply) nakedness, loss of teeth, or missed trains. Jung sought the meaning of these general symbols, not only in the fields in which Freud had researched but also in the study of comparative mythology and religion. Henceforth these archetypes would help to bring to light the universal dimension of individual problems.

Freud denied that dreams can reveal the future, their roots being found, according to him, in the past. However, he recognized that 'the dream can lead us into the future since it shows the realization of our desires. But

Dreams (1894) by Aubrey Beardsley (1872–98). The English painter and author's drawings in black ink emphasized the grotesque, the decadent, and the erotic.

this future, which is present for the dreamer, is moulded by indestructible desire to the image of the past.' Jung has been interpreted in slightly different ways, although his theory of the value of dreams in this respect does not differ greatly from Freud's. With regard to telepathic dreams, Freud was less reserved. But it is significant that he did not choose to publish the conclusions he had reached during his lifetime. Jung strongly affirmed the reality of telepathic feats that he called 'synchronies,' while at the same time emphasizing the difficulty of finding a satisfactory theory to explain them. Some psychoanalysts have taken note of phenomena of a telepathic or clairvoyant nature that often arise during psychoanalytical treatments.

Chickens Dream Inside the Egg
In the '50s the US physiologists Kleitman (1895–1999 and Dement (1928) attempted to establish an 'objective' method for the study of dreams. Specializing in the physiology of sleep, they rediscovered what the Hindu treatises described 3,000 years ago: the existence of two distinct sleeping states. The one is endowed with dreams, the other deprived of them. This distinction between dreaming sleep and deep sleep became evident thanks to the discovery of rapid movements of the eye that occur at the same time as remembered dreams and which are referred to as 'REMs.'

Physiologists were also able to show that everybody dreams, including those who claim they never do. They showed that dreams only became evident during certain periodical phases of sleep and that these phases became less with age; with babies eighty percent of the total sleeping time is taken up with dreams, falling to thirty-five to forty percent with children and twenty to thirty percent with adults.

This showed that dreams, far from being only the relics of the previous day's memories, as Freud had claimed, are predominant at a time when these memories are nonexistent. In the case of chickens, physiological signs of dreaming were apparent before the hatching of the egg and in the case of kittens, before their eyes opened. This suggests that dreams occur before memory is able to nourish them.

The experiments conducted by Dement and Kleitman in 1959 seem even more significant. They prevented subjects from dreaming by waking them up when their eyes began to move. These people exhibited such alarming psychotic characteristics that the experiment had to be discontinued. Meanwhile the physiologists thought they had discovered the 'seat' of dreams, or what we prefer to call their 'relay station,' at the level of the pontine reticular formation in the most primitive part of the brain.

Newborn babies spend eighty percent of their total sleep time dreaming.

In France, Dr. Jouvet and his colleagues at Lyons also established that the prevention of dreaming in human beings resulted in alarming psychotic symptoms, and produced death 'while in perfect health' in cats and rats. They came to the conclusion that dreams are an essential function of life and that it is less dangerous to undergo hunger and thirst than to be deprived of dreams.

They thus came back through their laboratory experiments to the belief of Jung and others that the dream expresses a self-regulating and compensatory function of the organism. Dreams are indispensable to life. Indeed, physiologists of sleep are incapable of providing us with a guide to the meaning of dreams in general or of particular dream images. In this respect the analytical and symbolic method remains privileged. But apart from the possibility that physiologists may one day achieve this, it is essential to understand that their discoveries strike at the root of all Freudian views and throw light on the general function of the dream in a remarkable way. This function cannot be the realization of a particular desire, since it is at its height in infancy, at a time when the desire has not yet been born and when dreams can be nothing other than the expression of an ancestral desire, and it diminishes with age. The 'seat' of dreams may be situated in the most primitive part of the brain and not in the cerebral cortex, confirming the ancestral, hereditary, and collective bases of the dream, which Freud found so difficult to admit.

RAYMOND DE BECKER

FURTHER READING: C. Evans. Landscapes of the Night. *(New York, NY: Viking, 1983); E. R. Dodds. The Greeks and the Irrational. (Berkeley, CA: University of California Press, 1951); A. Guillaume.* Prophecy and Divination among the Hebrews and Semites. *(New York, NY: Harper & Row, 1939); M. Kelsey.* God, Dreams and Revelation: a Christian Interpretation of Dreams. *(Minneapolis, MN: Augsburg, 1974); J. S. Lincoln. The Dream in Primitive Cultures. (London, UK: Cresset Press, 1935).*

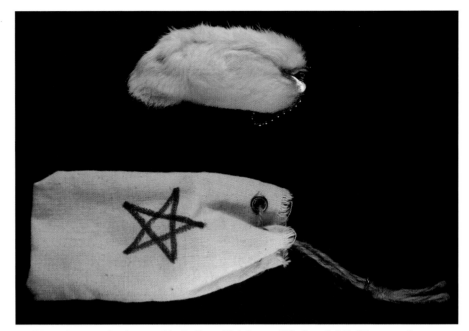

A rabbit's foot amulet for good luck. From Mal Corvus Witchcraft & Folklore artefact private collection, owned by Malcolm Lidbury (aka Pink Pasty) Witchcraft Tools.

Gambling Rituals

Fortunes have been won and lost through gambling whether at the racecourse, the casino, sports betting, or on the stock exchange. Taking a chance, undertaking a course of action that may, or may not, result in individual or collective gain, seems to be integral to human nature. The degree of willingness to trust to luck varies between individuals and 'attitude to risk' is a question posed to potential investors.

The eighteenth century in England was a heyday for games of chance, and for many people it became a drug that they were drawn to time and again, running up huge gambling debts. The age of the Puritans was gone; those who had the means were drawn to the gaming tables even though they might soon become those without means. Georgiana Cavendish (1757–1806), the wife of the fifth Duke of Devonshire, accumulated enormous gambling losses and, at the age of twenty, was forced to ask her parents to settle her debts. A type of uniform was sometimes adopted at the gaming tables: fashionable coats would be exchanged for coats made of a coarse plain fabric, or instead players would turn their own coats inside out for luck; masks were worn for one particular game that was entirely dependent on chance so that the expressions of the players could not be read; and broad-brimmed hats were worn to shield the eyes from light.

The irrational belief that there may be a link between a specific behaviour and the outcome of a game of chance persists very strongly and can be readily observed in casinos today. If a piece of clothing, a colour, an object or an action has been once linked to a successful result, it is likely that the individual will adhere to this in the belief that the 'luck' will persist. In this way a superstition arises, and from the superstition a ritualized behaviour.

ELIZABETH LOVING

Gemini

The sun enters Gemini, the third sign of the zodiac, on May 20 or 21, leaving on June 21 or 22. Gemini, the 'heavenly twins,' is traditionally held to be ruled by Mercury, and the combination of the mercurial quality of this planet with the natural duality represented by the twins is supposed responsible for the elusive and contradictory nature exhibited by those born under this sign.

Gemini natives are said to be naturally two-faced: no matter how hard they try to be straightforward and honest, their self-interest will always tempt them to be unscrupulous. In good times they can be charming, happy, and imaginative; but they are likely to fall without warning into sullen stolidity and pessimism; this is because they can reflect every change in their surroundings. On the whole, however, they adapt well to change, which they are constantly seeking; and as a result they seldom lose control of themselves, or of a situation, employing their ingenuity to cope with any sudden crisis.

At their best, Geminians make very entertaining companions and compelling conversationalists; but when they become concerned only for themselves, they grow cunning and evasive, and able to talk their way out of any situation. Indeed, it is their versatility that can be their downfall: they find it difficult to devote themselves to anything for long, whether a profession or a loved one, for while they may be deeply involved with one side of their nature, with the other they will immediately begin an intellectual analysis of their motives. It is perhaps this that has given them the reputation for never taking things seriously. Among careers that prove successful for Geminians are those of broker, journalist, lawyer, or diplomat—in

Carving of Gemini appearing on the facade of the Cathedral Amiens, France

brief, whatever combines a need for quick-wittedness with the probability of a constant change of surroundings. A military career has no attraction; as the Roman astrologer Manilius wrote, they 'wish war and trumpets far away.'

Gemini children must be supervised with care, for although they have good intellects they will always try to find a way round the labour of learning. Parents and teachers find it difficult to be severe with them because they can be so charming, and very soon they adopt bad habits that are almost impossible to eradicate.

When Gemini is the ascendant sign it traditionally determines a tall, upright body, with a long face and piercing eyes; movements, particularly of the hands, are quick and active. The constitution may be weak, with a tendency to respiratory infection.

The moon in Gemini is not taken as a good indication, for it is said to portend a nervous, restless temperament, which can reveal itself in ceaseless chatter and fidgeting. However, with other more favourable aspects, the moon in Gemini can denote a

quick imagination and practicality; the sort of temperament which can make a good actor or a romantic novelist.

Geomancy

Geomancy is the practice of divination from random marks made on the earth or by pen on paper. These marks are combined in a binary fashion to produce one of a selection of sixteen possible geomantic figures. The answer to the divinatory question is then drawn from this selection of figures and their arrangement.

The word comes from the Greek *gaia*, meaning earth, and *manteia*, meaning divination. The totally unconnected Chinese system of house and land siting known as *feng-shui* has been erroneously translated as 'geomancy.' The term has also been associated with the location of 'ley lines' but should strictly be applied solely to the traditional western mode of dot-divination.

The practice of geomancy can be reliably traced back to the ninth-century Islamic divinatory practice of *khatt-al-*

raml, which means 'lines in the sand.' The diviner first posed the question with a rhymed Arabic incantation. Then with the utmost haste he drew a quantity of lines or ripples in the sand, without counting. He then wiped out groups of two ripples at a time, leaving an odd or even number of ripples. These formed the basis of the geomantic figures.

This practice had its earliest focus in Egypt and in the Muslim-ruled southern shore of the Mediterranean in the ninth century AD. There are earlier references to an Indian origin, which is probably spurious, and to Archimedes (278 BC–212 BC) reputedly drawing geomantic figures in the sand during the siege of Syracuse to determine its outcome.

From its origin in ninth-century North Africa, where it is still practiced today, geomancy traveled south across the Sahara with the camel trains into Nigeria, Dahomey (Benin), Togo, and Ghana. Under the Yorubas it became part of the divinatory technique called *ifa*, which used chains of cowrie shells or a handful of palm nuts on elaborate wooden divining trays, to generate the same sixteen figures that the Arabs generated in the sand. The practice of *ifa* divination was later taken, as part of indigenous religious practices such as Voodou, to the Caribbean, South America, and the United States by the victims of the slave trade in the sixteenth and seventeenth centuries.

Geomancy also traveled with Arab traders down the east coast of Africa to the island of Madagascar in the late ninth century; there it became mixed with the Malay practice of *vintana*, resulting in 'sikidy' divination, which retains the same geomantic figures but gives them new names and interpretations. A third migration of geomancy went, probably in the fourteeth century, from the Arab world to the Byzantine Greek world, where it was called *rabolion*.

The last and most interesting line of transmission was via the Arab conquest of Spain. Although Muslim invaders entered Spain first in 711, the practice of geomancy does not seem to have been recorded there before the twelfth century. At this time Arabic manuscripts were beginning to be translated into Latin, and geomancy became, after astrology, probably the most popular form of divination in Europe. Here its sandy origins were forgotten, and it was practiced purely with a pen on paper or parchment.

The first geomantic text translated into Latin, some time between 1119 and 1157, was Hugh of Santalla's *Ars Geomantiae*. Soon after, Gerard of Cremona (c. 1114–87) translated a number of important works from Arabic into Latin, including a geomantic text. These texts set off a flood of works in Latin by writers such as Plato of Tivoli, Robert of Chester, and more famous scholars such as Michael Scot (c. 1175– c. l235) and Albertus Magnus (1193–1280).

The art of geomancy was developed by Ramon Lull (1235–1315), a Majorcan monk who invented a kind of cog-wheeled logic machine based directly on the binary nature of geomancy. By the thirteenth century, kings such as Wenceslaus of Bohemia (c. 1205–53) and Richard II of England (1367–1400) had their own geomantic reference manuscripts prepared for them.

The practice reached its apogee with Henry Cornelius Agrippa (1468–1535) and the Englishman Robert Fludd (b. 1574). Late in the eighteenth century interest in geomancy revived, and again in the late nineteenth century with its inclusion in the syllabus of the Hermetic Order of the Golden Dawn.

Each geomantic figure is made up of four levels, each level containing either one or two dots. This means there are sixteen possible combinations. The names of the figures, although originally Arabic, are usually given in Latin. They range from Via, which consists of four single dots one above the other to Populus, which consists of four levels of two dots.

The name of the figure is partially a reflection of its shape, Via meaning a road or journey, while Populus means a crowd, it being the 'fullest' possible figure. The other fourteen characters consist of various combinations of one dot and two.

The sixteen geomantic figures are attributed to the twelve signs of the zodiac, with some double attributions.

Decoration on the Jokhang Temple, Tibet, the principal geomantic power place in Tibet

They range from Puer, the boy (attributed to Aries) to Laetitia, joy (attributed to Pisces), with the head and tail of the moon attributed to Caput Draconis, the head of the dragon, and Cauda Draconis, the dragon's tail, respectively.

The planets and elements are also allocated to the sixteen figures, and each is also given a 'ruling spirit.' From these attributions, geomantic figures were often projected onto astrological horoscopes, mainly to answer immediate 'horary' questions rather than to interpret birth charts.

The technique of geomancy is best explained by following the steps of a theoretical divination. Whichever medium is used, sand or paper, the question must first be framed to avoid ambiguity in the answer. The diviner then makes sixteen lines of dashes or dots, with whatever instrument he has chosen, while concentrating on the question.

In the first row of dots the total is determined and, depending on whether the resultant number is odd or even, one or two dots are marked on the first line of a fresh piece of paper. The same observation is made for each of the subsequent fifteen lines.

The resultant page has sixteen lines, each containing either one or two dots. These are divided into four groups of four, called the 'Mothers.'

A chart showing geomancy and the corresponding signs of the zodiac

♈	⁞	Puer	♎	⁞	Puella
♉	⁞	Amissio	♏	⁞	Rubeus
♊	⁞	Albus	♐	⁞	Acquisitio
♋	⁞	Populus	♑	⁞	Carcer
♋	⁞	Via	♒	⁞	Tristitia
♌	⁞	Fortuna major	♓	⁞	Laetitia
♌	⁞	Fortuna minor	♌	⁞	Caput draconis
♍	⁞	Conjunctio	♌	⁞	Cauda draconis

The first group of four lines might look like this

odd number of dots	•
even number of dots	• •
odd number of dots	•
even number of dots	• •

This geomantic figure is named Amissio, meaning loss. The subsequent Mother figures are derived in the same way from the remaining lines and the results placed beside the first figure.

Let us suppose that the four generated Mother figures in this case happen to be Amissio (loss), Fortuna Major (great fortune), Puella (girl), and Fortuna Minor (lesser fortune). Immediately the diviner can derive a preliminary answer to his question: 'there will be a loss of some sort, followed by considerable luck which will come through a girl or woman connected with the proposed venture.'

The next step is to combine elements of the four Mother figures into four Daughter figures, and from these are derived four Nephew figures, which in turn produce two Witness figures. The combination of these last two geomantic figures produces the Judge figure, by means of which the diviner attempts to judge the outcome of the whole question. Suppose that the final outcome of these manipulations is:

• •
• • Albus
•
• •

This is considered a good figure, confirming the diviner's earlier conclusions. An added interpretation might be (from the planetary correspondence) that the venture will be mercurial and a little unstable.

The technique of geomancy does not need elaborate equipment, and can be practiced with limited preparation. It is easy to see why such a style of divination might have appealed to the Bedouin of the ninth century.

Modern practice lays more emphasis upon the astrological aspects of geomancy, but the practice is otherwise the same as it was more than 1,000 years ago.

STEPHEN SKINNER

FURTHER READING: Agrippa. Fourth Book of Occult Philosophy. (London, UK: Askin, 1978); W. Bascom. Ifa Divination. (Indianapolis, IN: Indiana University Press, 1969); F. Hartmann. The Principles of Astrological Geomancy. (London, UK: Rider, 1913); S. Skinner. Terrestrial Astrology. (London, UK: Routledge, Kegan Paul, 1980); S. Skinner. The Oracle of Geomancy. (New York, NY: Warner Destiny, 1977).

Edmund Gurney

A founder of the Society for Psychical Research (S. P. R.) and one of the most important pioneers in the scientific investigation of ostensibly paranormal phenomena, Edmund Gurney was born on March 23, 1847. He entered Trinity College, Cambridge, in 1866 as a Minor Scholar in Classics. His undergraduate career was prolonged, owing to spells of ill health, but he succeeded in being elected to a Trinity Fellowship in 1872.

Gurney was more interested in music than in classics, but after years of dogged application, he had to admit that he could never have been more than a moderately competent performer. However, he continued to reflect on the theory of music, and in 1880 published The Power of Sound; the great US psychologist William James (1842–1910) considered that when it appeared it was 'the most important work on aesthetics in the English language.'

Gurney decided to become a doctor and studied medicine partly in London and partly in Cambridge, from 1877 to 1881. Throughout his life he was intimately aware of, and unusually sensitive to, the sufferings of men and animals, and early in 1881 he abandoned medicine. In May 1881 he became a student at Lincoln's Inn in London, but within a year had abandoned his law studies. In 1877 he married Kate Sara Sibley. They had one child, a daughter, born in 1881.

The foundation of the S. P. R. in February 1882 supplied the occasion and the motive for the astonishing output of first-class work that he achieved, in the few years that remained to him. He was Honorary Secretary of the Society from October 1883 until his death in June 1888.

Gurney's main achievements, after the publication of the *Power of Sound*, were concerned with philosophical and ethical reflections, and with psychical research. The former are mostly collected in the first volume of his two-volume book *Tertium Quid*, containing an essay on 'The Nature of Evidence in Matters Extraordinary,' which is directly relevant to psychical research and it is probably still the best critical treatment of this fundamental topic. The main subjects in the other essays in this volume are Gurney's doctrine of pain in general, and the ethics of vivisection in particular; his contempt for the idealization of natural science and its practitioners, and for the optimism associated with it; and his grounds for thinking that survival of bodily death is at any rate abstractly possible.

Gurney's position may be summarized roughly as follows. He held that the notion of survival is not inconceivable, and that it is not so improbable as to be unworthy of further consideration. He himself had little if any de-

sire to survive. He realized that even if survival was a fact, things might possibly be as bad as, or even worse than, they would be if no one survived. But he felt certain that if no one survives, and there is therefore no possibility of the evils and injustices inevitable in this life being redressed, then the world is so predominantly bad that a reasonable man in a cool hour would desire the early and complete cessation of the human race.

Gurney's work in psychical research deals mainly with hypnotism and phantasms of the living. His research into hypnotism falls into two main

> A 'phantasm of the living' is experienced if, and only if, a person has a hallucinatory apparent perception as of seeing, hearing, or touching someone else . . .

divisions. The first is a study, theoretical and practical, of the purely psychological features of hypnotism, without regard to any paranormal phenomena that may be associated with it. The second is an experimental study of ostensibly paranormal features in connection with some cases of hypnosis, for example, in the telepathic induction of the hypnotic state, in community of sensation between operator and subject, and in some of the feats performed by subjects under hypnosis.

Overdose of Chloroform
Most of Gurney's experiments were done in Brighton, England, with a Mr. G. A. Smith as hypnotiser, and with subjects chosen by him. Smith had been a stage hypnotist, and he subsequently became Gurney's secretary and trusted assistant. There can be no doubt that he produced genuine deep hypnosis in certain subjects. But he had formerly been associated with a

man called Blackburn who, very much later when he mistakenly believed Smith to be dead, alleged publicly that they had at one time been cooperating in the production of fraudulent (non-hypnotic) phenomena, and this has cast a certain shadow on all experiments in which Smith played an essential part.

A book called *Phantasms of the Living* was published under the auspices of the S. P. R. in 1886. The authors were given as Edmund Gurney, F. W. H. Myers, and F. Podmore. Myers contributed the introduction and an important note in the second of the two volumes, and Podmore (1856–1910) gave invaluable help in collating and examining the evidence. All the rest of the book is due to Gurney.

The essential factual basis of the work is the reports of 357 spontaneous cases, for all of which the evidence is first-hand and is regarded by the authors as being of first-rate authority. Some idea of the labour involved in producing the book can be judged from the following facts. Gurney often spent eight or nine hours a day writing fifty to sixty letters in his own hand, and almost every living person who gave evidence concerning the 'phantasms' was personally interviewed by at least one of the three authors. The chief part of this delicate work fell on Gurney.

A 'phantasm of the living' is experienced if, and only if, a person has a hallucinatory apparent perception as of seeing, hearing, or touching someone else, who is at the time out of range of the first person's actual sense-perception, and if the latter is alive in the flesh at the time, or was alive very shortly before. Such an experience is classed as 'veridical' (that is, coinciding with realities) if, and only if, the actual state and situation at the time of the person appearing corresponds in considerable detail with the hallucination. Otherwise it is 'delusive.'

Stories of such experiences, alleged to have been veridical, have been common in all ages and places. Many of these are no doubt false. Others, which may well be true, may reasonably be ascribed to mere chance-coincidence, or explained by a combination of normal causes and unusual circumstances. The question is whether or not there are nevertheless a substantial number of cases that fall under neither of these heads; and, if so, what is the most plausible kind of paranormal explanation of them.

The authors of *Phantasms of the Living* concluded that there was, in the cases that they investigated, a substantial residuum of well-attested veridical experiences of the kind in question, the veridicality of which cannot reasonably be assigned to mere chance-coincidence, and cannot plausibly be explained by any combination of generally acknowledged normal causes. The most probable explanation of the veridicality of these is in terms of telepathic communication of experiences between the two people concerned.

The book gave, for the first time, a clear formulation of the questions at issue and an extremely acute and fair-minded discussion of each of them against a background of relevant experimental work, and of a large number of carefully scrutinized reports of spontaneous cases.

Edmund Gurney died in June 1889 at the age of 43 at the Royal Albion Hotel, Brighton, where he had taken a room for the night. The next day he was found dead, with a sponge bag pressed over his nose and mouth. At the subsequent inquest the jury returned the verdict that death had been accidental, and that it had been the result of an overdose of chloroform inhaled to relieve pain. Very naturally, from that day to this, there has been some suspicion that he committed suicide. There is no good reason to doubt the evidence on which the jury reached their verdict; and there is no positive evidence for the view that Gurney had some special reason for committing suicide. Nevertheless in view of his known temperament and his published opinions, suicide seems by no means unplausible.

C. D. BROAD

Haruspicy

Haruspicy is the practice of divination by the examination of animal entrails. In Etruscan society, it was the function of the *haruspices* or priests to undertake this task, specifically to examine the liver of sheep. In a pastoral economy, the welfare of the flock was key to the success of the community both

In divination there is a distinction between signs that are requested from the gods and those that are given voluntarily.

animal and human, so haruspicy may have had a practical origin that became formalized into religious practice; the appearance of the liver would indicate the health or otherwise of the animal. In divination there is a distinction between signs that are requested from the gods and those that are given voluntarily. Haruspicy belongs to the former category.

ELIZABETH LOVING

FURTHER READING: *Jean Mackintosh Turfa*. Divining the Etruscan world: The Brontoscopic Calendar and Religious Practice. *(Cambridge UK: Cambridge University Press, 2012).*

Horoscope

In astrology, a horoscope is a chart or diagram of the heavenly bodies showing the relative positions of the planets at a particular moment in time: given an exact time and place of birth, an astrologer casts an individual's horoscope from which deductions are made concerning the person's character and fortunes, and advice given on future courses of action. Horoscopes have long been a feature of the popular press to the extent that, during World War II, the authorities in Britain considered banning their publication on the grounds that the families of serving members of the armed forces might have their anxieties heightened by reading a negative horoscope. A report written at the time considered that although about two-thirds of the adult population read horoscopes only ten percent took them seriously and these individuals were probably of a 'neurotic type.' A suggestion from a horoscope that more protection from air raids would be gained by sheltering in hollows in the ground rather than in air raid shelters wisely appears to have been disregarded. In the years since then, the popularity of horoscopes appears to remain undiminished, to the extent that the weekend magazine supplement of a newspaper includes a horoscope for its readers. Predictably, the internet has also provided ready access to horoscopes.

ELIZABETH LOVING

Portrait of the English writer Aldous Huxley during a stay in Italy, 1958

Aldous Huxley

In his novel, *Brave New World*, Aldous Huxley (1894–1962) created a vision of a world where advanced medical science and technology have become instruments of genetic and social engineering, powerful tools in the hands of a global totalitarian state that controls every aspect of life. Every human need, whether shelter, food, occupation, recreation, or mood-altering drugs is supplied by an apparently beneficent government, but any attempt to question the system is forbidden. The family unit has been demolished, and words such as 'family,' 'mother' and 'romance' are considered obscenities as hangovers from ancient discredited systems. Children are brought up collectively in state-run nurseries, brainwashed and conditioned from infancy to fulfil the economic and social role decided for them by the state

according to a caste system. Every inconvenient and negative emotion is repressed, considered inappropriate in a society where the duty of all is to be happy, to be essentially unreal, inhuman. The words of one character, Bernard Marx, who questions the culture of material fulfilment and permanent 'happiness,' sum up the deadening and dehumanising ethos: 'I'd rather be myself,' he said, 'myself and nasty. Not somebody else, however jolly.'

His Life

Aldous Huxley was the third son of Leonard Huxley, a classics teacher, and his wife, Julia, whose uncle was the poet Matthew Arnold (1822–88). His grandfather was the distinguished biologist Thomas Huxley; a brother and half-brother both became eminent scientists. By all accounts the young Aldous was a precocious and introspective child. He was educated in a way that was common for boys from the middle and upper classes at

that date—a way that included living conditions of extreme austerity as well as a culture of institutional bullying and beatings from older boys and masters. He experienced the British public school system in its full and dangerous flowering. (In contrast to their name, these schools are expensive private institutions.) He was sent to his first boarding school at the age of nine. At age sixteen his sight was badly damaged by an eye infection, the damage so severe that he left school to be educated by private tutors and learned Braille, a system of reading for the visually impaired. This catastrophe may ultimately have saved his life as it exempted him from military service during World War One. His sight remained poor throughout his life but recovered sufficiently for him to read English at the University of Oxford during which time he was he was introduced to the circle of intellectuals and artists known as the Bloomsbury Group, which included

Virginia Woolf (1882–1941) and Bertrand Russell (1872–1970). One of the Bloomsbury haunts was Garsington Manor in Oxfordshire, an easy cycling distance from the university. Huxley was first invited to Garsington in November 1915 and it was here that he met his first wife, Maria Nys (1898–1955). Another member of the group, the novelist D. H. Lawrence (1885–1930), became a lifelong friend. Huxley's first book, a collection of poetry, was published in 1916.

The need to earn a living after graduation included a brief and unsatisfactory stint as a master at Eton College, probably the most renowned of the public schools. One of Huxley's pupils there was the young Eric Blair (1903–1950), later to be known as the novelist, George Orwell. Huxley was spared life as a schoolmaster by being offered employment on *The Athenaeum*, a literary magazine, and became drama critic for a newspaper, the *Westminster Gazette*. In November 1921, Huxley's first novel, *Crome Yellow*, was published. One of its characters, Mr. Scogan, emulated the theme that was to be developed so dramatically a few years later by Huxley, the idea that the human race could be manipulated and categorized into separate 'species' and trained to 'perform those functions that human beings of his variety are capable of performing.' In January 1923, Huxley was given a three-year contract by his publishers—he would receive £500 a year in return for two new novels. He and his wife left London for Italy, the start of what was to become an eventual permanent departure from England; from 1937 onward, Huxley and his family lived in the United States.

Terrifying Predictions

Brave New World was published in 1932. It proved to be an extraordinarily prescient and disturbing book. Huxley describes a world where certain elements have become a commonplace of the Western world in the twenty-first century—a world where the instant gratification of desire and the promotion of the self is no longer seen as moral weakness; where the power of the mass media and consumer consumption have created a form of enslavement through aspiration; where sexual activity is separated from emotional commitment and reproduction; where babies can be manufactured in test tubes; where increasing urbanization has meant greater separation from the natural world; where the 'reality' presented by filmmakers and digital games manufacturers has become for many a substitute for social interaction; where the ageing process itself is seen as abhorrent and to be avoided at all costs.

No other publication has been nearly as prophetic in talking about the controlling effects of a consumerist society. The concept of controlling populations through pleasure and distraction is effectively how much of Western society is run today. Just as the high-tech high-price development of sports is important to the culture of *Brave New World*, so rises the importance of video game culture in our own world. Consumerism and production of GDP is paramount in Huxley's futuristic envisioning, just as it is now: in *Brave New World*, Henry Ford is elevated to the status of a deity, the sign of the 'T' made at the mention of his name. Huxley warns as much against the consequences of unbridled consumerism as against the manipulation of science in a dystopian universe.

Of course, perhaps the most subversive parts of Huxley's novel remain unfulfilled: the banishment of the family unit, the raising of children by institution, and the participation in mandatory group sexual activities. Yet, with the advancements in technology, the society of today can be sexually active with minimal consequences, occasionally resulting in the lack of commitment shown by the various lovers in Huxley's novel. As more family planning technology has become available, many couples are planning simply not to have children, perhaps a precursor to the lack of parenthood in *Brave New World*.

Most of all, Huxley's projections of a world of pleasure with few repercussions, of castes, and of consumerism eerily echo the current state of the world today. Perhaps in time his prophetic novel will continue to come true, changing our society into something totally unrecognizable.

ELIZABETH LOVING

FURTHER READING: Sybille Bedford. Aldous Huxley: A Biography. Volume One: 1894–1939. *(London, UK: Chatto & Windus in association with Collins, 1973); Sybille Bedford.* Aldous Huxley: A Biography. Volume Two: 1939–1963. *(London, UK: Chatto & Windus in association with Collins, 1973); Nicholas Murray.* Aldous Huxley: An English Intellectual. *(New York, NY: Little, Brown, 2002).*

Jupiter

Ever since the development of astrology as a study in itself in the seventh century BC, Jupiter, the largest of the planets, has been supposed by astrologers to be the most kindly disposed of them, and for that reason is often spoken of in astrological literature as 'the greater benefic,' the lesser being Venus, which is smaller. The zodiacal sign ruled by Jupiter, even when he was still the father of the gods and not yet a planet, appears always to have been Sagittarius.

Jupiter as a planet is constantly associated with wealth, high position, getting one's own way, promotion, prosperity, and all forms of status.

Anyone who wants to choose a time to begin an undertaking, to make sure that it shall not go wrong, would be advised by an astrologer to pick a time when the moon is going to be in a strong 'good aspect' of Jupiter. Similarly, if he chooses a time when Jupiter is fortified (that is to say, when he is in a favourable position), there should be no financial difficulties.

Although the chief association of Jupiter is with money matters, he is also concerned with social position, so that any question connected with snobbery can always be answered by examining the aspects of Jupiter. He is also 'the greater benefic' in an entirely general way, and signifies success of any kind, including the recovery of health. Success is always thought to be indicated by the influence of a favourable planet, so even if one were setting out to commit a burglary, say, or any other crime, it would be prudent to try to have Jupiter on one's side. Even if this precaution did not lead to financial gain, it might bring luck to one's illegal enterprise by causing a policeman to look in the other direction at the critical moment.

The signs ruled by Jupiter are Sagittarius (the Archer), which is regarded as positive and masculine, and Pisces (the Fishes), which has been described as negative and feminine, though the sexes symbolically allotted to these two signs should not be taken too seriously. Both signs have a touch of that happy-go-lucky optimism that is one of the most characteristic gifts of Jupiter to his natives.

Typically, a person born under Jupiter will be good-looking, if not handsome; like those born under Leo, although to a lesser extent, he will have the dignity of a natural ruler. He knows what is due to him and expects to receive respect accordingly. He will probably have an impressive

manner and in consequence is likely to be elected to official positions in clubs and other organizations. Such men are often successful businessmen or heads of companies, for they like making money. They usually uphold the established order and their dress is conventionally respectable.

People whose horoscope is dominated by Jupiter in his less favourable position spend their lives betting but are unlikely to meet with much success. Looking on the bright side, however, they may well win a competition, be promoted unexpectedly, or meet with some other kind of unforeseen good fortune.

I Ching

Probably the oldest extant book in the world, the *I Ching* or *Book of Change* is certainly one of the most extraordinary. This abstruse Chinese classic is known to English readers by several names. *I Ching* (pronounced Ee Jing) is the official romanized Mandarin spelling, while Yee King, Yik King and so on are spellings representing certain Chinese dialects. Often

> *It is indeed quite possible that the enigmas are intentional, that the* I Ching, *like many other mystical works, was written in a secret language whose significance was revealed only to initiates.*

called the *Book of Changes*, its title is better rendered in the singular form; either would suit the Chinese characters equally well, but its authors were concerned with the principle of everlasting change that governs the exquisitely balanced universal harmony; the transient individual changes that result are of secondary importance. Although this ancient work has long been used primarily for divination, it

is revered also as a source of religious wisdom and as containing in a highly cryptic form the quintessence of an ancient philosophy.

For well over 2,000 years, philosophers have been debating the purpose and meaning of the *I Ching*. The discrepancies in the various English versions are not inappropriate indication of the profundity of the Chinese text. Its hoary antiquity, its extreme terseness (remarkable even for an ancient Chinese text), and the mystical nature of its contents all combine to make it highly enigmatic.

Chinese scholars who have devoted whole decades to its study disagree on many fundamental points; and the scores of Chinese commentaries, both ancient and modern, are similarly at variance with one another. It is indeed quite possible that the enigmas are intentional, that the *I Ching*, like many other mystical works, was written in a secret language whose significance was revealed only to initiates.

Deserving Fifty Years' Study

That it was immensely important in ancient times is apparent from what Confucius (551 BC–479 BC) has to say about it. He tells us that the leather thongs binding the tablets on which his copy was inscribed 'thrice wore out' from constant use and that, could his life have been prolonged, he would have given fifty years to studying it, thereby perhaps becoming a man 'without grave fault.' What use he made of it is not recorded. While he may have loved it wholly for its deep insight into the mysterious workings of the universe, he may also have esteemed it as a practical book of divination. What is certain is that it came to be included among the 'Four Books' and 'Five Classics,' which for nearly 2,000 years were required study for Chinese candidates taking part in

A Chinese man practicing divination using *I Ching* sticks c. 1955

of the universe is a limitless, imperceptible void—T'ai Chi, the Absolute. In it, all objects have their being and each owes its transient individuality to a particular combination of Yin (negative) and Yang (positive).

A system of diagrams illustrating this concept is attributed to Fu Hse, who is said to have lived 30,000 years ago. Even assuming that he never existed or that so vast a stretch of time is a fanciful exaggeration, the fact remains that the diagrams are perhaps more ancient than any others in the world. Probably these diagrams had already existed for thousands of years when, if the traditional belief is accepted, King Wen (c. 1150 BC) and his son Duke Chou provided each of them with an explanatory text. Modern scholars believe the text to have been produced at a later period, but it cannot have been much later, as Confucius regarded it as belonging to high antiquity. This text, coupled with a commentary written either by Confucius or by some of his disciples, forms the work as it now stands. Since Confucius lived some 2,500 years ago, the main text must be somewhere between 2,500 and 3,100 years old and the commentary just about 2,500.

The main body of the book consists of sixty-four sections, each headed by a different diagram in the form of a hexagram (a figure made up of six broken or unbroken lines). The hexagram is followed by a short text attributed to King Wen. Here is an example: 'Integrity. Sublime success. Righteous persistence brings reward. Those opposed to righteousness meet with harm. It is not favourable to have any goal (or destination) at this time.' Next follows a terse Confucian commentary that amplifies the meaning of the text and usually explains how it came to be derived from the hexagram. Then comes a brief note on the symbolism and its implications: 'This hexagram symbolizes thunder

the all important Imperial Civil Service Examinations.

There have been stern scholars who believed that so lofty a classic was shockingly besmirched by being put to use by soothsayers. For all that, it is certain that it has been used for divination since before the days of Confucius. Certainly it owes much of its reputation—now swiftly extending to the West—to the surprising accuracy claimed for its predictions. Today in China, Japan, Korea, and Vietnam—the four countries where scholars readily understand the Chinese script—there are countless people, ranging from pious mystics to street fortune tellers, who peer into a future revealed by means of its curious diagrams.

The present Chinese government, in its campaign against 'ancient superstitions,' may well have banned its use

but it would not be surprising to learn that Communist generals and administrators still secretly seek its advice. They will know, for example, that in seventeenth century Japan, Yamaga (1622–85) built up the Samurai into the finest fighting force in Asia by teaching them a type of strategy that accorded with an interpretation of the *I Ching*. Though it is not a military book, it teaches how all activities benefit from being made to harmonize with the universal cycles of everlasting but orderly change, involving advance and retreat, progress and retrogression, each in due season.

A System of Diagrams

The *I Ching* is the product of a religion that predates both Confucianism and Taoism and goes back to the very beginning of Chinese civilization. According to its teaching, the womb

rolling across the whole Earth: from it all things receive their integrity. The ancient rulers gave abundant and timely nourishment to all.' So much for the hexagram as a whole. Next come notes on each of its separate lines, attributed to Duke Chou: 'Line 1. Moving onward with integrity brings good fortune.' Each note is followed by a Confucian commentary on the line text: What is willed comes to pass.'

Obviously a book containing so many sections, each composed of terse aphorisms, does not make for smooth reading. There are readers who, believing that an inner significance relates the parts to one another, read and re-read the book from cover to cover as regularly as devout Christians read the Bible. But mostly it is read in connection with the act of divination.

The soothsayer (who may be anyone at all) burns incense, prostrates himself thrice before the silk-wrapped book and, by a complicated manipulation of yarrow stalks (a plant also used for divination in the West) or by tossing three coins six times, receives in answer to the question in his or her mind one hexagram—or in many cases two of them, with the emphasis directed to one particular line.

As there are sixty-four hexagrams, each capable of giving seven answers (either with reference to one of the six lines or without emphasis on any of them), the total number of basic answers is 448. As two hexagrams are often drawn and more than one line may be stressed, the number of possible answers is much larger. They are considered sufficient to take care of any eventuality, though in one sense all of them are variations on just four themes—proceed energetically, proceed with caution, stop, or go back.

In another sense this is a gross oversimplification, for almost every word in the text, the commentary, the note

on symbolism, and the individual line or lines particularly stressed is carefully weighed for its bearing on the question and on the circumstances governing both question and inquirer. Because of the seemingly mechanical means of obtaining a hexagram, this method could be dismissed as fortune telling of the most arbitrary sort, were it not for at least two special characteristics.

First and foremost, the *I Ching* does not regard the future as fixed, so that ordinary fortune telling is out of the question. The answers tell the inquirer not what will happen, but how he or she should act. Second, the book's high moral tone makes it quite useless to people who intend to act from selfish motives. The answer 'cautious progress' does not mean that the inquirer will act in that way, which is what a fortune teller would be likely to imply, nor does it mean that to progress cautiously would be to the inquirer's immediate material advantage.

What it does mean is that, under the circumstances, it would be morally right to do so and therefore it would redound to his ultimate good and perhaps also to his immediate advantage, in the higher sense.

However, where impersonal objects, events, or forces are involved, there is indeed a powerful element of prediction, for it is assumed that normally all things, unless disturbed by deluded man, progress in accordance with the cycle of events to which each belongs. Yet even where such predictions do suggest fortune telling, the moral tone of the book still sets it quite apart from what is usually understood by divination. Again and again there are references to 'the Superior Man,' whom the inquirers are expected to take as their model.

The one seemingly crude aspect of the whole process is that, mathematically speaking, the manipulation of the yarrow stalks or of the three coins produces results apparently

Stone-texture background with the *I Ching* symbol

just as random as those that would be achieved by the ordinary tossing of a coin. However, Western sceptics who feel inclined to dismiss such divination contemptuously may be deterred by C. G. Jung's preface to Richard Wilhelm's German translation of the *I Ching*, in which it is apparent that the eminent Swiss psychologist was convinced of the value of its predictions. Unfortunately his explanation of 'how it works' is less satisfactory than his description of 'what it does.' One gathers he had faith in the *I Ching's* ability to foretell many of our actions quite accurately, and attributed this ability to the fact that the images it employs relate to the collective unconscious and make a powerful, though perhaps imperceptible appeal, to us to act or expect things to happen in a certain way. His attempt to explain the mechanics of the oracle is by no means clear. The traditional explanation is that what happens to the yarrow sticks or coins while held in or falling from the inquirer's hands is not at all accidental, but bears a relationship to the cycle of events to which the answer belongs.

As it is impossible to demonstrate such a relationship, there will always be scoffers—Chinese as well as Western. However, doubters open-minded enough to persist for a while in using the *I Ching* are, it is said, often astounded by the accuracy of the answers and by their sometimes extraordinary appositeness to the question and to the surrounding circumstances.

According to a commonly accepted belief, it does not take long to discover that the responses are random or even discourteous when the act of divination is performed for fun; whereas they are most likely to be strikingly correct when 'diviners' act in all seriousness and when, while putting questions and interpreting the answers, they allow their minds to enter a state similar to that reached in the

early stages of Buddhist or yogic meditation. From this one may infer that Jung (1875–1961) was perhaps right in supposing that the symbols and words that constitute the oracle convey messages directly to the mind, at a level beyond everyday consciousness.

It is apparent that the *Book of Change* is wholly concerned with the attainment of inner serenity and of harmony with man's surroundings and not at all with material success, except to the extent that, in a universe governed by moral law, material success may well be the ultimate result of righteousness. There are Chinese philosophers and mystics who read it for its spiritual counsel, using it less often (if at all) for divination, and they appear to be untroubled by the disjointed nature of the aphorisms. Perhaps they really are able to discern a sublime pattern hidden from ordinary readers. Chinese tradition claims that the book reveals the secret workings of the universe; also, that its careful study would lead a man to live a blameless life largely free from frustration, because all his thoughts and actions would be in serene accord with the mystical order of being that governs the activities of the ants and the bees, the smooth progress of the seasons and the majestic movements of the stars.

A Variety of Versions

Of several available translations in English, Legge's was produced about a century ago, under the inevitable handicaps of those days—lack of dictionaries and reference books, and of learned teachers fluent enough in English to check what he wrote. It is an extremely literal translation and thereby doubly puzzling. Richard Wilhelm's, rendered into English from his German version, is on the whole excellent; it is marred by a few sentences of which the sense is far from clear, but that is perhaps to be expected in a book designed for use as an oracle. His notes and explanatory chapters are most valuable. Blofeld's rendering is less scholarly and has much less detailed explanatory material; it is a popular version with introductory chapters specially written to make the book's use as an oracle as straightforward as possible. A comparison of all three translations reveals discrepancies on every page and there are research scholars, both Chinese and Western, whose interpretations agree with none of those published. Fortunately, faultless accuracy matters somewhat less than in most other books; there is often so little connection between the terse sentences that a mistake made in one is not likely to perpetuate itself in those that follow.

A remarkable observation frequently heard is that all three versions produce satisfactory results when used for divination. This is evidence in support of Jung's theory that the symbols make a direct communication to the unconscious mind. If this is so, it would seem that errors in the translation (and some small errors or divergencies in the various Chinese editions) are, as it were, by-passed.

JOHN BLOFELD

Each *I Ching* symbol has its own meaning. This Chun symbol represents a new shoot struggling to burst through the earth in the first days of spring.

Using the Yarrow Stalks

The traditional method involves the use of fifty sticks, preferably stalks of yarrow, a plant with sacred connotations, which may be found growing widely on common land in China.

1. One stick is set aside, and the remaining forty-nine are divided into two heaps with the right hand.

2. From the right-hand heap, one stick is taken and inserted between the ring and little fingers of the left hand.

3. From the left-hand heap, four sticks at a time are put aside until four or less remain; these remaining sticks are inserted between the ring and middle fingers of the left hand.

4. From the right-hand heap, four sticks are set aside in the same way, the residue being inserted between the middle and index fingers of the left hand.

The total number of sticks held in the left hand will now be either five or nine (1+1+3, 1+2+2, 1+3+1, or 1+4+4). These sticks are set aside.

The remaining sticks (either totalling forty-four or forty) are mixed and divided into two heaps, and picked up according to the same principles as before. In this operation, the total number of sticks taken will be either four or eight (1+1+2, 1+2+1, 1+3+4, or 1+4+3). They are set aside.

The operation is repeated a third time with the remaining sticks (which may total variously forty, thirty-six, or thirty-two), and these again yield a total of four or eight sticks.

Genghis Khan (c. 1162–1227) consulting his destiny (from *Grandeur and Supremacy of Peking*) by Alphonse Hubrecht (1928)

The combination of the three numbers of sticks picked provides one of four kinds of line, which can be represented as follows:

5+4+4	—0—	'old' yang line 'ritual number' 9
9+8+8	—x—	'old' yin line 'ritual number' 6
5+8+8		
9+8+4	———	'young' yang line 'ritual number' 7
9+4+8		
5+4+8		
5+8+4	—— ——	'young' yin line 'ritual number' 8
9+4+4		

This is the first (the lowest) line of the hexagram. The successive five lines are generated in the same way, to give one of the possible sixty-four (that is, 2x2x2x2x2x2, since each line is either yang or yin) hexagrams.

When the hexagram is made entirely of 'young' lines, its interpretation is limited to the judgment of King Wen, the Confucian commentary on the judgment, and the note on the symbolism of the hexagram.

However, 'old' lines must be thought of as 'moving,' or developing into their opposites. The latter part of the text for any hexagram is devoted to an explanation by Duke Chou of the significance of these 'old' lines, usually identified (in English translation) as—for example—'nine in the second place' or 'six at the top.'

Finally, these 'old' lines are envisaged as mutating into their opposites: an old yin into a young yang, and an old yang into a young yin. This results in a second hexagram, for which the judgment, commentary and symbolism should also be read.

The ritual that has to be gone through to generate a hexagram in this traditional way is time-consuming, and those who regularly consult the I Ching usually employ one of two quicker methods: coins or painted wands.

Ancient Chinese coins had an inscribed face and a plain face. If three coins are tossed on to a table, and a value of two given to the inscribed side and three to the plain side (or

respectively to the 'tails' and 'heads'), the total will be either six, seven, eight, or nine, corresponding to the 'ritual' numbers ascribed to the four kinds of line above. It is therefore a matter of moments—six tosses of the three coins—to generate a hexagram, complete with young and moving lines.

As an alternative, six flat wands may be painted solid black on one side (to represent a yang line) and with a white band on the other to represent a yin line. These are wrapped in a mat or cloth, which is then unrolled on a table so that the painted wands immediately form a hexagram. There is no way, however, of identifying 'old' or 'young' lines by this method.

The sixty-four hexagrams are regarded as being made up of two trigrams, of which there are eight in all. These each have a number of different symbolic connotations, so that each hexagram represents a combination of two meanings.

For example, the third hexagram, Chun, the symbol of initial difficulty, is made up of the lower trigram Chen, representing thunder and awakening, and the upper trigram K'an, representing water and obstruction. The Chinese ideogram for Chun is a picture of a new shoot, struggling to burst its way through the earth in the first days of spring. King Wen's judgment of this hexagram is:

'Initial difficulties are followed by success and prosperity, the result of acting firmly and correctly. Nothing should be attempted unless there is a possibility of success, and it is advantageous to appoint those who can provide appropriate assistance.'

The symbolic significance of Chun attributed to Confucius is that of a raincloud over thunder: the superior man therefore is inspired to put his affairs into proper order.

The Duke of Chou's explanation for any 'old' lines in this hexagram are as follows:

In the bottom line, nine signifies:
Obstacles and hesitation before action.
Perseverance is rewarding.

In the second line, six signifies:
Difficulties increase.
One of the horses breaks free from her wagon.
But he is not a highwayman,
He is one who wishes her to be his wife.
The chaste maiden rejects his advances,
And waits ten years before she bears children.

In the third line, six signifies:
He hunts deer in the forest without a guide,
And loses his way.
The superior man, understanding the situation,
Gives up the chase.
To continue brings humiliation.

In the fourth line, six signifies:
The horses break from the wagon.
She seeks the assistance of her suitor.
The time is auspicious for going forward.

In the fifth line, nine signifies:
Obstacles to generosity.
A little perseverance brings success.
Much perseverance brings misfortune.

In the sixth line, six signifies:
The horses drag the wagon back.
Tears of blood are wept.

It will be seen that, depending upon how many of the lines are moving lines, it is possible for this hexagram to mutate into any one of the remaining sixty-four, providing a further, complementary, interpretation.

Ch'ien ☰	Heaven	Sky	Ice cold	Early winter	Creative active strong light	Father	Head	Horse	Purple	Northwest
Tui	Pool	Marsh	Mist rain	Autumn	Joyful plaesurable	Youngest daughter concubine	Mouth	Sheep	Blue	West
Li	Fire	Lightning	Sun	Summer	Clear beautiful depending clinging	Middle daughter	Eye	Pheasant	Yellow	South
Ch'en	Thunder		Thunder	Spring	Active moving arousing	Eldest son	Foot	Dragon	Orange	East
Sun	Wind	Wood		Early summer	Gentle penetrating	Eldest daughter	Thigh	Cock	White	Southeast
K'an	Water	Cloud a pit the abyss	Moon	Winter	Labouring enveloping dangerous melancholy	Middle son	Ear	Boar pig	Red	North
K'en	Mountain		Thunder	Early spring	Stubborn immovable perverse	Youngest son	Hand fingers	Dog	Blue	Northeast
K'un	Earth		Heat	Early autumn	Receptive passive	Mother	Belly	Cow mare	Black	Southwest

The *I Ching* is probably the oldest book in the world. These are the eight trigrams of Fu Hse

The language in which the *I Ching* is written, and the difficulties posed by its translation, have been the cause of considerable misunderstanding in the West. It is not a predictive text. It is firmly based in Taoist philosophy, and the advice that it gives is much more along the lines of 'if you do this, then that will result.' The 'superior man' who features constantly in the commentary is not a Nietzschean *ubermensch* but a sensible person, male or female, who is prepared to accept this advice. Duke Chou's often enigmatic explanations reflect the organization of the Chinese state ten centuries BC, and their interpretation today must be performed with intuition, since they can no longer be taken literally. When these reservations are properly understood, the *I Ching* remains a valuable text for the present-day enquirer.

BRIAN INNES

FURTHER READING: Henry Wei. Authentic I-Ching. *(Newcastle, CA: Newcastle Publishing, 1987); James Legge. The I-Ching. (Mineola, NY: Dover, 1963); John Blofeld. The Book of Change. (NSW, Australia: Allen & Unwin, 1968).*

Leo

The sun is in Leo, the fifth sign of the zodiac, between July 23 to 24 and August 22 to 24, the period soon after the summer solstice when its heat and strength are at their height. As a symbol of splendour and pride, the lion was the 'natural signification' of kings and rulers. Those born 'under the Lion' often have a lordly bearing, and expect to be treated with the respect due to their status. Whether or not their position merits respect, they expect it, for they are confident of their own worth. They are natural leaders, and they love everything big in life.

It is impossible to overawe Leos, for they are only impressed by older persons or by those who are more powerful. They like titles and honours, and often reveal their feeling of importance by the wearing of ostentatious jewelry, although it seldom occurs to them that such adornments could be interpreted as a sign of vanity, and it would be uncharacteristic of Leos to give up using any title that they have earned.

They are brave in an emergency, but in some threatening situations they may appear too casual, for they do not readily believe that they are vulnerable to danger. When they are generous, it may not be genuine unselfishness, but simply a means to boost their own reputation. The Roman poet Manilius (48 BC–AD 20) wrote that Leo will spend on himself any wealth that he may acquire, and that he is too selfish to make a good trustee.

Leo is one of the more religious signs and in a temporal sense, too; typical Leos tend to respect those in power and authority. Their sympathies are always more likely to be with the established order than with the revolutionaries. In general appearance they are not often extravagant, for they are likely to think it more important to be conventionally respectable than to

Illustration from a copy of Al-Sufi's *The Book of Fixed Stars*. This copy was made in Prague in the fifteenth century and shows the detail of Leo. Held in the Royal Canonry of Premonstratensiens, Strahov, Prague

people with the sun in Leo have found an important career in the direction of social work and similar responsibilities. In the arts, typical careers are as orchestral conductors, organists, classical actors, or mural painters—those involving anything truly grand in scale or conception.

The ascendant in Leo is traditionally associated with a stature above average, a big-boned, and well-built body, lean in youth but tending to fleshiness in middle life. The head is big and round, and the sight is quick; and the carriage is upright and at times almost stately. In ill health the sight may be affected, and there is a tendency to suffer from heart disease, pains in the back, and lung troubles.

The moon in Leo is associated with a desire for self-dramatization. Everything has to be played out as if on a big stage, and everyone else must be drawn in as supporting players. Although this can prove almost unbearable, it is redeemed by the fact that it is genuine: such people need to be admired, to love, and be loved. They tend to dominate their children, insisting that they should be well behaved, this characteristic being reflected in their homes, which are usually clean and well kept.

Libra

The seventh sign of the zodiac is Libra, and the sun is in this sign between September 23 or 24 and October 23 or 24. When the sun enters Libra it is the midpoint of the zodiacal year, the end of summer when all the hard work that has gone into the first six months is balanced by the gathering in of the harvest produce, to be followed by its gradual consumption through the ensuing six months.

And once the harvest has been brought in, and the grapes crushed

dress in an ostentatious manner.

Trusting and good-natured, Leos may suffer disillusionment when someone in whom they have had faith does not come up to expectation, but usually they bring out the best in others, and frequently thrive in adversity. They are generally practical and relatively hard-headed: they can go straight to the heart of a problem, are capable of long-lasting effort, and can carry out ambitious schemes to their conclusion, particularly when in the command of others. They have strong willpower and a marked degree of self-control, and setbacks seem only to spur them on to greater effort.

Persons born under Leo are usually interested—and often involved—in politics, but nevertheless they are not duplicitous, and prefer everything to be brought out into the open. They like to delegate the less important aspects of life to subordinates, but

occasionally may be deceived, for their minds are straightforward rather than devious, and they are not as perceptive as they would like to think. Leos are self-confident, and in consequence an obvious choice for any job demanding leadership. Usually they are extremely robust and do not tire easily, but may at times be mentally and physically lazy. They may also be somewhat insensitive for, never having admitted weakness, they do not understand what it feels like to be at the mercy of someone else. Among other faults should be included a tendency to snobbish superiority, and considerable obstinacy in upholding as traditional what others may regard as absurd or out-of-date beliefs.

Leo natives tend naturally to take charge of others. In the political field, Napoleon (1769–1821), Benito Mussolini (1883–1945), or Fidel Castro (b. 1926), are typical Leo subjects; and

to make the wine, it is time to relax briefly, to enjoy the last of the summer sun and celebrate the successful culmination of labour.

So, by tradition, Librans are great lovers of pleasure and beauty, and fully appreciate elegance and harmony. In excess this can lead them into extravagance and indulgence beyond their means, but their natural politeness and good-fellowship serve to disarm those who might otherwise criticize them. Indeed, in ancient times they were held to be extremely trustworthy, those who could be allowed to handle other peoples' money, even if they had none themselves.

The Sign of the Balance

Libra is the sign of the balance, and the ability to compare things and reach an impartial judgment upon them is characteristic of those born with the sun in this sign. As a concomitant, they dislike argument, because it seems to them that the true merit of whatever is being discussed is obvious, and that there is no alternative worthy of consideration.

This can lead Librans to believe that they are the only competent judges of what is best in fashion or aesthetics, and at its worst such a belief can result in criticism of everything they see. As the English occultist Herbert T. Waite put it: 'their curiosity seems insatiable, and they will be found in their element at every sale, bazaar, church service, wedding, or funeral of note, observing and comparing every detail of their surroundings, always seeking to draw conclusions; fashion, ceremony, convention, family histories, and social scandal seem to be the breath of life to the Libran.'

Libra is ruled by Venus, and the best Libran type is full of charm, courtesy, and generosity—which frequently may be exercised in amorous pursuits. However, the Libran nature is flexible and easily swayed by feelings, and

likely to be affected by the necessity to please others. When the critical faculty is suppressed, Librans' attempts to satisfy everyone may sometimes make them appear rather dull and characterless, and in a bad situation the necessity to strike a balance can cause them to degenerate into fixed conventionality and fear of breaking away from it.

In general they do not like taking the initiative, preferring to have some rule or precedent that they can quote before making their judgments. But in this respect they can be very valuable, for they will always try to ensure that any justified claim is satisfied.

A Talent for Design

Libran natives reveal considerable intellectual ability, and can go far in their profession, but they seldom take a deep interest in subjects outside it. They show great talent as fashion designers, interior decorators, or show-business managers; poets, painters, novelists, and composers are also among Librans. Other typical careers are as lawyers or antique dealers: Librans often become expert in the details and origins of collectors' items.

Traditionally, the ascendant in Libra indicates a well-formed body, of average stature or above; the face tends

to be rounded, with a good complexion, even beautiful; and the eyes are full of feeling. The physical constitution of the average Libran is basically strong, but the health can be impaired by indulgence in excessive eating or drinking, which may result in kidney or bladder trouble.

Those who have the moon in Libra in their horoscope are likely to show an excessive tendency to be swayed by the opinions of others. They dislike extravagant display, and constantly seek to avoid unfriendly relationships.

Lots

It is said that when Jesus was dying on the cross, the Roman soldiers on duty at the execution cast lots to decide which of them should have his tunic (John, chapter 19.24). After the traitor Judas had killed himself, when his place among the apostles needed to be filled, the two leading candidates were Joseph, Justus, and Matthias. Lots were cast to decide between them and the lot fell on Matthias, which was taken as a sign that he was God's choice (Acts, chapter 1.23). Casting lots, in other words, is a way of reaching a decision that is felt to be fair—

Libra in a carving on the Palazzo Ducale in Venice, Italy

because it is beyond the participants' control—but which is also regarded as a way of ascertaining the wishes of a higher power. A person's 'lot in life,' it is implied, is apportioned by fate or the gods or whatever powers may be, and someone who 'draws the short straw' is felt to be the victim of fate rather than chance.

Making decisions by lot had a long history in Judaism, going far back beyond the time of Jesus. Land was divided among the tribes of Israel by lot (Numbers, chapter 26.55). The ritual of the Day of Atonement involved taking two goats and choosing one of them by lot to be the scapegoat, which symbolically carried the sins of the people and was sent out into the wilderness to die (Leviticus, chapter 16).

The high priests of Israel were equipped with the mysterious objects called the *Urim* and *Thummim*, which were used to divine the will of God in some way akin to casting lots. In Saul's time, the Urim and Thummim were used to divine who had sinned and attracted God's anger. The possibilities were whittled down until Saul eventually said: 'Cast the lot between me and my son Jonathan,' and the lot fell against Jonathan, who had sinned secretly by disobeying an order (1 Samuel, chapter 14).

The Urim and Thummim were kept in a pouch attached to the high priest's breastplate and later writers identified them as twelve stones, which they said shone with light to give a positive or favourable answer, but remained dark if the answer was negative. It is clear that when lots were cast, it was God who was believed to determine the

outcome, not chance. 'The lot is cast into the lap, but the decision is wholly from the Lord,' (Proverbs, chapter 16.33).

A related, but more complicated, type of divination mentioned in the Old Testament (and known as rhabdomancy) involved throwing sticks into the air and watching how they fell, or similarly observing the flight of an arrow. This has been practiced in many parts of the world. It is said that Salisbury Cathedral in England

> *So simple is the principle of casting lots, and so universal the need for help in making difficult decisions, that they have been used everywhere.*

stands where it does because, when the decision was taken to build it, an archer fired an arrow into the air and the foundation stone was laid on the spot where the arrow landed. This was a way of leaving the exact choice of site to God.

Going by the Book

Another traditional Jewish method of divination was to ask a child to quote a verse of the scriptures at random or say which verses had been studied in school that day, and then draw one's own conclusions. Or a passage could be picked out at random from the Bible or one of its books—the Psalms, for example—and taken as an answer to a question previously formulated in the mind.

The Greeks used verses taken from the *Iliad* and the *Odyssey*, while the Romans preferred to take theirs from Virgil's *Aeneid*. Such verses were inscribed on a number of discs that were strung together, called *sortes* (from the Latin *serere*, to string). Their popularity led to the title *Sores*

being added to the many names bestowed upon the goddess Fortuna.

At the famous oracular center of Praeneste, the sortes were inscribed upon tablets carved from sacred oak trees and housed in a chest or ark made of hallowed olive wood. To ascertain the ruling of the presiding deity, the inquirer received a tablet drawn from this chest by an acolyte, which could be done only on certain days of the year. The prophetic words found upon the tablet were then made clear or interpreted by a learned and pious priest. If the prediction proved to be favourable and was eventually fulfilled, it was the custom for the satisfied inquirer to present a votive offering to the temple of the goddess. Later, in Imperial Rome, the Virgilian *Sortes* of the Latin augurs were one of the most renowned and successful methods employed to divine the decrees of fate.

The high reputation that Virgil (90 BC–70 BC) enjoyed as a master magician and a prophet of Christ's birth —rather than as a poet—in Europe in the Middle Ages gave the *Aeneid* a long life as an oracle. However, Christians generally preferred to use the Bible; they would open it at random and prick out a sentence with the eyes shut to determine a course of action. Prayer books and hymn books were also employed. On especially solemn occasions the clergy would fast for two or three days, before putting a copy of the New Testament or a Mass-book on the altar of a church and using it to gain divine guidance. In the fourth century St. Martin was chosen as Bishop of Tours by this method.

In Muslim countries the Koran has been used in the same way and Buddhist scriptures are so employed in the East. In West Africa lots are used to select written verses that are considered significant.

These are not really random methods, of course, for behind all forms of divination is the conviction that all phenomena provide clues to the underlying pattern, and so the future events, of the universe. So simple is the principle of casting lots, and so universal the need for help in making difficult decisions, that they have been used everywhere. Geomancy has developed from simple methods of divination from the patterns made by scattered pebbles or grains of sand, while the greatly respected Chinese oracle, the *I Ching*, depends on the casting of sticks or—the method that has become more popular recently—coins.

In the *Nihongi*, the Japanese cosmological 'bible,' it is recounted how certain discontented princes in the year AD 658 sought to divine the future of their treasonous plans by drawing slips of paper that had been magically inscribed. Such a proceeding followed intoned incantations and the making of offerings to propitiatory spirits. Taking this book as the foundation for his divinatory art, the celebrated medieval Japanese seer Taka Shima Kaemon made prognostications with astonishingly accurate results. In Japan he is still held in high esteem, and many a modern politician or business man there consults those sages who carry on the tradition said to be transmitted from him, through his successors, to this day.

Peeling the Bark
Medieval Jews would peel the bark from one side of a piece of wood, but leave it on the other. The smooth, peeled side was called 'the woman' and the rough side 'the man.' The wood was thrown twice in the air. If it fell with 'the man' uppermost the first time and 'the woman' the second, that was a good sign, if the reverse it was a bad. Falling the same way twice was considered noncommittal.

Tibetan tradition used pebbles, coins, ears of grain, dice, or twigs as lots and many people carried a booklet with them that explained the meaning of different patterns.

In sub-Saharan Africa a way of casting lots uses the odd, even gruesome, collection of objects in the diviner's basket or bag. They are thrown down and conclusions are drawn from the patterns they make or the proximity of one object to another. The object that lands in the middle or one that falls by itself is considered very significant.

A modern method of divination from dice, which is not intended to be taken too seriously, is shown below. Choose a question from the list, or make up a question of your own. Concentrate on it while shaking two dice and throwing them within a circle that has been traced on the top of a table. Add the two numbers revealed. Then throw again, adding these numbers to the former. With this total consult the list of answers.

To seek to understand the supposed value of decisions or predictions arrived at by the casting of lots, it is necessary to abandon the Western theory of causality and to embrace what C. G. Jung (1875–1961) spoke of as 'synchronicity.' Cause and effect express the evolutionary aspect of both physical and psychological phenomena, while synchronicity stresses the random, the variant, the unique.

FURTHER READING: W. R. and L. R. Gibson. The Psychic Sciences. (New York, NY: Pocket Books, 1968); C. G. Jung. Synchronicity: An Acausal Connecting Principle. (London, UK: Routledge & Kegan Paul, 1972).

Destiny from the Dice
A simple method of divination from dice. Choose a question from the list below (or make up one of your own). Concentrate on it while shaking two dice and throwing them in a circle traced on a table. Add the two numbers shown, throw again, and add the second total to the first. With the combined total consult the list of answers.

QUESTIONS	ANSWERS	
Shall I fall in love?	4	Yes, if you are unselfish
Will happiness be mine?	5	No, if you are not prudent
Will danger threaten?	6	Yes, think of trees and gardens
Will I find what is lost?	7	Yes, if you rely on yourself
Shall I gain my wish?	8	Yes, if you co-operate
Will I be successful?	9	Yes, if you seek only the best
Will the debts be paid?	10	No, if you make difficulties
Is good fortune on the way?	11	Chance it
Will I get the expected letter?	12	If you are sincere
Must I wait for bad news?	13	Only if you distrust words
Must I wait for good news?	14	Of course, but make sure to conquer
Will I be found out?	15	Only if you insist
Am I being betrayed?	16	If you are yourself
Shall I try another profession?	17	Of course
Does my beloved love me?	18	If you work hard
Should I go to law?	19	Await a message
Can I trust my colleagues?	20	Only if you are very discreet
Should I move house?	21	Not if you refuse to take risks
Will I go on a journey?	22	Certainly, but change your habits
Am I to be married soon?	23	In an unlikely place or an unlikely way
Will I love more than once?	24	No, unless you are charitable.
Will I make him/her happy?		
Will I be rich?		
Will I have children?		

The Mayan calendar is famous worldwide for the misinterpretation of its meaning—that the calendar foretells the end of the world on December 21, 2012.

the zero point—the Long Count.

The calendar not only provided an orderly representation of events in time, but also indicated which days might be deemed auspicious or otherwise. The calendar was not only a measurement system but also an indication of good or bad fortune.

A popular misconception in recent years was that the date December 21, 2012 would herald a global change or catastrophe as it marked the end of a cycle in the Mayan Calendar. This was held to be a misrepresentation and scholars pointed out that there was no evidence that the Mayans had forecast the end of the world on this date.

ELIZABETH LOVING

FURTHER READING: William L. Fash. Scribes, Warriors and Kings: The City of Copán and the Ancient Maya. *(London, UK: Thames & Hudson, 1993).*

Mercury

The planet Mercury is not often seen with the naked eye, for it is never more than 28 degrees from the sun, and therefore seldom emerges from the golden glow of dusk or dawn. It is the smallest of the planets, and closely dependent on its parent, so it is inevitably associated with children. Childish vices—lying, fraud, and thieving, for instance—as well as childlike virtues such as ingenuous charm, are also attributed to Mercury. It is possible that masochists (using the word in a general sense to describe people who enjoy being treated severely as if by a stern parent) may be under the planet's influence.

Despite its childish qualities, simplicity was never a characteristic of this planet, for it was thought to influence the entire field of education, including all types of learning. Intellectual brilliance, quick-wittedness, and scho-

The Mayan Calendar

The ability to mark the passage of time was one of the distinguishing features of Mesoamerican societies that reached a high degree of development with the Mayan civilization. Mayan culture has been divided into a pre-classic period (2000 BC–AD 250) and a classic period lasting from AD 250–AD 900. Stone monuments from the latter period contain the incised hieroglyphs that document what is known as the Mayan Calendar.

The system was based on two main methods of time measurement, one (probably the older of the two) comprising twenty named days and the numbers one to thirteen: this combined gave a 260-day calendar—the *Tzolkin*. The second calendar—the *Haab*—was made up of eighteen periods of time each of twenty days' duration, plus five unlucky days at the end of the cycle to measure the length of a solar year. A specific day occurring in both calendars was repeated once every fifty-two years—the Calendar Round. There were, in addition, a lunar calendar, a repeating cycle of nine 'Lords of the Night' as well as another calendar comprising 819 days. The 'zero' point for the whole system was reckoned to be 3114 BC. The dating of individual events represented a calculation of the time period since

lastic ability are therefore considered to be typical qualities of people born strongly under Mercury.

Mercury rules trade and commerce, and those born under this planet are always intrigued by technical skills, and are often knowledgeable about trades such as carpentry and engineering. A Mercurian will always have an answer for any question; and although it may not always be correct, it will at least be glib and convincing. Although not all Mercurians are plausible rogues, the plausible rogue will almost always be a Mercurian.

The shy, timid, and tongue-tied people of this world need the Mercurians to speak up for them, and a discussion about whether or not the time is ripe for wages to be raised often turns out to be an argument between two Mercurians. It is likely that neither of them will become heated, for Mercury often appears to be rather cold and aloof, even in sexual affairs: unlike many other people, Mercurians think of these as just a part of the glorious game of life. When they marry, many of them do not really take their partners 'for better for worse, for richer for poorer . . . till death do us part'—as they think that, if the desire seizes them, the game can as easily be played with a different partner.

Among typically Mercurian professions is that of the journalist, for instead of being directly involved in life he is mainly concerned with viewing it objectively. A person born under Mercury may succeed in any learned profession, or as a schoolmaster who may have a wide general knowledge without being an authority on any one subject, or as a doctor. When a Mercurian is connected with the arts, it is often possible to discern a lack of the heavy, thoroughgoing seriousness that some artists seem to feel is the least that life deserves.

HANS BIEDERMANN

Numerology

Modern numerology is a popular type of fortune-telling. Lying behind it is a history of many centuries of speculation about numbers and their symbolism, and it is based on two extremely old principles. The first, which goes directly back to Pythagoras (c. 570 BC–c. 490 BC) and his followers in ancient Greece, is that numbers are clues to the real, underlying structure of the universe. The second is the deep-rooted belief that the name of a thing contains the essence of its being, so that the name of a person, properly analyzed and understood, will reveal the truth about that person's character and course through life. Linked with these principles is the tradition that the secrets of the universe are enshrined in the Hebrew alphabet.

Numerologists believe that the letters of your name contain the essential truth about you. You start by turning each letter of your name into a number (using the name by which you normally think of yourself), as follows:

A, I, J, Q, Y	1
B, K, R	2
C, G, L, S	3
D, T, M	4
E, H, N, X	5
U, V, W	6
O, Z	7
P, F	8

These letter-number equivalents come from the Hebrew alphabet, in which the letters also stood for numbers—aleph (A) for one, beth (B) for two, gimel (G) for three, and so on. Nougats are disregarded, so that S (shin 300) is three, while K (kaph–twenty) is two. There is no nine in the system because the Hebrew letters that stood for nine, 90, and 900 have no equivalents in our alphabet. Numbers for letters like E and X that do not exist in Hebrew are taken from the Greek alphabet, where the letters again stood for numbers.

Proportions of man and their secret numbers by Heinrich Cornelius Agrippa (1486–1535)

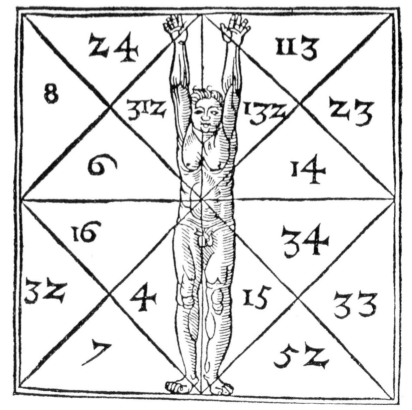

You write down your name with the number equivalents and add up the numbers. If the total has two or more figures, add these together and go on in this way until you reach a single figure. For example:

William Shakespeare
6133114 35125385125
Total 59: 5+9=14;
1+4=5

The number five is the number of the name William Shakespeare (1564–1616). Over the centuries a considerable body of symbolism has attached itself to the number five and Shakespeare's character and achievements can be interpreted in terms of it.

Any name can be turned into one of the numbers from one to nine, which means that the numerologist has a manageable quantity of categories, or broad personality-types, to work with. But he does not maintain, of course, that if your name adds to five you must have exactly the same character and talents as Shakespeare and the innumerable other human beings, past and present, whose names yield the figure five.

The number of your full name indicates your general personality-type. Within it, you can find out more about yourself by considering the total of the vowels in your name (the Heart Number, which reveals your inner self, the person you are at heart), and the total of the consonants (the Personality Number, which reveals your outer self and how others see you).

Open and Hidden

This distinction follows from the fact that written Hebrew, like other early alphabets, had no vowels. So the consonants, which were written down, show your outer shell, while the vowels, which were concealed, show

your hidden, inner personality. (Y is treated as a vowel only if there is no other vowel in the word: in Lynn it counts as a vowel, in Henry as a consonant.)

The same fact probably accounts for the old idea that vowels are particularly sacred and magical, more mysterious and important than the consonants that everyone could see written down; the 'soul' hidden in the 'body' of the consonants. Gnostic mystical theorists in the eastern Mediterranean area in the early centuries

If your Birth Number does not harmonize with the number of your name, then you are probably prone to fierce inner conflicts.

after Christ were sometimes peculiarly addicted to vowels. One of their versions of the name of God was, in English letters, Iaoouee.

You can also consider the numbers given by each letter of your name. The letters of William Shakespeare, for example, do not include a seven at all (suggesting the absence of the introspective and introvert qualities associated with the number), but contain the number one five times over (suggesting masterful creativity and originality, driving force, and egotism).

Again, you can consider nicknames and other variants of your full name, which are supposed to reveal you as you are in your relationships with those who use them. A married woman's maiden name should indicate her character before she married, and her married name should show how marriage has changed her.

Yet another important number is the Birth Number, found by adding

up your day, month and year of birth (for instance, if you were born on 15 August 1972: 15+8+1+9+7+2 =42, and 4+2=6). This number is believed to reveal the mould in which the workings of fate cast you at your birth, what you were destined to be. If your Birth Number does not harmonize with the number of your name, then you are probably prone to fierce inner conflicts.

The Number of God

If your number is one, you are thought to be an exceptionally powerful, positive, and dominating person, forceful, aggressive, and ambitious. You lead, pioneer, originate, and invent. Self-reliant, obstinate, and authoritative, you tolerate no rivals and you have few close friends. You can be kind and generous to people who do what you want, but you have a violent temper and no scruples if opposed. You are unlikely to find deep happiness in love and friendship, as you tend to look on other people as potential supporters or opponents rather than partners.

People whose number is one are daring and self-reliant. They stand on their own feet, resent anyone else's authority, rarely seek advice or follow it. They are strong leaders, good at getting things going, and should flourish as organizers, inventors, designers, planners, engineers, and technicians. They are single-minded, hasty-tempered, willful, and impatient, and take pride in being difficult to deal with.

Most of this follows from the fact that in Christian number symbolism one is the number of God the Father. The creativity, originality, and bent for organization of one are derived from the God who created the world, and many of the other characteristics, including dominance, initiative, leadership, loneliness, impatience

A concrete podium for the first three in a competition

of opposition, and generosity to supporters, are drawn from the God of the Old Testament.

This is reinforced by one's position as the first of the numbers, so that a year that adds to one is said by numerologists to be a time of fresh beginnings and discoveries, new ventures, an outburst of creative activity. The fact that the figure one resembles an erect phallus has not escaped the notice of numerologists and contributes to their view of the number's creativity, but also of its solitariness and independence.

That all things are essentially one thing, that unifying all the phenomena of existence there is a One that is also the Whole, is a belief found in many religious and mystical traditions. The number one has been revered by number mystics from the Pythagoreans onward as the First Cause, the Infinite God, the One that transcends all multiplicity. Whether one could properly be called a number at all was long in doubt, and until comparatively modern times it was generally thought of not as a number but as the essence or underlying principle of number, all other numbers being made of it (2=1+1, 3=1+1+1, and so on). It was

said to be neither odd nor even, but both, because if added to an odd number it makes it even and vice versa. So it combined the opposites of odd and even, and all the other opposites in the universe.

Two and the Devil

The human longing for unity and singleness, the tendency to regard oneness as good, multiplicity and diversity as evil, is deep and widespread. Many mystics have

> *. . . two, the first number to break away from one, is traditionally the number of evil and in Christian numerology belongs to the Devil.*

longed to become 'one' with God. In Judaism and Islam, God is One. In Christianity, God is Three, but also One. One is good, many bad, which is why two, the first number to break away from one, is traditionally the number of evil and in Christian numerology belongs to the Devil. It is also the number of woman, long regarded in male-dominated societies as fundamentally evil.

From the Pythagoreans onward, three has carried a connotation of evil, but modern numerology is reluctant to classify any number as inherently vicious and in its picture of two's characteristics, this ancient link is largely submerged. The link with woman has survived and two is still regarded as the number of femininity and as the opposite of one. Two is passive where one is active, negative where one is positive, weak where one is strong, receptive where phallic one is thrusting.

People with a name that adds to two are described as quiet, unassuming, and gentle. Tactful and diplomatic, they are followers rather than leaders, and they get their way by persuasion and cooperation instead of by the forceful, direct methods of one. Unambitious, disliking the limelight, they are content to stay in the background and since they are obedient, neat, modest, helpful, and discreet, they make good subordinates.

They are good-natured, sympathetic, and understanding, they get on well with people, but they may be rather shy and timid. They like detail and routine, and are worried by new departures, bold initiatives, sudden changes of plan. Twos tend to undervalue themselves and are always in danger of being trampled on by other people. They are likely to be fundamentally uncertain of themselves. Deep in their personality there may be a strain of malice, cruelty, and deceit, and at their worst they can be liars and mischief-makers, spineless, and sulky, cowardly and pessimistic.

All this is an old-fashioned stereotype of woman, not as the wife and mother and partner of man, which is more the preserve of six, but as man's opposite and subordinate. The characteristics apply equally to a year that adds to two, which numerologists expect to be a time of peace and quiet, of gentle progress by way of harmonious cooperation with others, of negotiation and reconciliation. As one numerologist puts it, the seed sown in a one-year grows quietly in the two-year.

Christian numerologists found confirmatory evidence of two's evil nature in the Bible, where Genesis does not say: 'God saw that it was good' after the second day of creation, though it says it about all the other days. And in the twelfth century Hugh of St. Victor said that, as the first number to break away from the unity of one, two is the number of sin, which deviates from original good. As the evil number that sets up an opposite of God, two naturally belongs to the Devil, God's arch-opponent. The reversed pentagram with two points upward is a symbol of evil and Satan. The cloven hoof is a mark of the Devil and so is the forked tongue of the serpent.

This link with the Devil accounts for the streak of malice and cruelty that numerologists attribute to two, and the characteristics of telling lies and making mischief come from the Prince of Darkness. The sense of two as evil and deceitful survives in several common expressions. To double-cross someone is to cheat or betray him, to be two-faced is to be insincere, and double-dealing is trickery.

Third Time Lucky

Three is traditionally the luckiest of numbers and belongs to lively, sparkling, charming people who easily make money and conquests in love, who are talkative and like to show off. Witty and talented, they adore the limelight and detest obscurity, though they are often more nervous and sensitive than their assured exterior suggests. They tend to expend their energies wastefully in too many directions and, since they love luxury and pleasure, to scatter money about. Though always the life and soul of the

party, they can sometimes be exasperatingly vain, gossipy, and superficial. Seldom worried or depressed, they are people to whom everything seems to come easily, who succeed without really trying.

Behind this picture of three several strands of symbolism converge. The number one, though potentially all-creative, is regarded as barren by itself, for however many times it is multiplied by itself it remains one. The number two introduces a pair of opposites, but two multiplied by one remains two. Three that fruitfully reconciles the opposites, to create more numbers (3x2=6). One is the number of God alone and unmanifested. In two something emanates from God's wholeness to create a pair of opposites. In three the opposites are reconciled, and God becomes manifest and comprehensible to human experience. Chiming with this is the sexual symbolism of three as the number of the

male genitals, which are threefold.

This is the basic numerological interpretation of the Trinity, the threefold godhead. As the number of the Trinity, in Christian numerology three is naturally linked with the most holy, the most perfect, the best. But the number's connection with the superlative is older, and the notion of the superlative itself involves the third term in a series of three—good, better, best. Three is not only linked with 'best' but also with 'all' as a number of completeness. Time is made of three ingredients (past, present, and future) and so is space (length, breadth, and thickness). All created things have a beginning, middle, and end.

The feeling that three is the basis of everything we experience may account for the belief that runs of luck tend to go in threes. 'Third time lucky' is a common phrase, and if two unlucky things happen one after the other, some people will deliberately break a

In three, numerologists say God becomes understandable to humans

dish or cause some other minor damage to end the run of ill luck. Three of anything is somehow 'all' or 'enough' of it, as in 'I'll give you three guesses.' The hero of a folktale often has three wishes or three tries at a task and the heroine has three suitors, while three often bobs up as a number of completeness in nursery rhymes: Goldilocks and the three bears, three little kittens who lost their mittens, three blind mice.

The medieval Christian numerologists remarked on various uses of three as a number of completeness in the New Testament, including the three gifts of the Magi, the three temptations in the wilderness, three denials of Christ by Peter, three falls on the way to Golgotha, three days between the crucifixion and the resurrection, three appearances of the risen Christ to his disciples. These could all be taken as foreshadowing's or reflections of the Trinity. Groups of three can also be found in Greek mythology, such as the three Graces, the three Fates, and the three Furies. They attracted the attention of Renaissance humanists, who connected them with the Trinity. Even the three heads of Cerberus, the dog of the underworld, became an emblem of the Christian doctrine.

Examples of divine triads come from the Celts, to whom three was a sacred number. They sometimes portrayed their deities in groups of three or with three heads or three faces, as a way of emphasizing their power and perhaps with the same basic idea of a single god making himself known in terms of three which underlies the stock numerological approach.

Down to Earth

Four, by contrast, is the number of the earth and is thoroughly gloomy. It is the number of people who are solid but uninspired, hard-working but plodding, steady, cautious, conservative, and conventional. They are calm and composed on the surface, but there may be violent eruptions of feeling underneath and also severe indigestion (earthquakes and eruptions). They are capable organizers and administrators, but four does not hold out high prospects of success.

The Pythagoreans linked one with the point, which in theory has no dimensions; two with the line, con-

Modern numerologists try to put a bright gloss on it, but four is fundamentally the number of poverty, disappointment, and defeat

necting two points, which has length but not breadth; and three with the triangle, connecting three points and creating surface, having length and breadth, but not height. To construct the simplest solid figure—a pyramid—a fourth point has to be added above the triangle, and the four points connected. This suggested that the basis of the construction of all solid objects is to be found in four.

Ever since, four has been the number of solidity and matter. According to the old theory, everything is made of the four elements (fire, air, earth, and water), and four is especially the number of Earth, a solid object bounded by the four cardinal points. People whose name adds to four are consequently described by numerologists as solid and stable, but sadly uninspired, like lifeless matter that lacks the divine spark, as respectable, stodgy, humdrum persons, who regard themselves as pillars of society. Four is traditionally the unluckiest of numbers because of its link with earthly existence, which medieval numerologists regarded as gloomy, laborious, sin-ridden, and filled with pain.

The connection of four with agricultural labour, toil on the earth's surface, and so with the traditional stereotype of the rustic, gave the number its connotation of relentless hard work for minimal and uncertain reward, and of conservatism, slowness, and caution. Modern numerologists try to put a bright gloss on it, but four is fundamentally the number of poverty, disappointment, and defeat.

Five and the Flesh

Five is quite different, a nervous and highly-strung number, associated with sensuality, fickleness, risk, and gambling. Fives are versatile and amusing people, clever and resourceful, good company, good at languages and with words, optimistic, and fun-loving. They make both friends and money easily. Jumpy, tense, and restless, they live on their nerves and they live for sensation and excitement. They enjoy adventure, travel, the new, and untried. They are highly attractive to the opposite sex and probably have active love lives. They hate to be tied down or in a rut. Impatient of rules, they are likely to be erratic, untidy, unpunctual, and irritable.

The restless, many-sided qualities of five follow from the fact that it comes halfway in the series of numbers from one to nine, so that it 'faces both ways' and has the characteristics of outgoingness, inability to concentrate, and unreliability. Liveliness, love of excitement and of sensual pleasure stem from the association of the number with the five senses (sight, hearing, taste, touch, and smell). This link, the principal clue to five in medieval Christian numerology, made it the number of the living flesh.

Five is made of the first male number (three) added to the first female number (two), and so it is the number of sex and marriage from the male point of view—an idea found in Hinduism as well as in the West. In five woman is added to man, in six she is multiplied by him, so six is the female marriage number. The association of five with man and the senses was strengthened by the fact that the human body has five extremities and, shown with arms and legs extended, can be fitted into a five-pointed star.

Five is also made of one (God) plus four (the earth, matter), and so it is the number of living things, the animate world of Nature, divine life infused into the inanimate. It is the number of man as a miniature image of the universe. It can stand for the four directions plus the center, represented in the symbolic decoration of Gothic churches by a five-petalled flower at the center of a cross.

Five is the number of the intersection of the earthly and the divine.

Six for Harmony

Six is fives's opposite number. Where five is jumpy, nervous, and erotic, six is calm and straightforward. It is the number of motherly, rather than sexual, love. Six is the only number in the first ten that is 'perfect,' meaning equal to the sum of its divisors other than itself (6=1+2+3), and so it is considered a specially balanced and harmonious number. People with names adding to six are expected to be well adjusted and peaceable, not racked by inner conflicts.

It was on the sixth day of creation that God created man and woman, which suits six as the feminine marriage number. It is essentially the number of the wife and mother, and those strongly influenced by it find their happiness primarily in love and marriage, home and family. Decent, tranquil, kindly, unselfish, and perhaps a bit humdrum, sixes are warm and affectionate, domesticated, and

thoroughly respectable. They also have the defects traditionally associated with the housewife, of being fussily preoccupied with trivialities, limited in outlook, sometimes unreasonably obstinate, and a trifle dull. A year that adds to six is supposed to have the same characteristics, as a time of harmony and balance, and is naturally a good year for marriages.

Contributing to the balanced picture of six is the hexagram, the six-pointed star made of two interlaced triangles, standing for God and man, male and female, fire and water, spirit and matter. On the sixth day of creation God made man 'in his image,' and where five is the number of man as microcosm, six is the number of the Universal Man, man as macrocosm. In the Cabala it is the sixth sefirah, Tifereth, which is the central, balancing, and harmonizing sphere on the Tree of Life.

The Mystic Seven

A glance at any concordance will reveal the frequency with which seven appears in the Bible, from the seven days of creation to the numerous groups of seven in the Book of Revelation—stars, angels, trumpets, plagues, thunders, seals, and vials of wrath among them. The Jews kept the seventh day, on which God rested from his work, as the sabbath, the day of rest and worship, which the Christians transferred to Sunday.

The key to seven is this connection with the week and the moon. It is an old and widespread belief that the cycles of life and death on Earth are connected with the waxing and waning of the moon in the sky, and each of the four phases of the moon's cycle lasts roughly seven days. This is the origin of the month of four weeks of seven days each.

It follows that seven is another number of completeness: seven days make a whole week, the whole world

Seven is a number of completeness.

was made in seven days, seven of anything makes a complete set. The planets known in antiquity, whose movements in the sky were believed to influence events on Earth, were seven, and they correspond to the seven days of the week, the seven metals and the seven colours of the rainbow or spectrum. There are seven notes in the commonly known heptatonic musical scale and seven vowels in the Greek alphabet.

As a number of completeness intimately linked with the inner rhythms of the universe, seven is powerful in magic and frequently used in spells and charms, often in association with three. In folk belief a seventh child has magical and clairvoyant powers, and the seventh son of a seventh son, even more so.

Besides being complete, seven is also numerologically solitary. It is not made by multiplication of any other numbers in the first ten, nor does it, multiplied, produce any of them. As a result it is considered a loner, isolated, and virgin. It follows that people whose number is seven are said to be withdrawn and solitary, introspective, given to reflection, interested in

spiritual matters. This is reinforced by the theme of the sabbath, the seventh day, the day of withdrawal from the busy world and concentration on the things of God.

So seven is the number of the mystic, the magician, the philosopher, the scholar, the recluse. It belongs to those introverted, quiet, thoughtful people who hold aloof from life's flurry and bustle. Secretive, proud, reserved, stoical, pessimistic, sensitive, they have no time for foolish, frivolous, and worldly things. Sevens may have a warmer heart than appears on the surface and may be deeply emotional while almost incapable of showing it. They are a law unto themselves.

Eight in the World

Eight is seven's opposite, as the number of worldly involvement. It is associated with business executives, efficient administrators, people of great organizing ability and dominating character, busy with worldly concerns, clever and realistic, cold and ruthless when necessary but not always unkind at heart. They are people who get on in the world. They are strongly influenced by money and power, and likely to be too self-sufficient and preoccupied with the main chance to make satisfactory partners in love and marriage. At the same time, eight's path is not an easy one. It is the number of outstanding success, but also of dramatic failure in worldly matters, and eight-people lead lives of constant strain and effort.

Lying behind this is the fact that four is the number of Earth and matter, and since eight is four doubled, eight comes to mean intense involvement in material things. In addition, the Cabala's eighth sphere corresponds to Mercury, the god of trade and commerce, and the figure eight resembles Mercury's wand or caduceus. The shape of the number, the two circles suggesting dualism—

success and failure—and the fact that eight is twice four, which is the unluckiest of numbers, account for the ominous overtones.

In a different line of symbolism, eight means 'a new beginning' and so 'new life.' In Jewish tradition a baby boy is named and so begins his life as a real person on the eighth day after birth. Baptism in Christianity is a new beginning and fonts in churches are frequently octagonal. As the number of new life, eight also means immortality and life after death. The early Christians associated eight with Sunday. They accepted that God made the world in six days and rested on the seventh, but they said that the Sunday on which Christ rose from the dead was God's eighth day, on which he renewed his work and gave humankind the possibility of everlasting life. As the number of life after death, eight stood for eternity and infinity, and the mathematical symbol for infinity is an eight lying on its side. The prospect of an eternity in heaven or hell has contributed to the modern numerologists' predictions of great success or dramatic failure with eight.

The Nine Bright Shiners

A human child is normally conceived, formed, and born in nine months, which has much to do with the character of nine in numerology. Nines are said to be people of great gifts, with a strong bent for service to humanity. They are often fighters for good causes, for the poor and unfortunate. Nine is the number of high mental and spiritual achievement, of inspired and inspiring people who have broad interests and wide sympathies. Generous and compassionate, they may be easily imposed upon and they are often criticized as wild, unorthodox, impractical, and rebellious. Passionate, romantic, and emotional, nines love to be on stage and need love and admiration. High-minded and idealistic, they fall in and out of love with great frequency. They enjoy the good things of life and relish beauty in all its forms.

Nine as the number of the humanitarian follows from the human gestation period. It is the number of love of mankind because of the child made flesh and born into the world. Another influence is the fact that nine is the last and highest of the sequence from one to nine and so it has the 'highest' characteristics. It is also seen as marking the transition from one scale (one to nine) to a higher scale (starting with ten) and so it is the number of initiation, which again parallels the birth of a baby after nine months.

Again, nine is a number of completeness. A complete circle has 360 degrees and 3+6+0=9. Christ completed his life on Earth and died at the ninth hour, and nine categories of people are called blessed in the Sermon on the Mount. It is also a circular and complete number because if it is multiplied by any other number it always reproduces itself (3x9=27 and 2+7=9, or 6x9=54 and 5+4=9, and so on).

Patterns in Time

One obvious and cogent objection to numerology is that your name is unlikely to be an index to your character because you acquired it by chance: you just happened to be born into a family named Shakespeare or whatever. Numerology, like other forms of divination, does not believe in chance. It sees the world as a design in which your name and the circumstances of your birth have their allotted place.

Time runs numerologically, of course. The year 1900 adds up to one, suggesting a time of new discoveries and inventions, and new and aggressive power groupings. Numerologists attributed the upsurge of interest in

mysticism and the supernatural in the 1960s to the fact that it was a seven-decade. Within the centuries and decades, each year brings a fresh number into play, and within each year, so does each month and day.

London's vowels add to five—resilience, versatility, sensuality. New York's add to three—brilliance, liveliness, glamour.

In theory numerology can be used to make your path through life easier and more successful. If your number is six, you should try to deal with important matters on a day that adds to six. You should also ideally live in a house whose number adds to six and a street whose name adds to six, or so

the numerologists recommend. In considering a city, the vowels that indicate its inner character provide the crucial number. London's vowels add to five—resilience, versatility, sensuality. New York's add to three—brilliance, liveliness, glamour. Those of Chicago and Los Angeles add to 9—high achievement (Chicago was the skyscraper's birthplace).

Music of the Spheres

Perhaps the most startling thing about numerology is its assumption that people and traits of character, periods of time, places, items of food, and everything that exists can be described in numerical terms or, to state it at its simplest and flattest, that everything is a number. The idea was bequeathed to Western numerology by the Pythagorean philosophers. Very little is known for certain about Pythagoras

Nine is linked to love of humankind as a result of the human gestation period.

himself, but Aristotle (384 BC–322 BC), an opponent of the Pythagoreans, gave his version of their views in his *Metaphysics*. He said that they believed that all things are numbers, 'such and such a modification of numbers being justice, another being soul and reason, another being opportunity and similarly almost all other things being numerically expressible.' The notion is hard to grasp but, to borrow Christopher Butler's analogy, to understand how 'opportunity' could be thought of as a number, it is helpful to remember that although we behave as if a table is what it appears to be, we can also think of it as being 'really' something quite different, a conglomeration of atoms or molecules. One reason why numbers attracted philosophical speculation of this sort is that they provide a principle of order in a seemingly chaotic universe. Numbers obey rigid laws but they also extend to infinity and have infinite possibilities of combination with each other. These characteristics recommend them to people who are in search of a basic pattern to the universe that will combine orderliness with infinite variety.

It may have been Pythagoras who discovered that the musical intervals known in his time—the octave, the fifth and the fourth—can be expressed in terms of simple ratios between the numbers one, two, three, and four. The discovery had a profound effect on Pythagorean thinking. Aristotle says that 'since, again, they saw that the modifications and ratios of the numerical scales were expressible in numbers; since, then, all other things in their whole nature seemed to be modeled on numbers, and numbers seemed to be the first things in the whole of Nature, they supposed the elements of numbers to be the elements of all things, and the whole heaven to be a musical scale and a number.'

This was the origin of the concept of the 'music of the spheres,' the harmony of sound made by the heavenly bodies as they travel their rounds in the sky, the basis of the modern numerologist's 'vibrations,' or cosmic rhythms that govern the universe.

The sixteenth-century astronomer Kepler endeavoured to calculate the orbits of the planets in terms of the proportions of a vibrating string to the octave.

> *Among these pairs were good and evil, male and female, and odd and even. Good and male were associated with odd numbers, evil and female with even numbers.*

The Pythagoreans were also impressed by the fact that the numbers one, two, three, and four added together, make ten. In other words, they create the decade, the first ten numbers which from this point of view are the essential numbers, the others merely repeating them at higher levels. That the first ten numbers are the essential ones is a conclusion naturally drawn from the worldwide practice of counting on the fingers. The fact that ten is produced by 1+2+3+4 suggested that these four numbers were the origin and basis of all numbers, and therefore the basis of everything in the universe. This was confirmed by finding the basis of construction of all solid objects in the same four numbers: one is the point, two is the line, three is the triangle, and four is the tetrahedron or pyramid, the simplest solid.

The Pythagoreans venerated a figure called the *Tetractys*, which is a simple demonstration that 1+2+3+4=10, and which looked like this:

This early way of representing numbers, by pebbles or dots, suggested or supported the distinction between male and female, numbers which has influenced numerology ever since. Like other Greek philosophers, the Pythagoreans regarded the existence of pairs of opposites as an important characteristic of the universe's construction. Among these pairs were good and evil, male and female, and odd and even. Good and male were associated with odd numbers, evil and female with even numbers.

When numbers are represented by dots, it is immediately obvious why the odd numbers are male and the even numbers female. The numbers three, five, and seven, for example are shown as:

The even numbers two, four, and six are shown as:

The odd numbers each have what Plutarch called 'a generative middle part,' while in each even number there is 'a certain receptive opening.'

Later philosophers followed the example of the Pythagoreans in seeing numbers as divine concepts, ideas in the mind of the god who fashioned the world. God was a great mathematician, who had created a universe of infinite variety and satisfying order to a numerical pattern. The same principle appears in the Cabala, where the *Sefer Yetsirah* describes the making of the world by means of numbers and letters.

In the Middle Ages numerology continued to flourish as a key to the nature of the universe and the mysteries of the Bible. One was the number of God the Father, two of his archenemy the Devil, three of the Trinity, four of matter and the earth, five of the senses and the flesh. However, Medieval numerologists were no more unvaryingly consistent than modern ones. On the contrary, a number could have several different meanings, and the one that best fitted a given set of circumstances would be applied to that particular context.

RICHARD CAVENDISH

Omens

'We suffer as much from trifling incidents as from real evils,' wrote the eighteenth century essayist Joseph Addison (1672–1719), 'I have known the shooting of a star spoil a night's rest . . . A screech owl at midnight has alarmed a family more than a band of robbers; nay, the voice of a cricket has struck more terror than the roar of a lion. There is nothing so inconsiderable which may not appear dreadful to an imagination that is filled with omens.'

That coming events cast their shadows before them is a deeply entrenched belief and an omen has been defined as 'some phenomenon or unusual event taken as a prognostication either of good or evil.' The rigorously fatalistic view that the future is determined in advance and cannot change has rarely been fully accepted in practice. Men and women have taken omens not so much as pointers to a predetermined future but as warnings of dangers to be avoided, or as signals of opportunities to be seized.

When the world of Nature is seen as an orderly system with a definite rhythmic pattern, any variation or disturbance of the established pattern tends to cause anxiety and to be interpreted as a sign of trouble ahead. In terms of climate change, recent extreme weather events have been seen as ominous indicators of what may lie

Window from the Holy Trinity Cathedral, Addis Ababa, Ethiopia, shows Noah giving thanks and a rainbow. Weather events were often perceived as omens.

ahead. For centuries, the sky, the scene of the orderly and regular procession of the stars, has been a fruitful source of omens of what is to come. Historically, the meteor, the eclipse, and the comet have perhaps created the greatest dread of all, the appearance of a comet being taken as a portent of the coming of the end of the world. Even in nineteenth century England, as Robert Hunt points out in his *Popular Romances of the West of England*, the lowering of tempest clouds could arouse great alarm among country folk. There was a folk tradition in the British Isles that a mighty storm usually heralded the death of a monarch. Known as 'the Royal Storm,' it paradoxically burst upon Republican England on the night when Oliver Cromwell (1599–1658) died.

In the Bible, Noah sees in the rainbow a sign that there will be no more flood; God says: 'I set my bow in

the cloud, and it shall be a sign of the covenant between me and the earth' (Genesis, chapter 9.13). In the Middle Ages considerable anxiety was frequently created by signs and portents that were taken to show that the Last Judgment was imminent.

It was this sense of apprehension, of impending disaster, which gave the word ominous its present meaning as a sign of future evil. In Nature this somber aspect predominated, a flower or plant blooming out of season portending trouble, or death.

Signs from the Animals

Among wild life, birds especially have been considered to have significance as omens. The cuckoo, as the embodiment of spring, indicated by its call what the future held. If the first call heard came from the right, the omen was good; if from the left, disaster was at hand. Birds have always been

Coccyzus americanus. The implication of the omen depended on the direction from where the cuckoo's call came.

regarded as messengers of the gods, the agents of communication between fate and ourselves.

Like the birds, other wild and domestic animals have made an immense contribution to omen lore, partly arising from the old belief that animals could be ancestral spirits animated by the desire to protect their descendants. Among communities as far apart as Africa and Lapland it is unlucky for a hare to cross one's path. The ill repute of the hare in the British Isles is derived from the tradition that this

animal was one of the forms that was assumed by the shape-shifting witch.

Both the dog and the cat figure very largely in the folklore omens of Northern Europe. Among schoolchildren the appearance of a spotted dog is a portent of good luck, while three white dogs provide an even happier omen. It is also extremely fortunate if a strange dog should follow you home and fawn on you. In China dog omens were drawn from the animal's physical characteristics and an official who happened to breed a white puppy with

tiger stripes could look forward to speedy promotion. For a cat to cross someone's path is a token of good luck but only if the animal proceeds from the right-hand side; an approach from the left can have the most sinister implications. It is also lucky if a strange cat enters the house of its own accord.

Modern animal omens rarely relate to horses, now that the horse plays a lesser role in the social economy. A host of other animal omens have survived, however, representing an old but far from extinct mode of thought.

A swarm of bees, the traditional bearers of the goodwill of the gods, which alights in one's garden, portends prosperity. For a ship at sea to be followed by a shark continues to have the most ominous implications for sailors.

Messages from Home

Within the self-created environment of man's home a special class of omen exists. The accidental falling of a picture or breaking of a mirror are ominous occurrences. In Devonshire, England, it was believed that if a rasher of bacon begins to curl up while frying, a new lover is on his way, while there was a widespread belief that to discover nine perfect peas in a pod promises a fruitful marriage. The hearth, once the shrine of the domestic god, remains the center of a whole class of omen, one of the best known of which is that a spluttering coal indicates a forthcoming quarrel. Some country folk hold any change in the rhythm of a clock to be a sign of death because it symbolizes a corresponding disturbance in the rhythm of the life cycle.

The human body itself involuntarily provides omens, in the form of shivering, sneezing, tingling, itching, and stumbling. Because of its association with the sensation of fear, a shiver running down the spine is immediately interpreted as a sign that 'someone is walking over my grave.' Sneezing was once supposed to indicate that the soul (which was equated with the breath) had been violently ejected from the body, hence the polite salutation of everyone in the vicinity of the sneeze: 'God bless you.'

Itching and tingling are happy or unhappy auspices, depending upon whether they are experienced on the right side of the body or the left. If the itching is felt in the sole of the foot, it means that you will soon tread on strange ground. The most common of all bodily omens, however, is provided by stumbling. To totter, to take a wrong step, or to fall indicates unhappy prospects for the project in hand and this is reinforced by the proverb: 'He who hesitates is lost.' William the Conqueror (1028–1087) is said to have tripped and fallen on landing on English soil, causing consternation among his followers.

The great crises of life from birth to death are occasions when omens are looked for and discovered. If a child is born with the incoming tide, the omen was deemed to be good but if at the ebb tide the portent was bad. For a woman, it is considered ominous if her wedding ring is accidentally broken, as this foreshadows the destruction of her marriage.

Among those who are unknowingly near to death there is sometimes an unconscious awareness of their condition.

In sickness it is a sign of forthcoming sorrow if a bird of dark plumage settles upon the roof. Certain psychic manifestations belong to the category of death omens, as for example the banshee, the Jack o' Lantern, and the phantom coach. The fetch, or psychic double of a person who is shortly to die, which manifests itself to someone near and dear to the individual, comes within the category of the omen since it represents a forewarning of death. Among those who are unknowingly near to death there is sometimes an unconscious awareness of their condition. They make their wills, settle their affairs, and make preparations for the end. As Jung (1875–1961) pointed out: 'Dying has its onset long before actual death.' Premonitions of death in the elderly are as much justifiable states of mind as they are omens. This kind of omen has an affinity with the prophetic powers that are so often associated with the dying.

The anxiety that mankind seems destined to suffer when contemplating the future was responsible for the system of omen interpretation known as augury. In Rome a college of priestly augurs interpreted the indications of approval or disapproval signified by the gods in relation to coming events. These signs might take the form of the flashing of lightning or the flight of birds. The augur stood facing South, with the East or lucky quarter, associated with the sun's rising, to his left and with the unlucky West to his right, and attempted to determine the meaning of the phenomenon from its angle of approach.

The augur did no more than stage a situation within which the laws of chance could operate freely, leaving the sign itself to be presented spontaneously by Nature. In an extreme example of this class of divination, called alectromancy, a circle representing the letters of the alphabet was prepared and upon each of the letters a grain of wheat was placed. A cockerel representing the nonhuman agency was introduced and began to eat the grains. The letters corresponding to the grains thus eaten were built into a word that supplied answers to the questions asked.

More directly associated with the natural type of omen however was extispicium, a system of divination based upon the examination of entrails, and oneiromancy, the interpretation of the symbolism of dreams. Another curious method, based upon the movement of the wind, was capnomancy, or divination by means of smoke arising from the burned sacrifice. If the smoke ascended perpen-

The Eve of St. Agnes, or The Flight of Madelaine and Porphyro during the Drunkenness attending the Revelry, (1848) by William Holman Hunt (1827–1910)

dicularly the omen was good, but if it spread in another direction, it was unfavourable.

Another system of omen divination involved placing a finger at random upon the open page of a Bible and deciding from the text thus marked out what the fates had in store. In this example, we see a reversal of roles, the human becoming the active agent while the omen, represented by the text, is passive.

The overlapping of the magical arts into the area of signs and portents can be observed in apotropaic actions (intended to avert evil) spitting or making the sign of the cross, or 'touching wood.' The magical principle of 'like curing like' can be called upon in some cases to annul an evil omen. This process was described by Sir James Frazer (1854–1941) as an attempt 'to circumvent destiny by accomplishing it in mimicry . . .

Public Portents

Belief in the power of omens has had a considerable influence on the course of history. Llodowick Lloyd (1573–1607) in 1602 described in his *Stratagems of Jerusalem* how 'The First King of Rome builded his Kingdom by the flying of birds and soothsaying.' It is also recorded that Emperor Constantine, while locked in battle with the barbarians, saw in the sky a shining cross with the words *In hoc signo vinces* (By this sign, conquer), which he then inscribed upon his banner and went forward to victory. The warriors led into battle by St. Joan of Arc found encouragement from the vision of St. Michael in the sky beckoning them onward, and from the white dove of the Holy Spirit which by alighting on Joan's standard provided a favourable omen.

In the reign of Henry II (1154–1189), Peter of Blois gave solemn warning to one of his followers: 'Do not entangle yourself in the false opinion of those who fear to meet a hare, or a woman with flowing tresses, or a blind man or a lame man . . . or if a wolf meets them, or a martin flies from left to right, or if on setting forth they hear distant thunder or meet a hunchback or a leper.'

The unsettled years of seventeenth century England were filled with ominous portents, among which were phantom armies marching through the clouds as if to announce the approach of civil war. When this did break out, it produced some very worrying signs, as at the trial of King Charles I when the head of his staff fell off. King James II was apparently alerted to the loss of his kingdom by an omen noted by John Aubrey who recorded 'the tottering of the crown upon his head, the broken canopy over it, and the rent flag hanging from the White Tower when I came home from the Coronation.'

By 1832 science had begun to intrude into the folklore of omens. By a reversal of the usual process the comet prophesied for that year was regarded as the cause, rather than the sign of forthcoming disaster. Vast numbers of panic-stricken citizens, particularly in Germany, at once refrained from all commercial activities until finally convinced that a collision between the earth and the comet was not inevitable.

Oracles

The main responsibility of priests in ancient Greece was to perform public worship, mostly by offering sacrifices to particular gods, but they had no pastoral function in relation to worshippers. At best they could decide technical questions of religious law, for example, whether a certain act had made the inquirer impure and how he or she could be cleansed. To meet the need for personal guidance there

substituting a mock calamity for a real one.' A common subterfuge of this type occurs when an individual defers to the superstition that casualties always occur in threes by snapping two matchsticks after breaking a piece of crockery, which is an expedient for making the omen run its course.

were oracles at a number of temples throughout the Greek world, to which the inquirer, whether a private individual or a state, could bring a question and receive an answer that was supposed to express the will of the gods. These temples were mostly dedicated to Apollo, whose cult had spread from Asia Minor to Greece.

The chief feature of the oracles was that the replies to questions were delivered by a man or a woman who had been put into a trance and who would answer from the subconscious. In the trance the medium would speak with a changed voice and personality, understood to be Apollo himself speaking through his instrument; this was apparently confirmed when the medium on returning to normal consciousness could not recollect what had been said. The modern psychologist finds no difficulty in explaining that such a trance is produced by suggestion. If a worshipper of Apollo were brought up to believe that on entering the innermost shrine of the god, after various elaborate ceremonies had been performed, he or she would be inspired, then by carrying through the appropriate ritual that effect would actually be produced. The priests who conducted the ceremonies need not consciously apply hypnotism to the medium. The suggestion implanted years before by the traditional practices would operate of itself.

Costly Consultations

The answers of the medium when in a trance might often be confused. This was satisfactorily explained by the belief that the gods, and particularly Apollo, did not answer man's questions candidly, but could be expected to bewilder and even mislead the rash inquirer by ambiguous and enigmatic answers. Actually the inquirer did not usually receive the medium's utterance direct. He was allowed to listen when the question was put and then after the medium had spoken; but a priestly functionary would convey the official version of the answer, often in verse. One is inclined to suspect that this was the point at which human intelligence in the person of the priests took a part in the framing of the oracle. Particularly when the inquirer had not been a private individual, but an embassy from a state presenting a political question—such as the advisability of a given alliance or the outcome of a prospective war—the priests might very well have wished for reasons of policy to favour one particular line. The confused words of the medium would then be shaped by the priest to express the official view.

It is not surprising that this rather elaborate ritual of inquiry was expensive for the private individual

At Delphi, Greece, the Sacred Way lead past the Rock of Sibyl and Treasury of the Athenians

and could only be used rather infrequently. At Delphi, for instance, in the fifth and fourth centuries BC the minimum charge was the equivalent of two days' wages for an Athenian, with additional sums payable in free-will offerings, as well as traveling expenses. States were charged by the priests at ten times the rate of private individuals. This full-scale form of consultation was only available on one day a month—he seventh, which was traditionally Apollo's birthday—and the oracle was closed for the three months during the winter when Delphi was difficult to reach by sea or by the mountain roads.

On the actual day, consultations went on from morning to night. Two women, with a third in reserve, acted as mediums working a shift system. If there were many inquirers or if the ceremonies did not go smoothly, some applicants would be left disappointed at the end of the day before their turn had arrived. Because of this, the Delphians used to confer on some states or individuals an honorary precedence that evidently guaranteed them a high place in the queue. Otherwise positions were determined by a ballot.

Simpler and cheaper forms of oracle were also available. The commonest was by a process of drawing lots. This was also practiced at Delphi, but little is known of it there. Its favourite oracle center was in the West of Greece at Dodona, near the modern town of Jannina. There, an oracle of Zeus had existed from the second millennium BC. Originally it was associated with a sacred oak that was said to utter prophecies, which were interpreted by its priests, the Selloi, who observed the taboos of sleeping on the bare ground and not washing their feet. All this ritual is not typical of Greece as a whole. In fact its nearest analogies come from pagan Prussia where there were also sacred oaks and priests with these curious taboos.

Blood for Blood

Orestes has been instructed by Apollo through the oracle at Delphi to kill his mother and thereby avenge the death of his father

ORESTES: The word of Apollo is of great
   power and cannot fail.
His voice, urgent, insistent, drives me to
   dare this peril,
Chilling my heart's hot blood with recital of
   threatened terrors,
If I should fail to exact fit vengeance, like
   for like,
From those who killed my father. This was
   the god's command:
'Shed blood for blood, your face set like a
   flint. The price
They owe no wealth can weigh. 'My very
   life, he said,
Would pay, in endless torment, for
   disobedience . . .
                  But when, he said,
A father's blood lies unavenged, and time
   grows ripe,
The neglectful son sees yet more fearful
   visitations,
As, toward eyes that strain and peer in
   darkness, come
The attacking Furies, roused by inherited
   blood-guilt,
Armed with arrows of the dark, with
   madness, false night-terrors,
To harass, plague, torment—to scourge
   him forth from his city
With the brazen lash, in loathed and
   abject filthiness.
Banquet and wine, grace of libation, he
   may not share—
This was the oracle's word; his father's
   anger, unseen,
Bars him from every altar; no man may
   receive him
Or share his lodging; scorned, friendless
   and alone, at length
He lies a shriveled husk, horribly
   embalmed by death.

                Aeschylus *The Choephori*
                (trans. Philip Vellacott.)

Advice on Personal Problems

Consultation at Dodona was by drawing lots: inquirers were given thin strips of lead on which they wrote their questions. These were usually expected to be framed so that they could be answered 'yes' or 'no.'

The strip was then rolled up so that the questions could not be read, and the name of the inquirer or a number was scratched on the back. Thus the secrecy of the question could be guaranteed. The questions were put into a jar, and the priestess drew them out, one by one, while at the same time drawing a lot for each, probably a bean coloured black or white to show whether the god's answer was 'yes' or 'no.'

It is fortunate that this simple method was used at Dodona, as some hundreds of these lead strips have been found: some of them still folded, others showing signs of having been smoothed out after one inquiry and then reused for another. They illustrate the rich variety of questions posed to the oracle. A few are from cities: Corfu asked about goodwill among its citizens; a town in Thessaly whether it might invest the funds of its goddess; the people of Dodona itself 'whether it is on account of the impurity of some human being that the god is sending the bad weather.' Most of the questions were from private individuals, pouring out their own personal troubles: 'Gerioton asks Zeus concerning a wife whether it is better for him to take one.' 'Lysanias asks Zeus whether the child is not from him with which Annyla is pregnant.' 'Leontios consults concerning his son Leon whether there will be recovery from the disease on his breast which seizes him.' 'Cleotas asks Zeus if it is better and more profitable for him to keep sheep.' All the practical problems of life show up, and the confusions and anxieties of inquirers are revealed in their expressions and handwriting. The would-be sheep farmer, for instance, was visibly unused to writing.

For some centuries the oracles at Dodona and Delphi engaged in professional rivalry and competition. Dodona claimed to be the sanctuary of the 'father of gods and men,'

The Temple of Apollo in ancient city of Didyma, Greece

and the oldest oracle in Greece. Delphi asserted that Apollo who spoke through its medium was the chosen mouthpiece of Zeus. Both priesthoods claimed a share in Greece's legendary past. However, under the rule of the Roman Empire, Dodona was destroyed and Delphi continued but mainly only as a tourist center.

By this time, the center of population and wealth had shifted to Asia Minor. In what is now the thinly populated coast of western Turkey there were huge new temples dedicated to Apollo and equipped with oracles within easy reach of crowded commercial cities. The temples have recently been excavated, and some of their history revealed. At Didyma, for example, a colossal temple had been begun about 300 BC but more than four centuries later it was still not quite completed. It contained a magnificent staircase, designed for religious processions, and a huge window in the facade of the temple from which the prophet could announce the god's oracles. Some of the questions that Apollo answered are curiously modern. One was the settlement of a strike of workmen building the theatre at Miletus.

Guidance from a Fountain

Didyma's chief rival was Claros, about 100 miles north. The old Greek colonies favoured Didyma, but the new towns consulted Claros. Corresponding to this division, the oracle of Didyma spoke in classical verse while that of Claros went in for all sorts of lively meters in a new style.

The inquirer was brought by night to a passage in the temple leading to the subterranean vaults.

The cities that consulted Claros often did so annually, and this civic outing included a choir that sang a hymn to Apollo specially composed by one of the citizens. The consultation itself must have been an exciting occasion. The inquirer was brought by night to a passage in the temple leading to the subterranean vaults. There was only room to walk in single file guided by torchlight, and the mazelike corridor led by six right-angled turns to a hall, where the consultants could sit while the prophetic medium continued to

an underground fountain whose water was supposed to convey the inspiration. The experience must have been awe-inspiring. However, sometimes it may have been conducted rather hypocritically. The medium was supposed to get a list of inquirers' names and then, without knowing their questions, give the appropriate answers in verse. But a Cynic philosopher who received an ambiguous reply, promising him reward after toil, found on investigation that the same verses had been uttered to a number of other consultants who, as he grimly remarks, had all experienced the toil, but none of them the promised blessings.

At last, in the third century AD, the work of the various oracles seems to have petered out. It was a time of economic and political collapse in the Roman Empire. Individuals were abandoning official religion and seeking refuge in private cults and magic. Christianity was gaining ground and was the chief critic of the oracles, which it regarded as the personal utterances of devils. In reply, the priests of Didyma tried to organize a combined front of all pagan beliefs and supported the Roman Emperor Diocletian (284–305) in his persecution of the Christians. But Christianity triumphed, and devastations in the inner sanctuaries at Delphi and Dodona bear witness to the impact of the new religion.

The oracles had fulfilled a need that was thereafter to be satisfied by other methods. The evidence from ancient times is not sufficient to prove whether in any instance they had really used supernormal or super-natural powers. No doubt the trances of the prophetic mediums were genuine enough. The answers that they gave, or were said to have given, for centuries convinced the majority of inquirers. This belief was chiefly produced by the oracles conveying the assurance that the gods were guiding the human questioner in the problem that he had laid before them.

H. W. PARKE

FURTHER READING: H. W. Parke. Oracles of Zeus. (Cambridge, MA: Harvard University Press, 1967); H. W. Parke. Greek Oracles. (London, UK: Hutchinson, 1968); H. W. Parke. Chaldean Oracles. (Lynnwood, WA: Holmes, 1984).

George Orwell

George Orwell was the pseudonym of the writer, Eric Blair (1903–1950). Born in Bengal, the son of an official in the Indian Civil Service, he returned to England with his mother and older sister at the age of three and saw his father only once in the following six years. He won a scholarship to Eton College, where he was taught briefly by the young Aldous Huxley (1894–1963), and in 1921 joined the Indian Civil Service working as a police officer in Burma. He resigned this post and returned to England in 1927, having decided to make a career as a writer. His experience of life on the margin of society in both London and Paris, including several periods living on the streets as a tramp, formed the basis for his first book, *Down and Out in Paris and London*, published under the name of Orwell, a pen name he was to retain. His book documenting the harsh poverty of the industrial heartlands of Britain published in 1937—*The Road to Wigan Pier*—contained a long essay on socialism, which was both a political analysis and a personal statement. By the time of its publication, Orwell was in Spain having volunteered to fight with the Republicans during the Civil War, which he would later use as the basis for *A Homage to Catalonia*. By its

publication in 1938, Orwell was established as a journalist and writer, and during World War II, he took a job at the BBC producing propaganda. However, it was only with his book *Animal Farm*, a satire on the Soviet state and Stalinism in particular, published in 1945, that he achieved wide recognition and financial stability. In 1947, while working on his final book, *1984*, he suffered from the tuberculosis that would eventually kill him.

Portrait of George Orwell (c. 1940s). Among his many books were *1984* and *Animal Farm*.

1984 is a nightmare vision of a dystopian future. Totalitarian control over a population is achieved through political power, power that is violently and indiscriminately exercised. But another force is also at work—that of propaganda and the manipulation of history, which Orwell had observed first hand. Propaganda had been used in Britain during World War II as a means of persuasion and control, together with the suspension of democratic government where the replacement coalition had wide-ranging emergency powers. *1984* describes a brutal society where any expression of individual or original thought is held to be a threat to the state, and must be destroyed. Its citizens are under constant surveillance from electronic monitors positioned in their homes that also pump out a stream of information and commands. Craft skills and the arts have disappeared and even the simple act of writing with a pen on good paper is unknown. When the novel's protagonist, Winston Smith, surreptitiously settles down to write his diary—itself a dangerous and subversive act—he finds it difficult. 'Actually he was not used to writing by hand.'

Orwell in this novel had predicted developments that were at the time almost unimaginable. As the Cold War began, the propaganda machines of the two opposing sides roared into action, with the United States and its allies pumping out films and pamphlets on the evils of Communism just as the USSR exercised its political influence over Asia and Eurasia. Also, the witch hunts of the McCarthy era that took place in the United States in the 1950s so closely mirrored the actions of the Thought Police of Orwell's novel, that one may call *1984*prophetic.

Even as the Cold War ended, surveillance such as Orwell described in *1984* became more and more a reality. CCTV, or closed circuit television, was embraced by Britain as a deterrent to crime, and by 1994, most of Britain was under constant surveillance by video cameras on every street corner. Suddenly, privacy was a luxury, and, like Winston, the public was constantly being watched.

As the Internet transformed the world, soon a new type of invasion of privacy and control was introduced.

The proliferation of electronic media and the technology used to access it has transformed both communication and the acquisition of information. However, it has also made detailed personal data about the individual available to corporations and government alike. In the post 9/11 world, the threat of terrorism enabled governments to tear down many rights to privacy. Edward Snowden (b. 1983) and other whistle blowers have proven that governments use this technology as a useful tool to monitor the

> *. . . the concept of 'Big Brother watching you' has become more of an accurate depiction of the present, but no less a nightmare for many.*

activities of citizens indiscriminately. Just as every comrade in Orwell's novel was considered a threat, so are those who use their phones or browse the Internet today. As governments continue to redefine the boundaries of privacy in the name of national security, the concept of 'Big Brother watching you' has become more of an accurate depiction of the present, but no less a nightmare for many.

ELIZABETH LOVING

FURTHER READING: G. Bowker. George Orwell. (London, UK: Abacus, 2003).

Palmistry

Palmistry or chiromancy is a method of divination through studying the lines and contours of the palms of human hands, together with the shape, size, and texture of the hands.

A highly developed subject in India, which was perhaps its birthplace, palmistry was known in China, Tibet,

Persia, Mesopotamia, and Egypt; it flowered, more or less in its present form, in Greece. The Athenian philosopher Anaxagoras (500 BC–428 BC) is said to have practiced the art, saying: 'The superiority of man is owing to his hands.' Aristotle (384 BC–322 BC) added that 'The hand is the organ of organs, the active agent of the passive powers of the whole system.'

Palmistry still continues to flourish in some parts of the world such as China. It is probable that graphology, the practice of assessing character traits by studying handwriting, was an offshoot of palmistry. During the Renaissance these skills were considered a legitimate part of natural science, even when condemned by the Church.

Mind and Body

The tradition that every line, star, point, cross, square, island, and triangle in the hand is significant has therefore been perpetuated for countless generations, and the modern palmist, like other practitioners of the art before him, believes that there is a relationship between these physical features and man's nature. The claim by the twentieth century German psychologist Ernst Kretschmer (1888–1964) that there is a connection between physique and psychotic illness, and the increasing conviction among medical men of the psychosomatic nature of many diseases, supports the view that there is an interaction between body and mind.

The occultist goes further and says that there is a constant interplay, not only between the physical and the mental, but also between these and the spiritual. The palmist stresses the importance of the apparently haphazard markings and formations of the hands as indications of character, but believes in addition that, in these, the past and the future may be read.

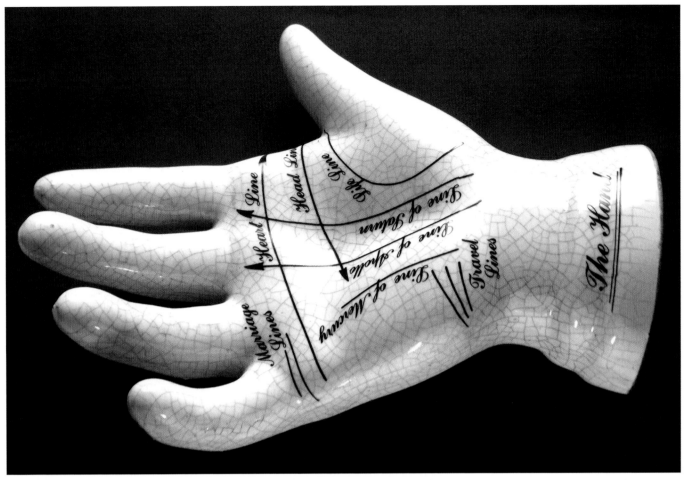

Porcelain hand used in palmistry to divine the future, from Mal Corvus Witchcraft & Folklore artefact private collection owned by Malcolm Lidbury (aka Pink Pasty) Witchcraft Tools

There are those who regard palmistry as a rational science, and others who believe that clairvoyance must be brought to bear when an interpretation is made. A number of ancient books on palmistry exist, as well as many contemporary ones together with a number of websites. There are also societies that instruct students in palmistry.

The superficial reader of hands is content to flatter the person who consults him by stressing such virtues as courage, straightforwardness, and warmth of heart; he or she speaks of sadnesses experienced only in the past, and paints a picture of a successful and happy future.

Palmistry may be studied under three headings. Firstly, correlation between the hands and physical or mental states might be called medical or therapeutic chiromancy,

and some palmists are extremely good at diagnosing the nature of an illness. Secondly, correlation between the hands and character could be called psychotherapeutic chiromancy. The palmist will describe the consultant's character in detail, praise the good qualities, and point out the weak ones. Thirdly, there is correlation between the hands and the past, present, and future. This is divinatory chiromancy. What the palmist has to say about the past may be verified, the present is of course clear, but that which is predicted for the future may well be taken with several grains of salt.

The danger so far as prediction is concerned is that the consultant may accept that a tragedy is inevitable and may allow this to prey on his mind. Some people are so suggestible that they themselves may unconsciously bring about a predicted disaster.

Therefore a high-minded palmist will never foretell misfortune or death without very carefully qualifying the reading and showing how the tragedy may be averted.

When preparing to read a hand it is necessary to be analytical with each detail being described separately; but in the actual reading it is essential to interrelate all the features. Each line should be studied in conjunction with all other markings on the hand, or the reading will be out of focus. In addition, both hands must be brought into relation with each other, for the left represents a person's inherited disposition, while the right reflects what he makes of himself; that is, his positive or negative reactions to his fate.

The titles and placing of the lines, bracelets, mounts, valleys or plains, of stars, points, squares, triangles, and islands, must be mastered by the student of palmistry. The diagrams and information follow give only a brief indication of their significance; a detailed study of palmistry is necessary to appreciate the vast amount of information that may be obtained from reading hands.

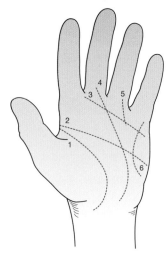

THE PRINCIPAL LINES

1. *The Life Line:* *General picture of the subject's destiny and the dates of outstanding events.*
2. *The Head Line:* *Intellectual capacities.*
3. *The Heart Line:* *Concerns the sentiments.*
4. *The Fate or Destiny Line:* *This should be checked carefully with the 'life line' as it indicates the subject's pattern of life.*
5. *The Apollo or Sun Line:* *Artistic trends, chances of success.*
6. *The Intuition Line:* *Insight.*

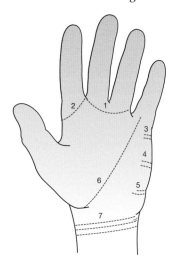

THE SECONDARY LINES

1. *The Girdle of Venus:* *The passions.*
2. *The Cross Line:* *Power to govern.*
3. *The Lines of Union:* *Marriage, children, divorce.*

4. *The Martian Lines:* *Military glory, personal triumph.*
5. *The Travel Lines:* *Journeys, discoveries.*
6. *The Mercury or Health Line:* *Bodily, mental, and spiritual well-being.*
7. *The Three Bracelets of Health, Wealth, and Happiness*

Because a person's inherited character and disposition are reflected in the shape of his hands and fingers, the texture of the skin and the shape of the fingernails, chirognomy, the study of hand formation, is an essential part of palmistry.

Large, straight, and well-shaped hand: Expansive personality, lively, and possibly aggressive.
Long and slender hand: Fastidious and gentle personality.
Pudgy hand: The 'priest's hand'—mystical and unctuous.
Thin and dry hand: Nervous, intellectual, touchy, tenacious.
Hard and firm hand: Energetic, sporting, good memory, tending to violence.
Damp hand: Lazy, unstable but kindly.
Hot hand: Vivacious, bountiful but lacking in depth and sincerity.
Cold hand: Taciturn, secretly generous.

The size, formation and flexibility of the thumb, the shape of the individual fingers, and their length in relation to the palm of the hand, are all significant.

Large thumb: Strong-minded, energetic, given to command, liking work, self-controlled.
Thumb bent well in toward the palm: Moderate, tending to be mean.
Thumb bent outward: Open-natured and generous.
Thumb bent out and backward: The 'killer's thumb,' danger of brutality.
Long fingers: Polite, excitable, anxious, delicate, aesthetic.
Short fingers: Impatient, sensuous, creative, good-hearted.
Pointed fingers: Impatient, sensuous, creative, illogical.

Fingernails vary widely in shape and are said to reflect a number of different character traits. The care of the nails does not affect their basic type in any way; whether they are carefully manicured or broken by work, their significance remains the same.

Long: Gentle and kind, discreet, keeper of secrets.
Almond-shaped: Idealistic, tactful, serene, courteous.
Long and thin: Visionary, irritable, delicate in health.
Rectangular: Practical, sensible.
Long and large: Timid.
Short: Critical, scientific.
Very short: Lacking self-control, fanatical.
Short and large: Morbid, sad.
Short and straight: Rigid, jealous.
Short and rounded: Envious, covetous.

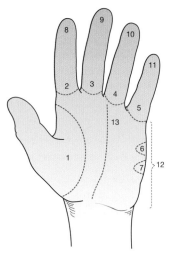

THE REGIONS OF THE HAND

1. *The Mount of Venus:* *Love, instincts, vitality, sensuality, fecundity, bounty.*
2. *The Mount of Jupiter:* *Religion, philosophy, ambition, leadership.*
3. *The Mount of Saturn:* *Stolidity, resignation, skepticism.*
4. *The Mount of Apollo:* *Artistry, exhibitionism, success, fantasy.*
5. *The Mount of Mercury:* *Finance, travel, inheritances, mental agility.*
6. *The Mount of Mars:* *Aggression, courage, fidelity, physical strength.*
7. *The Mount of Luna:* *Imagination, instability, clairvoyance.*

8. **The Finger of Jupiter:** *Domination, leadership.*

9. **The Finger of Saturn:** *Stability, conservatism, jealousy.*

10. **The Finger of Apollo:** *Artistic genius, musical, theatrical, cheerfulness.*

11. **The Finger of Mercury:** *Egotism, avarice, dissimulation, astuteness.*

12. **Range of Percussion:** *Signs concerning marriage, children, divorce.*

13. **Quadrangle of Heart and Head:** *Equilibrium, harmony, peace.*

A doctor may be able to tell, from a patient's physique, the type of illness he or she is likely to suffer, and in the same way the palmist claims that he can detect tendencies toward diseases such as cancer, tuberculosis, asthma, and heart disorders by studying the physical characteristics of the hand. The validity of such a claim is debatable, although much supporting evidence is offered by palmists who specialize in diagnosis. They also claim to substantiate or complement the findings of modern psychologists, and certainly, if specific physical characteristics indicate a predisposition to specific physical illnesses, they may well do the same where psychoneuroses are concerned.

The occult theory that the physical body is extruded or solidified from an etheric pattern-body called the astral suggests that the hands express in their form and configurations the subtle mental and spiritual essence, or core, of an individual. The driving power of the unconscious may be said to determine the outer or bodily appearance, and the palmist sees this force making itself apparent in the hands, as the phrenologist sees it in the configurations of the skull.

Palmistry classifies hands by type deducing personality traits and characteristics from their physical appearance and texture. A neurotic or nervous temperament is generally reflected in a small dry hand, either long and triangular in shape, or with distorted contours. The palm will be very lined, as will the thin, pointed fingers, and the Heart Line will be fragmented. A person with this temperament will tend to change occupations frequently, and to be emotionally dependent, but capricious in romantic relationships. He or she is likely to encounter tragedy of some kind, and to terminate marriage by divorce.

A person with a bilious temperament generally possesses a rectangular or square hand that is thin, firm, muscular, and warm, with yellowish skin. The lines are clearly marked and brown in tint, the fingers are long

Generally, the left hand is thought to indicate an individual's hereditary disposition, while the right hand shows what choices will be made . . .

and spatulate and the thumb big. The Head Line will be straight. The individual concerned will have a tendency to gastric troubles. Intelligent and enterprising, he or she will probably be successful although likely to encounter setbacks. Audacious, such an individual is likely to be impetuous in romantic relationships. Disliking discipline, this person is likely to marry for money rather than love.

A hand that is large and short, 'sticky,' red and hairy with a firm Mount of Venus, indicates a sanguine temperament. The thumb will be short and the hand will show few deep red lines. A person with this type of hand will be impulsive, unreflecting, and active in many ways, but will tend to be superficial in all undertakings. Optimistic and happy-go-lucky, he or she will enjoy life. Although people of

this disposition may be impatient with their marriage partners and children, they are very forgiving. Vain and easily taken in by flatterers, they enjoy public acclaim but may suffer from circulatory and cardiac illnesses.

An individual with a lymphatic temperament will have long, soft white hands with short fingers, the joints of which are somewhat dislocated, and large nails. There will be few lines, but those that there are will be well marked, if pale. There may be red spots on the back of the hand. Cold, calm, patient, and persevering, this kind of person has a gift for organization and will make steady progress in life. He or she will face difficulty and danger calmly, with a dislike of fighting and quarrels, preferring the good things of life. Dogmatic so far as religion is concerned, these people rarely seeks divorce.

The hands of a young person will reveal the direction his life is likely to take, and will also indicate future choices and difficulties. Generally the left hand is thought to indicate an individual's hereditary disposition, while the right hand shows what choices will be made, and what defeats and successes lie ahead, although some palmists do not admit this division of information between the two hands.

By studying their hands, young people may be guided to choose a suitable career. As a result of learning about character traits, predilections, propensities, and strong and weak points, they may be to able to orientate themselves in a positive way toward family, partners, and society; such knowledge gained from the hands is invaluable. Self-knowledge may help in the selection of a partner, and foreknowledge of financial success or poverty enable them to face the future thankfully or bravely as the case may be.

For the mature man or woman, the past can be reviewed by means of the hands, and errors investigated, understood, and forgiven. The present can be illuminated, and if it is found to be unsatisfactory changes may be indicated that will lay the foundations for a more promising future. The opportunity to profit by past mistakes, and to perfect the character, is always there.

In old age, studying the hands can recall past memories; thanks can be offered for dangers past, hurdles overcome, and successes gained. The hand should reveal depths, serenity, and an ever-expanding vision of the wholeness of life, of that which is the Eternal.

Significant Handshake

A palmist will start interpreting the characteristics of a client's hand almost from the moment that they first meet. To start with, he notices what kind of hand he, or more usually she, possesses, and what kind of handshake they exchange. Is the hand firm and friendly, or is it weak or flabby? The first key to the client's personality is there, indicating that she is strong or weak, nervous or assured, pampered or hardworking.

Having made these observations, the palmist holds the client's hands and studies their shape. If they are long, a gift for detail and deliberation is indicated, while if they are small the individual is likely to be intuitive and impetuous. If the client constantly withdraws his or her hands and gesticulates gracefully, it means that he or she will be successful at social gatherings; if the gestures are violent, the individual is likely to be aggressive and high strung.

Someone who clenches their hands is a restless, frustrated, but self-reliant and dynamic person. If the hands remain relaxed, the individual is a confident and practical person with many interests, but may be a little over-trusting.

The man or woman who try to conceal their hands have secrets to conceal; they may be extremely shrewd about money matters, and are likely to change their views on life frequently.

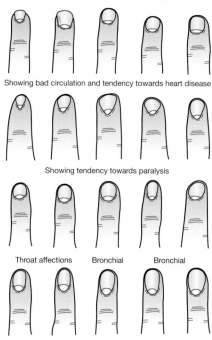

Showing bad circulation and tendency towards heart disease

Showing tendency towards paralysis

Throat affections   Bronchial   Bronchial

Delicacy of lungs   Consumptive tendencies

Sign of Strength

The way the client holds his or her fingers is another key to character. Close together suggests a leader, while someone who holds them slightly apart is primarily a good friend, and has a trusting nature. Unconventional or extravagant people spread their fingers wide, while those whose hands are held in a clawlike position are avaricious and untrustworthy.

The basic character is revealed in the left hand, on which the inherited pattern is shown. (Although palmists have debated whether the order of inspection should be reversed if the client is left-handed, no final decision has been reached.) A series of small lines and chains on the Life Line tells of physical weakness, but may also indicate a varied, nomadic, or unstable background. A double line gives added strength to the one that is duplicated. Triple lines are rare, but when they occur they can indicate genius, passion, fame, and riches; but if the surrounding lines or marks show

counterindications, deceitfulness or obsessional sexuality is likely. A meandering line suggests that the client lacks a clear goal in life, or that she may be the victim of troublesome minor illnesses or worries.

The way in which the Life Line terminates is significant. A forked terminal may mean feebleness in old age, which is to be expected, but it may also indicate lack of security because of improvidence in earlier years. If it ends with many tiny lines, financial loss or some tragedy may be forecast.

However, the depressing future foretold by these indications may be mitigated if the client deliberately strengthens herself both physically and mentally. Success in doing this will be reflected in the ever-changing configurations on the right hand. Regular inspection will show that, once practical steps have been taken toward improvement, harmful lines and marks, or distorted mounts, will disappear completely or be modified.

Once the palmist has interpreted the innate qualities and tendencies shown in the client's left hand, he or she will read the right one, making comparisons with the other from time to time. This will show whether the right hand shows modifications for better or worse, and enable the palmist to give advice as to what kind of action the client should take.

Plain hands showing scarcely any marks are rare, but do occur occasionally. What can be a strange and alarming blankness to the person concerned does not indicate death or an isolated existence nor does it mean that the individual is without significance.

BASIL IVAN RAKOCZI

FURTHER READING: Cheiro. Cheiro's Language of the Hand (Arco Books, 1968 reprint). M. Anderson. Palmistry. (York Beach, ME: Weiser, 1980).

Pisces

Those born between February 19 and March 20 fall under the sign of Pisces, the Two Fishes, the last sign of the zodiac. This sign may be of Egyptian origin, for there were two fishes among the Egyptian constellations, in the proximity of the Square of Pegasus, whereas the Babylonians described this part of the sky as either the Giant, the Tails, the Great Swallow, or by the name of a goddess. The ruling planet of the fishes was once said to be Jupiter, but from the 1840s onward, astrologers have become inclined to prefer Neptune as ruler of this sign. Pisceans, like Neptunians, do not mind being overcome by emotion, in fact, they enjoy it. They excel in any profession in which they have to act up to a situation.

Because of their genial, pleasure-loving temperament, Pisceans will always make the best of any situation; and they more often find themselves in situations rather than deliberately contrive how things are to turn out. They often succeed as journalists, actors, or in any profession where it is an advantage not to keep too close to reality. They are kind, good-natured, generous, but often rather weak-willed.

Pisceans are attracted by strange and exotic places, and a few may take the trouble to go there; a feeling for remoteness is thus the common element of the mystics, the travelers, and the astronomers with whom this sign abounds. Typically they are not interested in having problems too clearcut; they prefer to leave things vague and allow them to solve themselves. They are often and easily taken in by advertising rackets and other bogus 'opportunities.'

Versatility is another quality of Pisces; for though it is an advantage to have a family tradition, for example in music or architecture or acting, a Piscean often ignores pressures that urge him toward a particular career. Although he is, 'the average sensual man,' he is also more than that. Having decided that he will never 'set the Thames on fire,' one may be astounded to find him suddenly doing something quite remarkable.

It is tempting to write off the Piscean as nothing more than a pleasant companion, only to discover later to one's surprise that he is quite capable of hard work and devoted service. He is normally too fond of gossip to be properly discreet in conversation, and with increasing age becomes too casual to dress with normal care. He gets on well with people, and is popular. He is supposed to err in the direction of Mr. Micawber's weakness, always hoping that something will 'turn up,' but perhaps the Piscean is not quite so casual as he is represented.

Precognition

Knowledge of what is going to happen in the future; ways of gaining such knowledge, really or allegedly, have been legion and include astrology, palmistry, and many other methods of fortune telling, prophecies, oracles and omens, summoning up spirits or ghosts, trance states, dreams, premonitions, and 'intuitions;' much work has been done on precognition as a type of psi ability.

Premonitions

During World War II, Winston Churchill (1874–1965), as Britain's leader, often went out by car at night during air raids to see things for himself. He usually sat in the back seat, behind the driver. On one particular occasion, however, he changed his mind and went round to the other

A stained glass window showing Pisces, Notre Dame Cathedral, Chartres, France

side of the car. Later that night a bomb fell and the blast tilted the car up on two wheels, but then it righted itself. If it had not, both Churchill and his driver might well have been killed. When Mrs. Churchill heard about the incident, she asked her husband why he had changed his usual seat in the car. He replied that he didn't know, but, when she persisted, he said that 'something inside' him had told him not to sit in his customary place.

Churchill's premonition may have changed the course of history, it seems, but most presentiments or forebodings are not on so dramatic a level. A premonition is a mysterious awareness of a future event, often of an unwelcome nature —death, danger, ill luck, or a mishap of some kind— not arrived at by rational calculation, but coming into the mind unbidden in some way as yet unexplained. It can range from a clear prevision of a specific future occurrence—'X is going to be killed in a road accident tomorrow'—to the vaguer 'X is going to die soon,' on to a still vaguer but powerful foreboding of some impending, but unspecified, evil.

Even when they hit the main target, premonitions frequently seem to get details wrong. J. W. Dunne (1875–1949), author of the celebrated book *An Experiment With Time*, was in South Africa in 1902 when he had a vivid nightmare about an island that was threatened by a volcano. In the dream he was desperately trying to get the authorities to take action to save the island's 4,000 inhabitants. He knew that the figure was 4,000 and the number preyed on his mind in the dream. Several days later Dunne read the newspaper accounts of the eruption of a volcano on the island of Martinique that had killed 40,000 people. However, Dunne mistook the number of dead, reading it as 4,000, and he only discovered long afterward that the reported figure had

Artist Claire Fearon painted a picture of the 2011 Japanese earthquake terror after a premonition a year before the disaster struck.

really been ten times as many. As a result, he came to the conclusion that his precognition had been of himself misreading the newspaper stories.

Warnings of Doom

Premonitions may occur in dreams or in the waking state. They are among the most commonly reported experiences of an apparently psychic nature, and perhaps there are not many people who have not had a premonition at some time or other. There are many occasions when a premonition turns out to be wrong and the expected event does not happen, but these do not make the same impression on the mind as the ones that are borne out.

Writing in the *Journal of the American Society for Psychical Research*, W. E. Cox reported an analysis of the number of passengers riding in a train involved in an accident, compared with the normal number. He found a

significant reduction: for example, the Chicago & East Illinois Georgian carried only nine passengers on the day it was involved in an accident, but a typical sixty-two, five days before. Cox concluded that potential passengers had had an unconscious premonition to make them change their plans.

Not all premonitions are of misfortune, by any means. It is quite a common everyday experience, for instance, to hear the telephone ring and 'know' who is going to be on the other end before you pick it up.

Disaster Ahead

It is the premonitions connected with disaster, however, which hit the headlines. Like the dream in which Countess Tuchkov saw her father giving her the news of her husband's death at the battle of Borodino, also in 1812. The dream came three months in advance of the event—Borodino being an unknown place to both her husband and herself at the time. A few nights before he was assassinated in 1865, President Abraham Lincoln (1809–65) is said to have dreamed that he saw his dead body lying in state in the East Room of the White House.

After the sinking of the *Titanic* in 1912, there were stories of premonitions and prophecies of the liner's fate. The novelist Graham Greene (1904–1991), then a small boy, dreamed of a great shipwreck the night before the tragedy. A businessman named J. Cannon Middleton canceled his passage on the ship after dreaming two nights in succession of her floating keel upward on the sea with the passengers and crew swimming around her. On the other hand, the celebrated professional palmist and fortune-teller Cheiro (1836–1936) had told a well-known journalist of the day, W. T. Stead (1849–1912), that April 1912 was going to be a time of danger for him: 'So don't travel by water then if you can help it.' Stead took no notice and went down with the liner.

There were numerous reports of premonitions after the disaster at Aberfan in Wales in 1966, when a coal tip slid down a mountainside and crushed the village school, killing 128 children and sixteen others. Dr. J. C. Barker, a psychiatrist, collected seventy-six accounts of premonitions allegedly foreseeing the disaster. Of these, thirty-six had occurred in dreams and twenty-four premonitions had been witnessed by another person before the event. Some of the stories were impressive. For example, a woman in Plymouth, England 'saw' a mountain of coal hurtling down and burying a school in a valley and described what she had seen at a meeting on the day before the disaster occurred. This was confirmed by six witnesses who had been at the meeting.

A particularly sad example was the case of a ten-year-old Aberfan schoolgirl, who told her mother the day before the tragedy that she had dreamed of going to school and the school not being there because 'something black had come down over it.' The little girl

Like other examples of precognition, or inexplicable foreknowledge of the future, premonitions are vexingly difficult to pin down.

went happily off to school as usual next day and was killed in the disaster.

Dr. Barker helped to set up a short-lived British Premonitions Bureau in the following year, 1967, backed by a London newspaper. Nearly 500 examples were sent in during its first year, though most of them came from only a small number of people. In May a Mr. Hencher told the Bureau of his premonition of a plane crash with sad deaths of children and something to do with the aircraft's tailfin. In the following month a plane duly crashed at Stockport with substantial loss of life, including a number of child

fatalities. The tailfin, which was the only part of the plane undamaged, was pictured in many of the newspaper stories. In 1968 a bureau of the same kind was set up in New York, with similar results. In 1969 a man sent in a premonition of the crash of a light plane, with a number something like N129N or N429N. A few months later the world heavyweight boxing champion Rocky Marciano (1923–69) was killed in the crash of a light aircraft numbered N3149X.

Dr. Louisa Rhine, the distinguished US researcher, commented that 'if imperfect ESP impressions, especially those suggesting disasters ahead, could be clarified, intelligent preventative action could follow to the untold advantage of mankind.' Among many interesting cases she investigated was the example of a long-range premonition in which a mother 'saw' her son dead in his bath. This haunted her and two years later, when she heard him singing in the bath and then he fell silent, she felt thoroughly uneasy and went in, to find him exactly as she had seen him in the premonition. Fumes from the

View of Merthyr Vale and Aberfan. Aberfan cemetery can be seen on the hillside

gas heater had knocked him out and if she had not found him in time, he would have died.

A Pig in the Palace

A case worthy of one of the stories of P. G. Wodehouse (1881–1975) was reported to the Society for Psychical Research in 1895. It involved the wife of the Bishop of Hereford, who dreamed that after reading family prayers in the hall of the bishop's palace she opened the dining room door and saw an enormous pig standing between the table and the sideboard. The dream amused her and in the morning she told it to her children and their governess before reading prayers in the hall. She then went into the dining room and there, to her astonishment, was the pig as large as life. It had somehow got out of its sty and wandered into the house.

Like other examples of precognition, or inexplicable foreknowledge of the future, premonitions are vexingly difficult to pin down. Most of them are revealed only after the event has occurred, which makes them useless as evidence, and of those that are independently recorded before the event all too many are unsatisfactorily general and vague. Those specific enough to be impressive, on the other hand, at once attract intense suspicion and hostile criticism, because they seem to threaten our common-sense ideas of time and our cherished belief in human free will.

RICHARD CAVENDISH

Miriam's Dance (1360/3 by Tarnovo literary and art school), as in Exodus (chapter 15)

Prophecy

A word of Greek derivation, prophecy means 'speaking before.' In modern English it usually implies foretelling the future. Originally, however, this was not a prophet's essential function. He was the human spokesman of a god (preeminently of Yahweh, the God of Israel) and therefore a transmitter of divine messages, which might concern the future or might not.

Even in English the idea of prediction has not always been present. When St. Luke's gospel describes the beating and taunting of the blindfolded Christ, his assailants say, 'Prophesy! Who is it that struck you?' (Luke, chapter 22.64). What is demanded here is proof of such supernormal knowledge as a true messiah ought to possess.

The Old Testament sometimes employs the term 'prophet' very loosely. For instance, Abraham is a 'prophet' because he is the friend of God. Moses and his brother Aaron are called prophets, and their sister Miriam a prophetess, each for a different reason: Moses as the appointed mouthpiece of divine laws, Aaron as their translator into practice, Miriam as a leader of song and dance in God's praise. The common factor in these four instances is a special relationship with Yahweh.

Miriam's song of triumph over the Egyptians (Exodus, chapter 15.20–21) may be the oldest thing in the Bible, a kind of 'spiritual' made up on the spot. It proves the antiquity of 'prophecy' in some sense. However, the Hebrew prophesying that led up to the poetry of Isaiah and Jeremiah had a more specific character. It took place in a state of ecstasy. The prophet was a *nabhi*, a 'called' person. The Holy Spirit of Yahweh breathed upon him, and he leaped and sang and saw visions, and burst out into oracular sayings. Nabhi enthusiasm could be contagious, like the dancing mania of the Middle Ages, attacking people not normally subject to it. It appears first in chapter eleven of the book of Numbers, where seventy Israelite elders undergo a temporary collective seizure in the presence of Moses. In 1 Samuel (chapter 19) the rapture engulfs its victims against their will.

Men or women could prophesy. However, when prophets began to combine in guilds, membership was apparently confined to men. The full-time nabhi who had the gift was often a strolling player with a flute, harp, or tambourine. He wore a skin mantle with a leather belt. In the early period when Samuel and Saul flourished (c. 1050 BC–1015 BC) the nabhi might appear to be hardly more than a fortune teller, offering 'inspired' messages in return for presents and hospitality. But a graver theme always underlay his vocation, even at its most debased. Ostensibly at least, he received the word of Yahweh.

Profeta Osea. Depiction of a nabhi prophet

A Vessel of the Spirit

When we search for parallels outside Israel, we should recognize a distinction. The nabhi might look like a soothsayer or medium, but in fact he was not. Saul knew the difference, and banished persons of the latter type while respecting prophets (1 Samuel, chapter 28.3). Soothsaying and mediumship in the ancient world were based on techniques. Diviners had their pseudo-sciences of dream interpretation and omen-reading. Even the priestesses of Delphi, who succumbed to possession by Apollo, put themselves into a drugged state that induced the prophetic process and brought the oracle.

The Hebrew nabhi, if true to his calling, did not seek answers to questions by any similar art. He might make himself receptive by prayer or fasting, but he could not compel the Lord. It was the Holy Spirit that came, or did not come, with an imperiousness beyond the prophet's control. The prophet might deceive others, and himself, into thinking the Spirit was upon him when it was not—as in the remarkable story of Ahab and the battle of Ramoth-Gilead (1 Kings, chapter 22)—but he never pretended that his message was extracted from God by some technique of his own.

The sounder parallels with the Israelite tradition are to be found in the realm of ecstatic religion. There is an account of a Canaanite fanatic becoming possessed by a god, c. 1100 BC, chronologically between Moses and Saul. Closer still to the nabhi excitement, and better documented, is the frenzy accompanying the cult of Dionysus. But while the outward symptoms may have been much the same everywhere, Hebrew prophecy had a unique capacity for growth and enrichment. Yahweh was more than Dionysus. To faithful Israelites he was not merely a god but supreme, the only higher power that mattered, at least to them; and his cult had an ethical content, both for the community and for the individual. The nabhi experience could and did mature, over the centuries, into a solemn disclosure of the divine will through inspired speakers.

Its Greek counterpart passed from the fiery Dionysiac phase into Orphic mysticism. Hebrew prophecy went on growing as a phenomenon in its own right, even after it transcended its nabhi origins. In the end it transformed Israel's religion without losing its identity.

So profound were its effects that some scholars have claimed what is certainly too much. They have contended that the later, literary prophets—Isaiah and the rest—actually invented Israel's religion, and that Old Testament history is largely fiction, concocted to give a pedigree to their teachings. This theory is now out of favour for several reasons, but chiefly because of what the history says, and the tone that the prophets take.

We get a picture, first, of a priestly cult of Yahweh as the God who rescued his people from Egyptian bondage and settled them in the Promised Land. The nabhi prophets have only a subsidiary role. Then, after many years, come the literary prophets. They do not speak like innovators founding a new religion; they appeal to a pure ancestral faith, which they say has been corrupted by monarchy, material wealth, a court priesthood, and flirtation with paganism. The priestly political tradition and the prophetic tradition are two aspects of the same religion. It is incredible that either party would have invented the other in just this way. But having recognized the fact, we should also recognize that it was the prophets, rather than the priests, who gave Israel's faith its eventual grandeur and permanency.

The Prophetic Succession

Between the nabhi and the authors of the later Old Testament books stands the transitional figure of Elijah. He denounced paganism and tyranny in the northern Israelite kingdom under Ahab (875 BC–853 BC). A memorable event in this prophet's career is a visit to Mount Horeb in Sinai, where Moses had received Yahweh's commandments. Elijah witnesses much the same portents— wind, earthquake, fire—but 'the Lord was not in' them. The Lord speaks to him in a 'still small voice.' Here Israel's religion is moving toward a new spiritual level.

Elijah left no writings, apart from a doubtful fragment preserved in 2 Chronicles (chapter 21.12-15). About 760 BC, however, literary prophets began to be active, in a succession that went on for centuries and has had no parallel in any other religion. Even these were speakers rather than authors: they harangued crowds, recited verses, and told stories in public, underlining them with symbolic gestures, such as smashing a pot in token of a city's ruin. Some of their doings and

. . . While the prophets' main objects were to teach, warn, and encourage, they did foreshadow future events: hence the notion of prophecy as prediction.

utterances were set down on sheets of papyrus, either by themselves or by their disciples. The sheets were glued side by side to form a continuous roll; these rolls are the books of the prophets, as we have them in the Bible after many transcriptions.

The literary prophets were still men on whom the Spirit breathed as it had on the nabhi. Habakkuk seems to have regarded himself as a nabhi still, and to have made himself receptive with conscious purpose (Habakkuk, chapter 2.1). But in both respects he was unusual. Generally, ideas and images surged unbidden into the prophet's mind; visions forced themselves on him, in sleep or waking; and now, instead of pouring them out in a raw state, he reflected on them and gave them poetic form.

The most important literary prophets fall into two groups. The first quartet comprises Amos, Hosea, Isaiah, and Micah. Amos was a shepherd and labourer. His book of divine messages is notable as the earliest known left-wing manifesto. It denounces the

complacent nobles of Israel, and foretells a 'day of the Lord' that will bring retribution on an unjust society. Hosea attacks religious corruption. Isaiah and Micah scan a broader horizon, seeing the Lord as ruler over other nations besides Israel, and foreshadowing a worldwide peace when he will be worshipped by all mankind, if his chosen will only be faithful.

Ideas and images surged unbidden into the prophet's mind; visions forced themselves on him, in sleep or waking

A second quartet of prophets arose in the late seventh century, after the northern Israelite kingdom had been destroyed by Assyria. These were Zephaniah, Nahum, Habakkuk, and Jeremiah. Jeremiah, the most important, was a priest; there was no inevitable clash between the two callings. He speaks darkly of the sins of Jerusalem and its impending fall. However, he looks farther ahead to a restoration and a 'new covenant,' which the Lord will write upon the hearts of his people.

Jeremiah, in fact, envisaged a future when the purified religion of Israel would develop into something greater and nobler. So did the unknown author of the mistakenly attached portion of the book of Isaiah that begins at the fortieth chapter. This 'Second Isaiah' prophesied in Babylon during the Jews' captivity. He hails their deliverer in the person of Cyrus the Great, who will conquer Babylon and let the captives go home. He calls Cyrus the Lord's Anointed, or Messiah. By launching that momentous theme, and predicting a universal reign of righteousness under the One God of all mankind, the Second Isaiah takes a further step toward the expansion of Israel's faith into a world religion. So, in another way, does the book of Jonah, which depicts that prophet bearing God's word to the Gentiles of Nineveh.

Ezekiel, like the Second Isaiah, belongs to the Babylonian exile. He is the least spontaneous of the prophets, the nearest to being a composer of planned essays. His book closes with a description of a Utopia. Afterward come a few post-exilic prophets who add little. Judaism regards prophecy as ending with the Old Testament canon.

Hints of the Future

It will be noticed that while the prophets' main objects were to teach, warn, and encourage, they did foreshadow future events: hence the notion of prophecy as prediction. But the divinely revealed hints at the future are never the whole message. Some, moreover, are conditional and not absolute: 'If you do this, such and such will happen,' not simply 'Such and such will happen.'

Yet with every allowance made, the predictions raise difficulties for their religious interpreters. If inspired, they must be right. But how should they be construed? On a literal reading, some have been fulfilled (the repeated promise of Israel's return to Palestine, very impressively indeed); but several of

Mysteries of the Rosary, sixteenth century, by Campi Vincenzo (c. 1536–91). Oil on canvas. San Bartolomeo Collegiate Church, Emilia Romagna, Parma, Italy. The image shows Mary and the apostles experiencing the Pentacost.

the more grandiose have not. There is, for instance, no sight of the prophets' Golden Age.

Here Christians and Jews part company. The orthodox Jewish view is that the Golden Age and similar consummations still lie ahead. They will come with the Messiah. Christians have sought to gather the prophetic loose ends together by applying them to Christ and the Church. Often the application is figurative, but not always. The gospel of Matthew insists on Jesus's literal fulfillment of various cryptic texts in the prophets, from his birth at Bethlehem onward.

Many of the Christian interpretations involve a species of hindsight. In the light of Christ the prophetic text may seem to make sense, and sometimes it manifestly does. Yet a person reading the text beforehand would seldom have been able to predict the fulfillment. The strongest argument for the Christian view is probably Isaiah, chapter 53, which describes a suffering 'servant of the Lord' in terms that fit no historical person but Jesus. An episode in the Acts of the Apostles (chapter 8.27–35) shows how readers were driven to speculate about this passage in Jesus's time, and how quick the Christians were to apply it.

Christianity counts John the Baptist as the last prophet of the old dispensation. Christ himself assumes the prophetic role when he foretells the fall of Jerusalem and the Temple. His words raise the same problem as the other unfulfilled prophecies, because they suggest that the world will end when the Temple falls, or soon after, and that some of his contemporaries will live to witness both events. The Temple fell in AD 70, but the world did not end. One explanation is that Jesus was simply wrong. Another is that he spoke of the nearer event as a type or symbol of the more distant,

and his sayings on the two topics have not been clearly enough distinguished. Another is that the prophecy was conditional like Jonah's, and the condition, whatever it was, has been left out of the gospels.

Christianity pursues the prophetic theme in the story of Pentecost (Acts, chapter 2), when the Holy Spirit descended on the disciples. Christian prophecy ends with the Apocalypse, the last New Testament book.

Has valid prophecy occurred since? Jews deny this. Roman Catholicism asserts, as a matter of faith, that the Holy Spirit abides in the Church, pre-

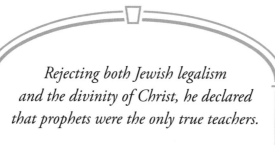

Rejecting both Jewish legalism and the divinity of Christ, he declared that prophets were the only true teachers.

serving it from error but never adding to the content of revelation. The main Protestant bodies have taken the same stand, often more firmly.

Nevertheless, several extremists of the Reformation period claimed to be, in effect, prophets; and the term has since been applied occasionally to leaders of sects. The Mormon Church refers to its founder as 'the Prophet Joseph Smith,' on the ground that he was a vessel of special revelations. Roman Catholic theologians have argued that such events as visions of the Blessed Virgin are Christian equivalents of the pre-Christian prophetic experience. Mary's appearances at Fatima in Portugal in 1917 are said to have been accompanied by predictions of future happenings.

The Prophet of Islam
Islam, the third great religion with Old Testament antecedents, places prophecy at the heart of its scheme.

Mohammed was and is *the* Prophet. Rejecting both Jewish legalism and the divinity of Christ, he declared that prophets were the only true teachers. His mission was to restate and perfect the teachings transmitted from Allah by five predecessors—Adam, Noah, Abraham, Moses, and Jesus—all of whom had been misconstrued. The Koran, dictated to him by the angel Gabriel, is frequently spoken of as the Islamic Bible; in fact it is more like a single prophetic book of the Old Testament. While no Muslim can ever supersede Mohammed, Islam has allowed a kind of prophecy to continue, in such cults as Sufism. The predictive element has always been less conspicuous than in Judaism and Christianity.

In other religious contexts it is doubtful whether the word 'prophecy' should ever be used. There are no close parallels to the Jewish literary genre. As for the more primitive excitements that are reminiscent of the nabhi, these are better discussed in terms of 'ecstasy' or 'possession.'

Can any safe conclusion be drawn about the prophetic experience? Visions, voices, and so on can doubtless be explained away, but does the explanation dispose of the message? Bertrand Russell (1872—1970) once alleged that we can draw no objective distinction between a man who eats too little and sees heaven, and a man who drinks too much and sees snakes. However, such dismissals cannot be final, because prophecy never took place in isolation. It was a factor in the life of Israel, or the Church, or the Muslim community. The depth and durability of the prophets' insights, the effects on history, are a matter of record. The alcoholic does nothing comparable with his delusions.

Nor does Russell refute the one modern genius who professed to be a prophet himself and, in some sense, demonstrably was: William Blake (1757–1827). It is thought that Blake's visions and revelations may have come to him in a hypnagogic state, between sleeping and waking. But the prophetic books that he based on them are not mere 'automatic writing.' They are highly-wrought works of unique literary stature, profound and far ahead of their time. As with Blake, so with Isaiah or Ezekiel. Wherever the experience came from, the resulting work cannot be exorcised by pseudo-scientific incantations about mental unbalance or physical disorder. The prophet may have been subject to either or both. Even so, he still has a secret that escapes his critic.

Colloquial use of the word 'prophecy' to mean 'prediction' raises the question whether people who profess to foretell the future should ever be called prophets because of that alone. As in antiquity, so today, the practitioners of such arts as astrology and dream interpreting cannot normally qualify. Seeking knowledge through a technique is a different thing from being invaded by divine inspiration. Still less should the term 'prophet' be attached to racing tipsters, pollsters, or forecasters of economic trends.

One query does persist. There are cases where a person who seems to be simply a fortune teller like other fortune tellers is strikingly more successful than most. The classic historical instance is the astrologer Nostradamus (1503–66). When all wild claims have been discounted, it remains true that a handful of his bizarre quatrains scored astonishing hits. The US crystal-gazer Jeane Dixon (1904–1997), whose forecasts were a regular feature in the United States press, was a modern counterpart. In such cases we may feel that the technique is superficial, and the soothsayer has been touched by more mysterious influences.

The final judgment should turn, perhaps, on the nature of the messages. Where they carry a spiritual or moral charge, it should seriously be considered whether something like Hebrew prophecy is occurring again. With Nostradamus that element is slight. Jeane Dixon, on the other hand, has made predictions about the future of religion, including the rise of a new messianic figure born in February 1962. It is noteworthy that although she is a devout Catholic, she concurs with two other Catholic seers in expecting an early end to the papacy as we know it. Such a forecast, against the forecaster's presumed beliefs, certainly suggests an idea forcing its way in from outside the conscious self.

Multiple Time

Few attempts have been made to explain prophecy scientifically, except in the sense of explaining it away. The Holy Spirit's visitations are explained in psychological terms; the predictions are swept aside as guesswork, wishful thinking or, when correct, as forged after the event. Among rationalists who have admitted that knowledge, including knowledge of the future, may indeed come from 'beyond,' the best known is J. W. Dunne (1875–1949), author of *An Experiment With Time* (1927). Dunne had noticed that stray images entering his mind—either in dreams or in passive receptivity—fitted into experiences that he underwent later, yet could not have foreseen. He persuaded twenty-two experimental subjects to write down their dreams immediately on waking, and watch for fulfillments within a limited time. Several produced images and motifs, some highly unlikely, which figured later in their waking experience. None was associated with any important message or meaning. Still it might fairly be urged that some features of biblical prophecy were being reproduced.

Dunne proposed a theory of multiple time. The human mind stretches away back from ordinary consciousness into an inner self that can observe other temporal dimensions. This sometimes pushes through into the conscious ego with glimpses of what that ego may eventually see for itself, but has not seen yet, because it has not reached that point on its own time-track. The deeper self is immortal and might, one gathers, look indefinitely far ahead.

Possibly the main interest of Dunne is that while he sets up a kind of unconscious in place of God, he concedes that this unconscious must be more than psychoanalysts recognize. If it is to fill its ambitious role, it must have its own methods of cognition. Much the same view has been advanced, as the logical conclusion of Jung's system, by the Catholic psychologist Victor White (1902–1960). In any impartial study of prophecy, the most fruitful approach may well be to say: 'Yes, I agree with any Freudian or Jungian that these things come from the unconscious. But how did they get there in the first place?'

GEOFFREY ASHE

FURTHER READING: D. Aune. Prophecy in Early Christianity and the Ancient Mediterranean World. *(Grand Rapids, MI: Eerdmans, 1983); J. Blenkinsopp.* A History of Prophecy in Israel. *(Louisville, KY: Westminster John Knox, 1983); John Alden Williams ed.* Islam. *(Upper Saddle River, NJ: Prentice-Hall, 1961); Mona Wilson.* The Life of William Blake. *(New York, NY: Oxford University Press, 1950).*

Psi

Greek letter, used in parapsychology to denote 'psychic' abilities or phenomena; clairvoyance, precognition telepa-

Mr. and Mrs. James Coates conducting an experiment in psychometry. Mrs. Coates is seeking to read the content of the envelope by extra-sensory means.

thy, and psychokinesis are generally regarded as effects of a single, unified ability, called 'psi.'

Psychometry

The use of an article, called an 'inductor,' as a means of receiving extra-sensory impressions is known as object reading, psychoscopy or, most usually, psychometry. Extra-sensory perception (paragnosis) is a broad term covering various concepts, of which the most important are telepathy and clairvoyance. Clairvoyance, the ability to see objects not actually present, may be in time—seeing into the past, present or future—or in space (telaesthesia), in which case it should be considered as synonymous with clairvoyance in the present.

One experiment has been reported of a psychometric test the results of which depended upon telepathy. The subject of the experiment, a woman, was handed an envelope containing a photograph sent by a man known personally to the researcher. She put her right hand briefly into the partially open envelope without looking at the photograph, which served as an inductor but contained no clues for practical purposes. She commented as follows: 'Someone who reads and writes a lot. He is at home in any field. He performs journalistic work. He is quickly stimulated. He leads a hurried and irregular life. I see him writing while seated in a train. He picks up every scrap of news. This is not just curiosity—he has to keep abreast of

everything that happens. He can be curt at times. Stacks of papers lie on his desk in a complete jumble. He has a good sense of humour. He speaks foreign languages. Machines form part of his environment. I hear a regular thumping sound. The air reeks. I smell a peculiar, vile scent. The uproar is awful. He himself does not work among the machines, but he walks between them. He sits at a desk. He has a feeling for poetry. He gets a lot of books sent to him.'

It was totally unknown to the subject that this man was the managing editor of a provincial newspaper. This case was therefore a direct 'hit.' The researcher was in frequent touch with the editor at the time, and had visited his office several times, where his desk was covered with papers.

From time to time during their talks, he would stroll into the composing room to give various instructions. The room smelled of printer's ink, and there were the familiar noises of a printing plant.

As a journalist, the editor was always in search of news, and traveled a great deal by train. He possessed a good sense of humour, was a lover of poetry, and was accustomed to receiving books for review. From this it appears that the subject of the experiment was able to pick up in her mind the thoughts that crossed the researcher's when he saw the editor's photograph. In other words, when touching the portrait, she had the power to bring to mind what to the researcher remembered when seeing his picture.

The nature of telepathy now becomes apparent. It is the reception in one's mind of thoughts that emanate from another person's mind. The picture was no more than a prerequisite for the researcher remembering all sorts of things about the editor. The same can be said regarding the picture as an inductor to the psychometrist's 'upwelling' of thoughts that rise from within the mind, coming, as might be said, 'out of the blue.'

When psychometrists are observed during experiments and questioned about their ways of working, it appears that they usually get their impressions in the form of images coming to them or being 'forced' upon them: this is how the various thoughts connected with the object handed to them are experienced.

A Flood of Tears

Psychometrists often show an inclination to compare themselves with those who have difficulty trying to recollect a forgotten word or name. If anyone tries to bring to mind such a 'missing' word he or she will often observe that, at first, names or words that have some kind of associative connection with the forgotten word seem to be 'thrust' upon him.

The same thing happens in psychometry, as is obvious from the following example pertaining to the well-known Gerard Croiset (1909–1980). One day he asked a student about his Oedipus complex: 'Have you an Oedipus complex or are you interested in it?' When the student denied his involvement, Croiset continued: 'And yet you have something to do with it.' The student again denied this. Then there was a moment of silence, during which Croiset seemed to wait

Experiments with psychometrists have shown that, not only are they not affected in their functioning by distance between experimenter and subject, but they can also break through the time barrier.

for complementary impressions. Then he said: 'Now I see other pictures. Did you see a person this morning in a flood of tears that could not be stanched?' The student answered that he had seen that morning a patient in the eye hospital who had an excessive flow of tears. When the question is asked how Croiset came to talk about an Oedipus complex, it is not difficult to give an answer. Croiset's brother Max was a famous actor, who had many times played the principal character in Oedipus Rex. At the moment that Oedipus plucks out both his eyes, pieces of red beet were put over the actor's eyes, causing a flood of tears. So, for Gerard Croiset, a flood of tears was associated with Oedipus and whatever was connected with this drama.

In Bits and Pieces

Conscious memory recall may occur gradually or as a whole. Every event is built up of a number of various elements. The same difficulty in obtaining a complete 'picture' can be observed in psychometrists. Often they will get only a few letters of a first or last name 'thrust onto' them in a paranormal way, or they very often 'see' only a few elements of the totality of events occurring in the past of people with whom they are in telepathic rapport.

In one psi experiment the subject, on being introduced to a woman unknown to him, suddenly 'saw' the image of a pair of long white gloves and long ear-rings. The sensitive told the woman that both images went together and had something to do with her, but he did not know what the connection was. She then explained that as a member of a theatrical group she had recently played a part in which she had to wear long white gloves and long earrings. For the second act she had to change costumes, and one evening one of the gloves got caught in an ear-ring. This agitated her a great deal especially since she had so little time before going on stage again.

G. E. Müller (1850–1934) who contributed a great deal to the development of the psychology of memory, has pointed out certain signs that he called 'exactitude criteria'—standards by which the accuracy of memory may be gauged—and which together form the 'total exactitude-consciousness' or certainty about the thing remembered. These criteria include the exclusiveness and the persistency with which the reproduced fact or name is brought to mind. A very important exactitude-criterion is the 'fullness of ideas,' by which is meant the awareness that ideas which are brought to mind are connected with others.

In experiments with psychometrists it is very often found that the impressions they receive are coupled with a firm exactitude-consciousness.

When questioned them about how their minds work, and especially about this exactitude-consciousness, the same criteria occur as the ones found in memory research.

A lowered state of consciousness, that causes the person to be less inhibited, is evidently favourable to Psychometry. In observing psychometrists, their level of consciousness during the experiments is seen to be lowered totally or in part. In most cases this lower level is so slight that it can only be detected with special instruments. With a few subjects this lowering of the level of consciousness goes so far, that one may speak of trance and auto-hypnosis. The state of lessening of inhibition resulting from the auto-hypnosis enhances the flow of telepathically received impressions.

Through the Time Barrier

Experiments with psychometrists have shown that, not only are they not affected in their functioning by distance between experimenter and subject, but they can also break through the time barrier. Some of their experiences show that they are able to get impressions from persons they will meet— by chance—in the future.

In 1946 a test was developed that is known now as the chair experiment. This test consisted of two steps. First the subject (Gerard Croiset) gave a description of the characteristics and certain outstanding experiences of a person whom he expected to occupy a certain chair in a lecture hall. Next, often some weeks later, the person who by chance occupied this chair was questioned, to see to what degree Croiset's description fitted or deviated from the personality and experiences of this individual. These chair experiments were carried on for many years and in many parts of Europe.

Experiments in the Parapsychological Institute of the State University of Utrecht showed that some individuals

Portrait of Dutch ESP Expert Gerald Croiset

were able, under certain circumstances, to furnish data about lost persons, thefts, and murders. This discovery raises the question of how far these gifts might be used for practical purposes. However, it must be emphasized that to the science of parapsychology the question of whether ESP can have a practical application is only secondary. There are parapsychological 'hits' of tremendous theoretical value but with little practical implication.

The man in the street tends to think, incorrectly, that sensitives are

able to see anything and everything. Nothing is further from the truth. Continual research has taught us that in nearly all such persons we find a more or less specialized interest determined in part by their own experiences. A psychoanalytical approach should, then, provide a knowledge of the urges that motivate them toward the direction of their interest. One example is the case of a sensitive who regarded it as almost his holy mission to detect thieves and succeeded repeatedly in doing so. Talks with this man showed that, when he was about seventeen, his father wrongly suspected him of having stolen some money. This suspicion caused quite a lot of difficulties for him that stopped only when his father received proof that his brother, who was always supposed to set an example, was guilty of the theft. The urge that this sensitive showed to solve thefts was clearly related to the psychical trauma which this suspicion had caused.

In contradistinction to the urge to see certain things, there exists also the urge not to see certain things. It is self-evident that this negative urge ought to interest the researcher just as much as the positive one: the more so because many of the blind spots that are considered to be shortcomings are closely linked to such negative urges.

The following case is a starting point. In October 1958, a Mrs. A. B., who had often given evidence of psi abilities, was visited by a woman. In the course of the visit, Mrs. A. B. spontaneously asked her visitor whether her father was possibly interested in the play *Gijsbrecht van Amstel*, as she got the impression that in some way or other he had something to do with this tragedy. On receiving a negative answer, Mrs. A. B. did not pursue the matter further.

On January 17, 1960 the visitor's father died. The family inserted the announcement of his death in the newspaper the following day and Mrs. A. B.'s visitor signed the announcement. Under this insertion, at a distance of about 6 inches, there was an advertisement of a forthcoming performance of the tragedy *Gijsbrecht van Amstel*. Because both announcements were coincidentally associated in space as well as in time, and both were read by the visitor, we may accept that we have here a case of a so-called 'displacement' or substitution based on 'defense' mechanism which certainly originated in a repression.

A Childhood Guilt

Some years ago a researcher came into contact with a 23-year-old student who was gifted with psi abilities to some degree. A series of psychometric experiments followed, which on the whole produced satisfying results. One day, when handed a cap to be used as an inductor, the subject said that this object gave him a very unpleasant feeling. The cap, which had been made available by the police, belonged to a man sought in connection with the murder of the new-born child of his unmarried daughter. The student said that he felt terrified. Suddenly he threw the inductor away, stating that he did not get any impressions.

Some days later, although not given any information about the origin of this object, the test subject asked whether it had something to do with the murder of a new-born child. When the researcher asked him why he put this question, he replied that he had had a dream about a man who had put a newborn child under a heap of pillows. At that point the researcher replied that this 'picture' was correct.

Afterward a conversation followed about 'displacements' in time as observed by Whately Carington (1892–1947), S. G. Soal (1889–1975), and others. Suddenly the subject exclaimed: 'Now I know why I did not get any impressions a few days ago.' He began to talk in detail about an event in his childhood. His mother gave birth to a second child and gave so much care and attention to the new baby that it aroused feelings of hate and repugnance in him. One day, an aunt who happened to visit them saw him deliberately throwing bricks into the cradle: his aunt consequently gave him a sound spanking.

When he was asked him if he could find any connection between this experience of his youth and his not being able to tell anything about the inductor (that is, the cap) given to

him a few days previously, the subject answered: 'It's quite clear. Unwittingly I identified myself with the murderer of the child. Something within me told me: "You might have done the same thing: you are capable of doing something like that." Therefore I did not want to see it.'

When he was asked if he could account for his anxiety when he took the inductor in his hand, the subject answered without hesitation that he was sure that this anxiety must have resulted from a deep repression. 'Evidently, I knew at once when you handed me the inductor that this had to do with the murderer of a child. Because I identified myself with the murderer, however, I must immediately have repressed these impressions, which caused anxiety. During my sleep, when censorship was weakened, the story loomed up in me.'

Condensing Space and Time

In the dreams and hallucinations of experienced by sensitives the phenomenon of condensation or compression has also frequently been noticed. One such case concerned a sensitive, W. Tholen, who, like Gerard Croiset, succeeded innumerable times in supplying details by telephone about missing persons, animals, and objects. In August 1964 he was consulted on the telephone by a doctor, unknown to him, whose wife had mislaid three trinkets. Mr. Tholen gave a description of an antique cupboard that was supposedly in the consultant's home. He 'saw' the missing objects in this cupboard. Since the doctor did not possess such a cupboard he paid no further attention to the sensitive's words. Subsequently he found the three trinkets, but in three different cupboards. He then realized that the sensitive had amalgamated elements of these three cupboards and visualized an entirely new piece of furniture.

Similar compressions and condensations have been recorded in which situations, both from the past and from the future, blend with situations from the present into a new and at first unrecognizable whole. Croiset, for instance, when asked to indicate where a missing person might be found, described a stretch of river where ships were moored. The ships were at that time no longer there but had been moored there some days previously. It was the place where the missing person had drowned, and Croiset had wanted to indicate where to look.

W. H. C. TENHAEFF

FURTHER READING: J. H. Pollack. Croiset the Clairvoyant. *(New York, NY:* *Doubleday, 1964); W. H. C. Tenhaeff.* Telepathy and Clairvoyance. *(Springfield, IL: Charles C. Thomas, 1972).*

Pyromancy

Pyromancy is the practice of divination by the use of fire. The Roman writer, Marcus Terentius Varro (116 BC–27 BC) classified it as one of the types of divination deriving from the four elements—fire, air, water, and earth. The practice was known to the Greeks, although its use goes even further back in human history. The behaviour of a flame resulting from a sacrificial fire was deemed significant—whether it smouldered or burned clear and high. Pyromancy was also used in Asia in conjunction with animal bones: the appearance of burned bone—the colour and resulting cracks — providing the means by which supernatural signs could be interpreted.

Sagittarius

The sun is in Sagittarius, the ninth sign of the zodiac, between November 22 or 23 and December 21 or 22. Sagittarius is associated with flying and journeys to distant lands, and Sagittarians are generally enthusiastic travelers. Idealism is another of their traits, but this can range from altruism

Mosaic on the floor of the Galleria Umberto I in Naples, Italy, shows Sagittarius

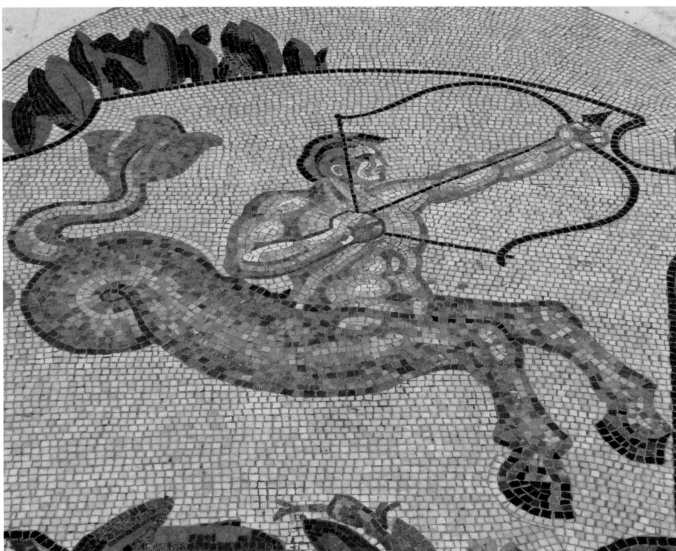

to dangerous fanaticism. Sagittarians can too easily become the worshippers of the law they preach, slaves of ritual and convention.

They may be rebels only for the sake of rebelling; hypocrites in religion; even political turncoats in pursuit of their ambitions. Yet they seldom betray a personal trust, and remain good friends, although their instinct to be outspoken on any subject may cause pain to those close to them.

A Sagittarian businessman will never be content with a monotonous job, however well it may pay; he is always eager to progress to something bigger or, supposedly, better. Ambition in Sagittarians varies, from the ruthless desire to amass a large fortune to the natural wish that any person has for success in life.

Hope is another quality that this sign exemplifies, and an individual under its influence will remain optimistic in spite of repeated disappointments. Sagittarians have a strong sporting instinct, believing that it is more fun to take a chance than to be prudent, and gambling is one of the vices that they find especially tempting.

People born with the sun in Sagittarius are usually interested in education, and they often enjoy teaching, particularly of games and sports, and are always pleased to see their pupils making the best of themselves. Other careers include the armed forces, advertising and dealing in horses.

People born under Sagittarius sometimes find it difficult to express affection. On the whole, however, generosity comes naturally to Sagittarians (provided they themselves are well-protected), for they believe that money and luck will never cease to flow toward them.

Traditionally Sagittarians, though sound in constitution, are inclined

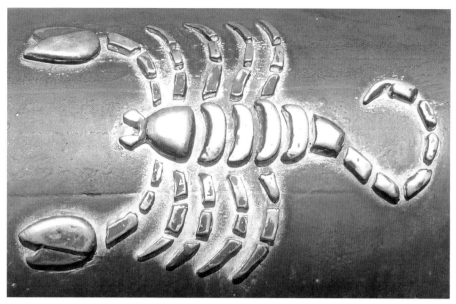

Scorpio—thought of as the most dangerous sign of the zodiac

to be highly strung, and may suffer a nervous breakdown. Hips and thighs are susceptible to diseases such as sciatica and rheumatism. The moon in Sagittarius denotes a lofty and idealistic nature, with a dedication to conventional religion or philosophy; with bad aspects, this may result in narrow-minded bigotry and a 'holier-than-thou' attitude.

Scorpio

The sign of the scorpion, according to the traditional zodiac, rules those who are born between October 23 and November 21. For many years it

Work should be a natural expression of one's energy, as it is with animals, and as it is with creative artists and craftsmen.

has been the custom to maintain that Scorpio is the most dangerous sign of the zodiac, with quite the most tricky character that one might have to deal with. It was accused of being the most

dark, secretive, treacherous, and generally vicious sign of any.

In fact, the genuine Scorpio person is governed by his energy, for this sign, like Aries, is ruled by Mars, the planet of courage, energy, and activity. He wants to act, not brood, and hence he is frequently uninhibited and impatient. To the true Scorpion nothing is too much trouble. His aim is to do, he sees no point in boggling or hesitation, little in compromise and none at all in shirking. He is admirably thorough.

Work, to him, is a pleasurable pastime: to work for money, from the Martian point of view, is slightly dishonest. Work should be a natural expression of one's energy, as it is with animals, and as it is with creative artists and craftsmen. Any attempt to turn work into a burden is offensive to the Martian spirit.

Human relations are made far easier by the positive attitude of the Scorpion, who is not perpetually on the defensive, not grasping, not full of forethought for self, though he may cause offence through too little sympathy for the timidities of others.

There is something very satisfying

in the thoroughness of the Scorpion. He does not merely play at doing things, but carries them through in a properly adult and professional manner, in contrast with those born under Gemini, Virgo, and Pisces. Another characteristic of Scorpio is wit and humour, which may be a socially acceptable safety valve as much as an overflow of good nature.

Any quality that confers benefit on others is a virtue, and the benefit to be derived from Scorpions is that they take on themselves the dark, dangerous, and risky tasks that others frequently do not dare to undertake. But by the same token, they would rather be active than do nothing and so may be tempted into impatience.

Scrying

The word 'scrying' means seeing, as in the slightly old-fashioned 'descry,' for which most people would now use 'discern.' Strictly speaking, scrying is the kind of divination that uses transparent materials—water, mirrors, crystals—in which are formed visions of the future.

Under the heading of scrying a startling range of techniques might be included. Scrying with water is properly called hydromancy: also using water are such secondary forms as cylicomancy (using cups of water), and leconomancy (using oil poured onto water in basins), not to mention all the forms that involve moving water, or indeed other liquids ranging from ink to treacle. Mirror scrying, or catoptromancy, also has its subsidiary forms, which include divination by the reflections in brass objects and on the backs of watches, and through magnifying glasses.

Today it is medicine rather than magic that suffers from over-special-

ization, and the seers have broadened their bases once again. The more obscure forms of scrying never had more than a limited application. Hydromancy and catoptromancy dominated the field, and instances of the use of cups of water, and variants, can be found in magical traditions

Sitting and staring into a glass ball is obviously a great deal less work than drawing up horoscopes or laying out Tarot cards.

from all over the world—ancient Egypt, Assyria, Persia, Tahiti, and southern Africa, as well as from the Graeco-Roman world and among later European peoples. Mirrors, too, were beloved by the prophets of the old civilizations, including that of the Aztecs, who held them to be a sacred emblem of the dark god Tezcatlipoca.

These interrelated forms of scrying maintained their prestige into fairly recent centuries, but then slowly began to die away. There may be a few determined hydromancers left, in the backwaters (literally) of modern occultism. But in our time the form of scrying that has pride of place is that which uses the crystal—properly known as crystallomancy, but more often and called crystal-gazing.

This process displays quite an impressive heritage. Groups in north Borneo, New Guinea, and Madagascar have such divination in their traditions, while the indigenous people of Australia venerate pieces of crystal quartz that are apparently sometimes used to provide visions. An Inca legend mentions a chief who owned a magic crystal that revealed the future. The Maya of Central America, and other groups in that region, believed firmly in divination from polished

stones. And in what is now the United States, the Cherokee Native Americans once looked for foreknowledge in bits of polished crystal, while the Apache used such stones to scry the whereabouts of lost or stolen property.

In Europe the crystal apparently began to come into its own among the Franks and Saxons in the early centuries of the Christian era. Small crystal globes were found—by excavators centuries ago—in the tombs of high-status individuals, and scholars eventually concluded that the objects were used for divination rather than as ornaments. Certainly many early Christians, including St. Patrick in the fifth century, denounced the practice strongly enough to indicate its spread. By the nineteenth century, crystallomancy had joined other popular forms of fortune-telling, along with palmistry and cards.

Do-It-Yourself Scrying
Some of the explanation for crystal-gazing's popularity must lie in its simplicity. Sitting and staring into a glass ball is obviously a great deal less work than drawing up horoscopes or laying out Tarot cards. Nor is there any prerequisite jargon to be learned. And yet, in the history of scrying, people have gone to a great deal of trouble to impose complication upon this basic simplicity.

The ball itself might be merely a sphere of glass. But past authorities often insisted that it should be the more costly kind, a specially rounded and polished sphere of crystalline rock. Quartz was always a favourite, though the wealthier scryers put their faith in the stone called beryl, of which aquamarine and emerald are variants, and which has certain valuable mystic

Opposite page:
The Crystal Ball **(1902) by John William Waterhouse (1849–1917)**

An Aztec mirror that passed into the possession of Elizabethan court alchemist and astrologer John Dee. Now in the collection of the British Museum, London, England.

connections. Beryl is usually green-tinted within its translucence, though John Aubrey (1626–97) in his *Miscellanies* (1696) suggests that for scrying it ought to have a tint of red.

No hard and fast rules exist for positioning the crystal. Most modern fortune tellers place it in a simple mount that holds it still on the table. In the past it has been pierced and hung from a string, or partly flattened so that it rested on a table by itself, or was simply held in the hand. However, the paraphernalia sometimes associated with the practice could be varied and abundant. One crystal owned by a scryer known to William Lilly (1602–81) was said to be set in silver, with the angelic names of Raphael, Gabriel, and Uriel engraved on the mount.

John Melville's account of scrying, first published in 1896, provides lists of much more involved trappings. The ball, says Melville, should be enclosed in a frame of polished ivory or wood and should stand on a crystal or glass pedestal. The frame should have 'mystic names' engraved on it, preferably in raised gold lettering—Tetragrammaton, Emmanuel, Agla, Adonai. The pedestal should have the name Saday inscribed on it.

Melville recommends the use of a special table called the 'Lamen,' circular and bearing similar mystic engravings. Otherwise, the scryer can make do with a small table covered with a white cloth, and perhaps a black handkerchief round the base of the ball to shut out reflections. In the scrying room there should be a place for a fire,

perhaps a brazier, to burn the 'usual perfumes' (probably incense, balsam, and so on). Also on the table should be two candles set in gilt or brass candlesticks with the names Elohim and Elohe engraved upon them.

Ritual Purity

A considerable amount of ceremony is apparently expected to precede successful scrying. The care of the crystal is crucial: it must be kept perfectly clean, and this cleanliness is without doubt a form of ritual purification. The crystal is washed with soap, rinsed with alcohol or vinegar, and polished with velvet or chamois. The table and the room must also be spotless. And the scryer himself comes in for a share of purifying, through careful washing, abstention, prayer, and the like. Melville recommends the occasional herbal infusion, of mugwort or perhaps chicory, to keep the scryer properly attuned.

Preparations for scrying must be made while the moon is waxing; the process itself works best when the sun is in its farthest northern declination, and also at sunrise, midday, or sunset. The zodiacal sign Libra is of crucial importance to scryers: Melville says that it rules the kidneys, which have connections with the eyes and with the intuitive faculties. Libra also governs the beryl, and the two herbs, mugwort and chicory, are mentioned for the infusions.

The sign Taurus, linked with the cerebellum, has some part to play as well. And the moon, as so often in the mystic realm, is said to be the dominant planetary influence, though it has no associations with either of the two signs of the zodiac mentioned.

Immediately before the scrying begins, the final preparations introduce more magical ceremony. Crystal-gazers are often described as making a few 'magic passes' over the globe, before getting down to business.

John Melville asserts the efficacy of such passes, which he says help to 'magnetize' the crystal. But other kinds of preserving magic involve much more elaborate procedures.

Many writers proffer lengthy, involved prayers or incantations as used by seers of the past. Melville tells the would-be scryer to follow the speaking of the prayer by putting a special ring on the little finger of his right hand, hanging a pentacle around his neck and drawing a magic circle with an ebony magic wand. Then, after more incantations, and the burning of the perfumes, the scryer can finally get down to some serious gazing.

In modern times, the crystal-gazer merely stares at the globe with a certain concentration. (Many writers believe that he enters, or must enter, a trance—others disagree.) F. W. H. Myers (1843–1901), the psychical researcher, recommended a dim light and about ten to fifteen minutes of gazing. But various scryers have claimed to be able to function quite well in bright light or in darkness, and each seems to have his or her own idea about how long it takes to see anything.

> *Modern Spiritualists sometimes use the crystal to get in touch with spirits, and there have been claims that visual contact has thus been made with 'the beyond.'*

Visions in the Glass

What, then, does one expect to see? Melville follows older magical handbooks when he says that the ceremonies will conjure up an angelic spirit in the glass, though medieval authorities were convinced that all scrying was demonic and that the spirit was either Satan or one of his devils. Modern Spiritualists sometimes use the crystal to get in touch with spirits, and there have been claims that visual contact has thus been made with 'the beyond.' In these cases, it seems, the prophesying or fortune telling was done verbally, by the visible spirit to the scryer.

But most crystal-gazers today claim to see visions, not supernatural beings. What they see may range from swirling, abstract shapes to sharp-edged, explicit scenes from reality. Most agree that before the vision appears, the crystal seems to become foggy and opaque from the inside. Then the mists dissolve to reveal the vision. From various scryers questioned by the Society for Psychical Research in the 1880s, come examples of things seen: a favourite but long-dead dog, a moving coloured light resembling an eye, beautiful landscapes from some unknown land—and, of course, scenes from the future.

Spectaculum photographed in 2011 in Wassenberg, Germany

Evil Black Clouds

The traditions of scrying have been partly systematized, so that even if the amateur never gets past the foggy stage he can still find meaning in the mists. White cloudiness, predictably, is a good portent, but black is evil. Green or blue cloudiness indicates coming joy; red, yellow or orange clouds herald disaster. If the clouds ascend, the answer is 'yes' to any question you have asked; descending clouds mean the answer is 'no.' And in a recent book on fortune telling, Basil Ivan Rakoczi (1908–79) explains that the vision of a globe within the crystal indicates travel; a skull indicates death or wisdom; a star, success or a warning; an eye, good luck or impending evil; a bird, some message or potential rebirth.

There are those who will say that crystal-gazing on any level is fraud and fakery. Others, more kindly, will suggest that the scryers are self-deluded—that they are hallucinated, thanks to all the magical preparations and their own suggestibility. Because many scryers have claimed to go into trance, it has been said that the visions spring out of their own unconscious minds,. But psychical researchers like Myers and Frank Podmore (1856–1910) found that many scryers remained fully and normally conscious. Their own explanation made reference to the form of ESP called clairvoyance.

Theodore Besterman (1904–76), in his scholarly and objective account of crystal-gazing, proffers several accounts (authenticated enough to satisfy him) of clairvoyance through the crystal. There can be little doubt that many people are firmly convinced that it works, that the crystal is a valid way of activating and focusing the scryer's clairvoyance. Sybil Leek (1917–82) goes so far as to say that, of all types of fortune teller

operating today, 'the crystal-gazer is the person most likely to have a genuine psychic ability.'

So in the end all the mumbo-jumbo of burning perfumes and mystic names can be swept aside; all that is necessary appears to be the simple crystal ball and the scryer's gift of clairvoyance. However, for those who are about to buy a crystal and try it for

> . . . the Trojan princess Cassandra, whom Apollo loved but could not win, so that he gave her the gift of prophecy . . .

themselves, a word of warning from John Melville. The crystal, he says (and Sybil Leek concurs), is a form of white magic. Use it with an evil purpose, and it will 'react upon the seer sooner or later with terrible effect.'

DOUGLAS HILL

FURTHER READING: *John Melville.* Crystal Gazing. *(New York, NY: Weiser, 1970); T. Besterman.* Crystal-Gazing. *(London, UK: Rider, 1924).*

Second Sight

Ability to perceive things not visible to ordinary sight, in the future or at a distance; modern psychical research suggests that some people have this ability to a marked degree, and it may be latent in all human beings and possibly in other animals.

Sibyls

The prophetesses who bore the title of Sibyl in antiquity are celebrated in literature, and many are mentioned in allusions scattered through Greek

and Latin texts, but their historical character is not easy to grasp. Some of their personal names are known, but even in ancient tradition these appear unimportant. The classical Sibyls originated in Greek Asia Minor and were probably of oriental origin. They are always connected with Apollo, the god of prophecy, who also originated in Asia Minor. However, they are not his ordinary priestesses, nor even his ordinary prophetesses, for by comparison with the Pythia of Delphi, who was protected and controlled by a skilful priesthood, they appear as freelancers in prophecy without regular succession in most places. They would be little more than a minor curiosity of classical lore if Virgil (70 BC–90 BC) had not assigned a crucial role in the *Aeneid* to the Sibyl of Cumae. Indeed, when the Sibylline books of Rome are added to this account, it is clear that the renown of Sibyls in later literature and art is Roman rather than Greek.

Sibyls do not appear in Homer and are not well established elsewhere in Greek epic. But one character who has the marks of a Sibyl and is occasionally called one, is the Trojan princess Cassandra, whom Apollo loved but could not win, so that he gave her the gift of prophecy, but always as a painful fit of inspiration, in which her utterances were never believed. In Lycophron's iambic poem *Alexandra*, written in the third century BC, Cassandra is made to give a long and exceedingly obscure prophetic monologue on the future fates and wanderings of the Greek chiefs returning from Troy, and of Aeneas, their opponent, who reached Latium in western Italy. This tradition reappears in the *Aeneid*, where the Sibyl leads Aeneas eventually into the presence of the dead Anchises to hear him foretell the future greatness of Rome.

Cassandra by Evelyn De Morgan. Cassandra is shown in front of the burning city of Troy at the peak of her insanity (1898).

In Greece the best-known Sibyl, typical of all of them, belonged to Erythrae on the coast of Asia Minor facing Chios. She is probably the one mentioned by Heraclitus (535 BC–475 BC) as quoted by Plutarch (AD 45–AD 120), who says of her, 'The Sibyl with raving mouth, uttering things without smiles, without graces, and without myrrh, reaches over a thousand years because of the god.' Sibyls were in fact believed to live for 900 or 1,000 years, and it was thought that sometimes even after death they could make their voices heard in the air. Other Sibyls, of whom little is known, were those of Marpessus of Alexandria in the Troad, of Phrygia, of Sardis, of Delphi, of Thessaly, of Egypt, and, in the West, of Cumae in Campania. Very little remains of their actual prophecies except for inscriptions such as one at Erythrae in the Sibyl's dwelling, and such late compilations as the book *On Long Lived Persons* by Phlegon of Tralles, who lived in the second century AD. In one utterance there a Sibyl claims a status between the human and the divine, and in another expresses jealousy or dislike of Apollo's priests or even of Apollo himself. The prophecies generally refer, like many others in history, to expected disasters such as war, plague, and famine. The Sibyls were very loosely attached to the pan-Hellenic Olympian religion and to local cults, and are often said to have been wanderers. Their prophecies were compulsive manifestations of a power to which they felt enslaved.

In the *Aeneid* Virgil makes the Sibyl a figure already established at Cumae at a time corresponding to the Greek heroic age. Such traditions at least suggest the antiquity of the influence of Greek religion in Italy, even if it is here exaggerated. The Sibyl, in frenzied inspiration, prophesies the terrible wars that will follow Aeneas's landing in Italy. She then conducts him through the entire extent of the infernal regions before leading him to meet his father, Anchises, among the blessed, and from there into the upper world again, through the ivory gate of dreams. No Sibyl of old Greece had a role of such grandeur.

The Sibylline Books

The celebrated legend of the Sibylline books, recorded by Varro (116 BC–27 BC) and Dionysius, is among the more historical of Roman traditions of Sibyls. These were offered for sale to King Tarquin of Rome (reports vary between Tarquinius Priscus and his son Tarquinius Superbus) by a mysterious woman who was perhaps the Sibyl of Cumae. Nine books were offered but rejected because the price was too high; then, when she had destroyed three, six were offered at the same price as the nine but were again refused. Finally on the insistent advice of the augurs, the last three were bought at the price of the original nine. They were kept by the

Roman state for centuries under the special care of a board of magistrates, were concealed from public view, and were consulted, with the help of Greek slaves, at moments of crisis or when alarming prodigies such as monstrous births occurred. They were used during the Latin wars and much later when Rome was threatened by the Gauls and Hannibal (247 BC–c. 183 BC). Exceptional sacrifices were

Like all ancient cosmic symbols which are but the reduction of natural law to the simplicity necessary for human use, the Tarot is of the utmost practical value. . .

ordered for the infernal powers after consultations and once in 226 BC the burial alive of a Gaulish and a Greek couple. Sibylline oracles had much earlier been mocked by the Greek Aristophanes (c. 446 BC–c. 386 BC) as texts of nonsense, but the Romans, perhaps following Etruscan tradition in such matters, regarded them as sacred texts giving practical rules for dealing with abnormal, uncanny, and perilous situations.

Apart from the classical Greek and Roman framework, a large collection of Jewish, Chaldean, and Christian prophetic poetry, in Greek hexameters, was formed in the eastern Mediterranean region in Hellenistic and Roman times. This collection is now known as the *Oracula Sibyllina.*

E. D. PHILLIPS

Sortilege

Divination by lots, from Latin *sors*, 'lot,' and *legere*, 'to read:' *sortes* is the type of divination that picks a passage at random from Homer,

Virgil (70 BC–90 BC), the Bible or some other work as a guide to the future: more generally, a term for magic, sorcery, and witchcraft.

Tarot

The uninitiated usually regard the Tarot as a system of fortune telling using a special pack of cards. However, this is the lowest, if not a debased, aspect of a method of communication by symbol that has behind it not only antiquity but also esoteric knowledge. It may be described as 'the cosmic method in universal creation or emanation, including its purpose and result.' As practiced by the Western user, it is generally associated with the Tree of Life of the Cabala but it has also affinities with the pyramids of Egypt and with Indian theosophical philosophy. 'Like all ancient cosmic symbols which are but the reduction of natural law to the simplicity necessary for human use, the Tarot is of the utmost practical value in all senses.'

The origins of the Tarot are not clearly defined. A. E. Waite (1857–1942) concluded that it had no exoteric history before the fourteenth century and the oldest examples of Tarot cards probably date from about 1390, while occult tradition places their origin at about 1200 AD. It is said that the gypsies are believed to hold the first set of cards and that they alone hold the secret of its meaning.

According to occultists, the system comes first from the East, probably from Chaldea. After the destruction of the seat of learning in Alexandria, the adepts of all countries converged upon Fez in Morocco and made it the pivot of their esoteric science; since they spoke in many tongues, they decided to create a set of common symbols

The Empress from the Visconti deck

that all could understand and in which their truths could be pictured. 'As a skeleton for their invention the wise men chose the relatively simple system of numbers and letters afforded by the Qubalah' (S. Mayananda, *The Tarot Today)*. The Hebrew alphabet consists of twenty-two letters and these placed upon the twenty-two Paths of the Tree of Life gave a combination of bases for correspondences. By this system of a pack of cards containing four suits of fourteen cards each and twenty-two trumps unconnected with the suits and called the Major Arcana, ideas could be exchanged without the necessity of the spoken or the written word.

The four suits are designated Wands, Cups, Swords, and Pentacles, symbolizing amongst other things fire, water, air, and earth: in each suit are four court cards: the King, the essential Self, 'Spirit,' in man; the Queen, the 'Soul' or inner pattern part of a particular human personality; the Knight, representing the special focus-

ing of energies and a personal sense of selfhood; the Page or Esquire, standing for the Body or personal vehicle. These four court cards correspond also to the four letters of the sacred Name of God in Hebrew theology—*Yod, He, Vau, He.* Yod is represented by the Kings of the four suits, and more especially by the suit of Scepters or Wands, and it stands for the First Principle—the origin of all things. The first He symbolizes substance, in opposition to essence, and this is represented by the four Queens and by the suit of Cups, the form that contains the Life and the Feminine Principle. Vau that indicates Affinity completes the Trinity, and is pictured by the bond of love and the mystery of union exemplified by the four Knights and the suit of Swords. To stop there would indicate Finality. So the fourth court card, that of the Page or Esquire, represents the second He, marking the transition from the metaphysical to the material world—God in manmade manifest.

The Fool from the Visconti deck

The Tower from the Visconti deck

This is the suit of Pentacles or Coins, the symbol of material gain but also the five-pointed star that leads man from the unreal to the real.

The Tarot in its Cabalistic form sets out to show the relation between God, Man, and the universe, and amongst other things it is a symbol of incarnation. It is one of those immemorial systems that were destined to convey this abstruse fact to mankind in a form that could be appreciated even by almost submerged awareness. Oswald Wirth (1860–1943) says that a symbol is designed precisely to awaken in our consciousness the memory of that which we have already known. In other words, the use of the Tarot evokes the associations that we have already formed in the past. In *Le Symbolisme Hermetique* he states that 'a symbol can always be studied from an infinite number of points of view and each thinker has the right to discover in the symbol a new meaning corresponding to the logic of his own

THE LOVERS

conception. Symbols are intended to arouse a thought by means of suggestion and thus cause the truth which lies hidden in our consciousness to reveal itself.'

P. D. Ouspensky (1878–1947) postulates that only a symbol can deliver man from the slavery of words and formulas, and allow him to attain to the possibilities of thinking freely: . . . occult knowledge cannot be transmitted either orally or in writing. It can only be acquired by deep meditation.'

Tarota or *Taro-Rota* means the Wheel of the Law and the Law of the Wheel, and is a widespread symbol of universal life; the same idea is found in Western symbology in the phrase 'spinning of the Web.'

Dance of Life

There are various methods of using the Tarot cards; reference has already been made to placing them upon the Tree of Life, they can be paired as opposites or complementaries, or they may be set out in a circle or wheel representing the universe.

There are no standard pictures on the packs of Tarot cards. While the pictures are basically the same, the presentation may vary. There is one known as the Marseilles or French pack that is probably the oldest in design and can be found reproduced in many books; generally speaking, the designs are crude and not well drawn. Manly P. Hall produced a pack drawn by Augustus Knapp (1853–1938) but this is no longer on the market. Paul Foster Case (1884–1954), founder

of the Builders of the Adytum, had a pack drawn by Miss Jessie Burns Parke, which was very similar to the one usually referred to as the 'Waite' pack, drawn by Miss Pamela Coleman Smith (1878–1951), under the direction of A. E. Waite; this, in turn, is generally held to be based on the Oswald Wirth symbolism, though it has been considered that in certain details Dr. Waite expressed his personal ideas

> *There is no reason why any interested student of the Tarot should not make his own pack, provided that he is prepared to undertake the necessary study to incorporate the correct symbols.*

of symbolism rather than the traditional esoteric ones. There is no reason why any interested student of the Tarot should not make his own pack, provided that he is prepared to undertake the necessary study to incorporate the correct symbols. Instructions for interpreting the meanings of the cards may be found either in booklets sold with the packs, or in the books on the Tarot written by authorities.

While there is an interpretation for each one of the fourteen cards in each suit, either right way up or reversed, the ordinary person is chiefly concerned with the Major Arcana, the trumps, since these are the only cards used in dealing with the Tree of Life or with the system of the Wheel.

There are twenty-one numbers on the cards, and a zero. This is the attribute of the Fool and its position has been the subject of much discussion. Where does one place zero and what is its significance? Taking the cards in numerical order it would seem clear that zero should precede one, yet Papus, one of the best known and most authoritative writers on the Tarot, places it between twenty and twenty-one, and takes it to refer to the

Animal Kingdom, that is the Kingdom of Instinct and not of Mind. If it precedes one the subsequent cards will fall sensibly upon their paths on the Tree, ending with the card called the Universe on the final path leading to Earth—the Plane of Matter. Israel Regardie (1907–85) says: 'Zero must precede one. This is the most logical place for it.'

If the method of the Wheel is worked, zero will be placed in the center as the hub; the remaining twenty-one cards will fall naturally into three segments of seven apiece, and when studied their mutual correspondence, either complementary, fulfilling or opposing, will be clear. There is a legend that once upon a time a man made a magical table and placed on it statuettes of the major trumps modeled as small golden figures. By his own great knowledge of the mysteries he was able to set the figures in motion and they wove in and out of the figures of the Dance of Life, so that he could see the pattern of evolution. But it was not given either to that adept or to his disciples to be able to move the twenty-second figure—that of zero or the Fool; for if the Fool joins in the dance the world is completed and there is an end to all things as we know them.

In this case the Fool represents the mystery of the Divine Love; when that is understood and he takes his place among the dancers, there will be no more sorrow and no more misunderstanding, for the former things will have passed away. It will be the Golden Age in reality; we shall see ourselves in proper relation to God and man; we shall indeed be united with the Highest and therefore there will be nothing left for which to struggle.

The trumps of the Major Arcana, their sequence and their general meaning are:

0. **The Fool:** the picture is of a young man, a bundle over his shoulder, a dog at his heels, gaily treading a cliff edge with no regard for where his steps are leading him. To those who have begun to perceive the esoteric meaning of the cards, this carefree attitude is significant of the man who has followed the Divine Law and become as a little child. In German the title of the card is *Der Sill*, which means the Holy or Innocent one.

1. **The Magician:** in exoteric packs this card is sometimes labeled 'The Juggler'; in the Marseilles and other French packs it is called *Le Bateleur*, which means 'the holder of a small farm or estate' in Old French; no previous origin of the word is known, but it could be that the card is intended to represent a lesser sun. The man in the picture has a figure-eight-shaped device over his head, a lemniscate, the sign of Universal Life. One of his hands points upward and the other down, while before him lies a table on which are displayed the four suits of the Tarot pack.

2. **The High Priestess:** she sits between two pillars in the place of Equilibrium; partially veiled, a book upon her knees, she is typified in the Book of Wisdom and in the mystical poets; she is the feminine aspect, the reflection of God. In Egypt she represents the Isis of Nature whose veil must not be raised by the profane.

3. **The Empress:** this shows a fine woman with flowing hair; she wears a crown with twelve points, signifying the diffusion of the First Principle in the same way that the twelve signs of the zodiac are disseminated and yet form a perfect whole. The card signifies the basis of Reality.

4. **The Emperor:** he represents the positive or active form of the Empress; he wields a scepter which

has always been taken as an attribute of the progenitor.

5. **The Pope or Hierophant:** this is the complementary opposite of the High Priestess, who is the instructress of the initiates to whom she imparts occult knowledge. The Hierophant gives this knowledge to ordinary people in a practical and oral form that they can understand.

6. **The Lovers:** this card represents on one hand the dual nature of man: when the child is first conceived its sex is not determined; the potentials of both sexes are carried by every embryo and one sex is finally assumed in the material world. The lovers also symbolize the most powerful of all the emotions; love properly expressed brings unity with the beloved, so that this dual card is both an analysis and a synthesis.

7. **The Chariot:** this portrays the man who has vanquished the elementary forces. It is the final card of the first seven into which the twenty-one numbered trumps are divided when they become a triad in the Wheel system; on the Tree of Life in the Hebrew version the card corresponds with the Hebrew letter *Zayin*, which signifies Victory in All Worlds.

8. **Justice:** this card stands for equilibrium in all worlds and in all forms. Occult science has been taught in word and indeed; the sword and the balance are the reward of a man's acts, whether they be black or white. As a man sows, so shall he reap. (In the Waite pack, and in several later ones, cards eight and eleven are transposed.)

9. **The Hermit:** this card sometimes pictures an old man and sometimes a young one. If he is old he is thought to be the managed in years who yet has a young heart; if he is a young man, he is one who has already learned to walk in the right way. He wears the cloak

of protection, carries the lamp of wisdom, and is supported by the staff of righteousness. His quality is prudence, and some packs will give the card this name rather than that of the Hermit. His significance is silence regarding the Inner Knowledge.

10. **The Wheel of Fortune or the Wheel of Life:** this card does not denote anything in the way of chance but is the symbol of the eternal action of time, the continuous rotation of the aeons, the mutable laws each recurring in turn and then resting in Equilibrium.

11. **Strength:** this is the strength of the young girl closing the mouth of the lion; above her head is the lemniscate—the sign of spiritual life and virility. Here is the counterpart of the young child in the cockatrice's den; she is Sir Galahad in opposition: 'my strength is as the strength of ten, because my heart is pure.' Galahad the boy knight is as sexless as this maiden.

12. **The Hanged Man:** this most curious of all cards has been given different interpretations by different writers but it is generally accepted that it stands for Equilibrated Power. In the Hebrew alphabet the letter *Mem* accompanies this figure on the path of the Tree and is one of the three 'mother letters,' standing for water. In all occult matters the element of water signifies a change of plane or of consciousness. This man has come far enough on the road to find absolute submission to the Will Divine.

13. **Death:** death is the culmination of life in the exoteric sense; in the esoteric meaning it is the passing from one stage of progress to the next. Death has been termed the Negative of Realization, the universal link between material and spiritual. Nearly all versions of this card are based upon a skeleton,

and include the ancient phallic symbol of the sickle or curved blade.

14. *Temperance:* here man is individualized. The water of life is being poured out and he has the power to accept or reject it for himself.

15. *The Devil:* this is a card that has puzzled many people but if it be looked at carefully it will be seen to represent number one, the Magician, in reverse. The power is now misused. The right hand, the hand of power, points sometimes downward and sometimes upward, and those he has taken in bondage are in chains at his feet. The card is sometimes referred to as Pan, unbridled Nature, and his lighted torch is the symbol of destruction. He is to be feared and to be conquered. To allow him to gain the mastery is to allow Matter to overcome Spirit.

16. *The Tower Struck by Lightning:* This card is usually said to be symbolic of the Fall of man; here is the Tower of Babel; man is being hurled into materialism; as he proceeds down the Tree of Life he becomes more man and less God. It must be noted that in two French versions, this card is considered to be a divine happening; one refers to it as 'The Fire of Heaven' and the other as 'The House of God.'

17. *The Star:* this picture represents the Word in action in Nature. The butterfly or ibis symbol is a sign that the spirit is not lost though man may have far to go; the spirit will survive and the Fall is not irreparable.

18. *The Moon:* here again is comfort for the soul in involution. The material world is only a reflection; man can descend no lower, and the Spirit is now immersed in Matter from which it must eventually start to climb again. Yet other writers have other ideas. S. Mayananda says: 'The picture presented by this Trump is a terrible travesty of what should be shown, or rather it is but the negative half. It seems to have been dictated by sorcerers or the Church in whose teaching the "world" is merely an evil condition to escape from to "heaven."' And an Indian writer, Govinda, says of this card 'the symbolism of the elements moves on many planes.'

> *. . . represents in one form God in man at the foot of the middle pillar of the Tree of Life. . .*

19. *The Sun:* this picture represents the first of the elemental kingdoms beginning its slow progress by development back to God. Spirit is renewed in a different form; man is freshened for his evolutionary climb and the mineral kingdom is slowly individualizing.

20. *Judgment:* life is progressing a little farther up the stairway, for this trump governs the evolutionary development of the vegetable kingdom.

21. *The Universe:* here in this last card, the macrocosm and the microcosm have met. Here the earth of matter is represented in the four quarters—the four Worlds—and here the four animals of the Apocalypse and of the vision of Ezekiel are depicted. It is the reconstruction of the synthesis of all and the figure of the androgyne is lightly veiled; as with the Lovers, sex is undefined. This represents in one form God in man at the foot of the middle pillar of the Tree of Life.

These are the major trumps of the Tarot pack. Only one suggestion of meaning can be given by any one person in a limited space; and it must be remembered that there are meanings to each trump according to the understanding of each student, and that they are intended to act as stimuli to the imagination. Each and every writer on the Tarot will have something different to say, will develop another aspect; all anyone can do is to suggest an approach. This is a system of universal communication by symbol and therefore it must be sufficiently fluid to allow each man to use it as an expression of his ideas on the Absolute. The more that is read about the Tarot; the more the cards are meditated upon, the greater will be the flow of understanding and the wider the comprehension.

CHRISTINE HARTLEY

The Origins of the Tarot Pack

'If one were to let it be announced that there survived to this day an ancient Egyptian work, a book that had escaped the flames which devoured their superb libraries, and which contained, unsullied, their teachings on important matters, everyone, no doubt, would be in a hurry to acquaint themselves with such a precious and remarkable book. And if one added that this book was widely distributed throughout much of Europe, and that for many centuries it has been available to everybody, people's surprise would be vastly increased; and would it not reach its highest pitch when they were assured that nobody had ever imagined it to be Egyptian, that it was held to be nothing, that no one had ever attempted to decipher a single page, and that the fruits of infinite wisdom were regarded as a collection of fantastic pictures without the least significance in themselves? Wouldn't

it be thought that one was amusing oneself at the expense of the listeners' credulity? . . .

'Nevertheless, it is true: this Egyptian book, sole relic of their superb libraries, survives today. Indeed, it is so common that no scholar has deigned to concern himself with it; before ourselves, nobody has ever suspected its illustrious origins. This book is composed of seventy-seven or perhaps seventy-eight leaves or pictures, divided into five classes, each presenting objects as varied as they are entertaining and instructive: this book is, in other words, the game of Tarot.'

It was with these words that Court de Gébelin (1725–84) began page 365 of the eighth volume of his *Monde Primitif* (1781). He was an obscure Protestant theologian from southern France, who devoted ten years of his life to writing this untidy hodge-podge of unscholarly speculation on the survival of ancient myths, symbols, and primitive languages; and more than two-thirds of the way through such a vast work is scarcely the most prominent place to find a statement that will make an author's name—yet it is solely for what he had to say about the Tarot that Court de Gébelin is remembered.

The origins of playing cards are obscure. One theory is that they developed from the same source as the game of chess: the Indian game of *chaturange* has four groups of pieces, each comprising king, general, horseman, and a phalanx of foot soldiers; while one Chinese card game has the same name as Chinese chess, *keu-ma-paou* (chariots-horses-guns).

Tradition attributes the introduction of playing cards to Europe, either to the Crusaders or to the gypsies, but the first identifiable reference to cards is in the fourteenth century. A German monk named Johannes, writing at Brefeld in Switzerland, says that 'a game called the game of cards has come to us in this year 1377.' The last Crusade began in 1270, and the Christians were finally driven out of Asia Minor in 1291; and although there were a number of condem-

> 'In the year 1379 the game of cards was brought into Viterbo from the country of the Saacens, where it is called naib.'

nations of gaming and dicing during the following century, there was no mention of cards, which makes it improbable that they were brought by the Crusaders.

The chronicler Giovanni Covelluzzo, in his history of the Italian town of Viterbo (1480), closely confirms Johannes's statement: 'In the year 1379 the game of cards was brought into Viterbo from the country of the Saracens, where it is called *naib*.' Since the gypsies did not appear in Europe until the fifteenth century, they cannot be credited with the introduction of playing cards.

Covelluzzo's account is particularly interesting in view of the fact that cards are known to this day in Spain as *naipes*, and some scholars believe the word to be of Arabic origin. Taking into account certain other indications, it seems highly likely that cards came into Europe following the Moorish occupation of Spain.

However, packs of these cards, which have remained virtually

unchanged in design for six centuries, did not include the twenty-two cards, bearing curious symbolic pictures, which are known as the Tarot trumps. They comprised fifty-six cards, divided into four 'suits:' in addition to the King, Queen, and Jack (Valet) of the modern pack used in such games as canasta or bridge, there is a horseman or knight. The symbols for the suits vary from country to country in Europe: in Spain and Italy they are cups, batons or clubs, swords (*espadas* in Spanish, *spade* in Italian), and gold coins: in France, the cup shape has been distorted into a heart, the club into a clover-leafed form, the sword into a pike-head, and the coin into a diamond-shaped flooring tile; in Germany the heart is the same, but the clover-leaf has been further distorted into an acorn, the pike head into a leaf, and the coin into a round hawk-bell.

Nobody knows when the additional twenty-two cards were incorporated into the pack that is used in the games of *Tarocke* or *tarok*, in Germany and Eastern Europe, and *tarocchi* in Italy and along the Mediterranean coast. Court de Gébelin was familiar with the game from its popularity in the Languedoc, but he was the first to attribute mystical significance to the pack.

He wrote, with justification: 'The trumps, numbering twenty-two, represent in general the temporal and spiritual leaders of society, the principles of agriculture, the cardinal virtues, marriage, death, and resurrection or the creation; the many tricks of fortune, the wise and the foolish, time which consumes, all, etc . . .' The suits, he maintained—much less justifiably—represented the four classes into which Egyptian society had been divided: the pharaoh and military nobility, symbolized by the sword; agriculture, symbolized by the club; the priesthood, symbolized by the cup; and commerce, symbolized by the coin.

He also remarked upon the recurrence of the number seven: each suit comprised twice seven cards, and the numbered trumps (not counting the unnumbered *Mat* or Fool) made three times seven.

In Paris, a wigmaker named Alliette (1738–91) was particularly struck by these ideas. He had decided to practice as a fortune teller, under the title of Etteilla (the reverse of his name), and elaborated on Court de Gébelin's theories. He announced that the Tarot had been written on golden leaves in a temple near Memphis, 171 years after the flood; Hermes Trismegistos had planned the work—so that it should properly be called The Book of Thoth—and it had been carried out by seventeen magi over a period of four years. To substantiate his theories, he designed his own pack, which incorporated a number of 'Egyptian' elements, and differed in a number of respects from the traditional.

It was Etteilla, also, who first drew attention to the fact that the number of trumps equaled the total number of paths linking the ten *sefiroth* of the cabalistic Tree of Life. The French occultist Eliphas Levi (1810–75) claimed that this indicated that the Tarot cards were older, and of greater universal significance, than even Court de Gébelin suggested; in his first book, *Dogme et Rituel de la Haute Magie*, he promised to make public the original designs from which the popular cards were derived. He described these designs, but did not himself publish them, although the English freemason Kenneth Mackenzie wrote that he had seen them in 1861; and the closest indication we have is the pack drawn

by Oswald Wirth (1860–1943) to the specifications of Levi's disciple Stanislaus de Guaita (1860–98). These are in fact no more than a late nineteenth-century prettification of the traditional designs, with the addition of the twenty-two letters of the Hebrew alphabet.

Another of Levi's disciples, a librarian at the Ministry of Public Instruction named Jean-Baptiste Pitois (1811–77), wrote a *History of Magic* under the name of Paul Christian. Falsely, attributing his source to the Roman philosopher Iamblichus (245–325), he described the initiation rites of the Egyptian Mysteries, and the use of twenty-two paintings along the walls of a subterranean gallery in the Great Pyramid; his descriptions of these paintings are a highly-Egyptianised version of the traditional trumps.

With the growth of interest in the occult, both in France and in England, a wide variety of Tarot pack designs proliferated. In this respect, an important work was a slim volume published by Macgregor Mathers in 1888, and this was followed shortly, in 1889, by *Le Tarot des Bohemiens*, written by the French physician Gérard Encausse (1865–1916 under the name of 'Papus.' The English translator of this book, A. E. Waite, designed a distinctly different, pre-Raphaelitish, pack, which was executed for him by Pamela Coleman Smith; then came the Golden Dawn pack, similar to Waite's but with differences of detail, and Aleister

Crowley's *Book of Thoth*, painted for him by Frieda Harris (1877–1962), which was crowded with extra symbolism. Today, there are hundreds of different packs, each reflecting the obsessions of its designer.

All these later packs depart further and further from the 'traditional' pack as it was described by Court de Gébelin, and as it has survived in what is now known as the 'Marseille' design. There are small inconsistencies in the engravings and descriptions in *Monde Primitif* (particularly in the representation of the 'Hanged Man,' which Court de Gébelin turned upside down), but they are of minimal significance. What is quite obvious is that their source is not ancient Egypt.

The Memory Game

Indeed, there is evidence to show that the Tarot trumps are the surviving remnants of a late-medieval educational game. Before the invention of printing, the committing of knowledge to memory was of the utmost importance, and over the centuries a number of memory systems had been devised. The Roman orator Marcus Tullius Cicero (106 BC–43 BC) was one of the first to describe such a system: it consisted of visualizing a familiar room, and placing in it a succession of objects and images that represented the concepts to be remembered. The medieval mind was familiar with a vast repertoire of such images: saints with the symbols of their martyrdom, mythological characters, and so on. Even today, popular symbolism retains some of these images: Hope with her anchor, or Justice with her scales.

With the invention of printing toward the end of the fifteenth century, these memory systems were gradually abandoned, but it is significant that some of the earliest printed books

> *Today, there are hundreds of different packs, each reflecting the obsessions of its designer. All these later packs depart further and further from the 'traditional' pack . . .*

were still devoted to the art of memory, such as *Ars memorandi* (1470), or Johannes Romberch's *Congestiorum Artificiose Memorie* (1533), both illustrated with designs whose style bears a close resemblance to the Tarot trumps. Even more significant is Thomas Murner's *Chartiludium logicae* (1509), which describes, and illustrates, the cards to be used in a game for learning the essentials of logic.

It is to be expected that, as books became available for scholars, the use of memory images should have been diverted to the less educated and the young; pictorial card games, indeed, are an important part of early education to this day. There is a set of so-called *tarocchi*, sometimes attributed to the artist Andrea Mantegna (1431–1506), which is made up of fifty images, representing ten orders of society from the beggar to the pope, the nine muses and Apollo, the ten principal parts of knowledge (such as theology, philosophy, music, poetry, and arithmetic), the three sciences (astrology, chronology, and cosmology), the four cardinal and three Christian virtues, the seven planets, the stellar sphere, the prime mover, and the first cause.

This covers just about everything that a fifteenth-century youngster would be expected to learn. The forty-one or forty-two trumps of the Florentine game of *minchiate* are related, but include more popular concepts such as the Wheel of Fortune, the Tower (an image that comes to us from the *Golden Legend*) and the twelve signs of the zodiac. Fragments of a variety of various other fifteenth-century packs have also survived.

It is fairly conclusive, therefore, that the seventy-eight-card 'traditional' pack, as it was described by Court de Gébelin and elaborated thereafter, is an assembly of elements from a variety of sources, none of which has a mystical origin. It is interesting, however, that the iconography of the cards, deriving as it does from a long-standing tradition of memory-training, includes a number of elements that go back much further than the fifteenth century. For instance, card XV, the Devil, shows a winged figure, wearing a horned helmet, and standing on some kind of pedestal. A smaller devil stands either side, at a lower level, each fastened by a cord about the neck to a ring on the base of the pedestal. The whole card bears a striking resemblance to a statue of the Mithraic Zurvan, with two attendant torch-bearers *(dadophori)*, discovered in a mithraeum in Ostia. And, going even farther back—though it cannot be construed as lending any support to the theories of Court de Gébelin— the horned Egyptian god Set is represented in reliefs as leading two smaller attendants by ropes about their waists. Whatever their origin, the Tarot cards can evoke a sufficiency of images to satisfy any occultist.

BRIAN INNES

FURTHER READING: P. F. Case. The Tarot. *(Richmond, VA: Macoy, 1977); M. Dummett.* Game of Tarot. *(London, UK: Duckworth, 1980); S. Kaplan.* The Encyclopedia of Tarot. *(Stamford, CT: U.S. Games Systems, 1978); Gareth Knight.* Practical Guide to Quahalistic Symbolism. *(York Beach, ME: Weiser); R. Cavendish.* The Tarot. *(New York, NY: Harper & Row, 1975); Papus.* Tarot of the Bohemians. *(York Beach, ME: Weiser); A. E. Waite.* The Holy Kabbalah; The Pictorial Key to the Tarot. *(New York, NY: Citadel); Michael Dummett.* The Game of Tarot. *(London, UK: Duckworth, 1980); Stuart R. Kaplan.*

Taurus

The second sign of the zodiac, Taurus the Bull was identified by the Greeks with Zeus's transformation into a bull when he abducted Europa; to the Babylonians he was the heavenly bull whose rising marked the beginning of spring.

Taurus is ruled by Venus, and people born under this sign are governed by their affections; they will go out of their way to avoid ill feeling. Modest, they do not seek popularity. Because he is associated with the earth, Taurus has been described as hefty, clodhopping, obstinate, lazy, and the opposite of intellectual. However, these adjectives are no longer thought to apply to the constellation. The following description, by the first century AD Roman astrologer Manilius, has similarly been superseded:

> *Dull honest Taurus to manure*
> *the field*
> *Strong Taurus bears, by him the*
> *Grounds are till'd:*
> *No gaudy things he breeds, no prize*
> *for worth,*
> *But blesseth Earth, and brings her*
> *Labour forth.*

According to modern astrologers, although Taurus is not ambitious his rewards are the fruit of his toil, and not the result of getting others to work for him. Valens, a classical writer of the second century AD, says: 'Those born will be good handicraft men, hardworking, good at keeping things, fond of pleasure and music, and generous: but some of them will be labourers, planters, and builders. And if the benefices (that is, Jupiter and Venus) aspect the ascendant, or the ruler is well placed, they become high priests or athletic trainers, and are awarded wreaths and purple robes, statues and busts, and are given charge of sacred rites and become notable and famous.'

This is the origin of the association that Taurus is supposed to have with money. In fact, this sign actually symbolizes not money but real wealth, the result of the material forces of production. However, music is also a Taurean art, and people born under Taurus are competent musicians and singers. The influence of Venus means that the Taurean is fond of pleasure, generous, and more than usually amorous. The bull is naturally highly sexed, but his attitude to sex is uncomplicated and he does not need to be stimulated by artificial glamour. Taurus's keynote is devotion, to a person, an ideal or simply to his work. His love is deep, lasting and undemanding. Humble by nature, he feels that he has no right to ask anything for himself.

Faithful Friend

Because he is ruled by Venus there is nothing heavy or unimaginative about Taurus. Although sensitive and keenwitted, the Taurean is not afraid of hard work or dirt or the unpleasant aspects of life, but accepts them as part of living. He enjoys beauty, however, and tries to avoid ugliness.

Emotionally truthful, the person born under Taurus is good-natured, reliable, and a faithful friend. He is inclined to brood, and needs encouragement. If religious, he is not necessarily conventional in his beliefs even though he is strong in faith and devotion. The Taurean gift for profound study makes scholars, philosophers, and artists, and people born under this sign excel at work that requires patience.

Depiction of Taurus the Bull from Palazzo Schifanoia, Ferrara, Italy. This fresco and others created alongside it are related to the calendar illustrations that appear frequently in Northern European manuscripts.

Tea-Leaf Reading

Although telling fortunes by consulting the patterns formed by tea-leaves on the base and sides of a cup is often regarded as drawing-room entertainment, it is not purely an amusement. The tea-leaves can act as a medium through which the clairvoyance of the reader is stimulated so that he or she is able to reveal truths that would otherwise remain hidden; or the figures formed by the leaves may be believed to reflect patterns that exist in the astral.

The method used in tea-leaf reading is time-honoured and simple. The client inverts her cup, turning it round three times; she places it on the saucer and then taps the bottom three times with her left index finger. The clairvoyant, who is in a light trance, picks the cup up and turns it round so that the leaves can be inspected.

All tea-leaf readers have their preferred methods of interpreting the patterns made by the leaves, and only some general indication of their meaning is given here:

Chain of small leaves: a journey, travel; if two larger leaves are in close proximity, the excursion is mental and not physical.

Serpentine chain of small leaves: a visit to the mountains; if two larger leaves are in close proximity, there will be ups and downs in daily life; inability to settle down.

Three small leaves close to one leaf: a man.

Two leaves close to a small leaf: a woman.

Group of small leaves in a triangular pattern: a child or children.

Heart: love; a heart broken or crossed by a chain of leaves represents a broken love-affair or a divorce.

Triangle: emotional involvement; jealousy; rivalry. If pointing downward this shape indicates a ménage à trois, if upward, ambition and success are suggested.

Square: several different possibilities are suggested by this formation; it may mean that the person concerned is well established, conservative, and a solid character. It can also imply a need for protection, or the client's failure to excel in his career.

Star: great success; a sign of genius; spiritual enlightenment. However, if it falls on or near a heart formation, the passions may be crushed and replaced by a life of asceticism.

The appearance of more complicated symbols or geometric signs needs profound study; because of their rarity they are extremely significant.

Many leaves spread all over the cup: a rich or confused character; extravagance; negligence; generosity.

Very few leaves in the cup: clarity; direct action in the future. However, this also indicates poverty in emotional life, and if the leaves arrange themselves in a provocative way they must be read with great care so that they offset the poverty of the all-over pattern.

Cross: this means that the client is at a crossroads in life, and that a personal sacrifice may be necessary. If this pattern is in conjunction with one large leaf, it can signify death. However, care and tact should be exercised in making such an interpretation, and it should be remembered that the possible death is not necessarily that of the client. Other leaves close by will ward off danger, and show a remedy for whatever ill is likely to befall him.

Circle: marriage; a close partnership; fame. A good omen.

Circle with a cross on it: enforced confinement, possibly in a hospital, prison, or other institution.

Two parallel lines of leaves: a propitious journey; dreams that will come true; a long and happy life. Reinforcement of all else seen in the cup.

Dots: letters; messages; thoughts.

Stars: good luck.

Dashes: surprises.

Flowers: joy; an engagement; marriage.

Dregs in the Cup (1838) by William Sidney Mount (1807–68). Oil on canvas

Fruit: good fortune; children.
Daisy: simple happiness.
Gun or dagger: danger; strife.
Scythe: good harvest; a death warning.
Musical instruments: good company.
Scales: justice; success at law.

Ladder: increasing success.
Key: secrets revealed; knowledge.
House: stability.
Bottle: excess; flirtation at a party.
Envelope: news.
Fan: an indiscreet love-affair.

Teapot or kettle: good cheer; contentment.
Pair of scissors: angry words.
Hammer: hard work.
There are other general indications:
Time is represented by the differ-

ent levels of the cup. The rim is the present, and below this lies the near future, while patterns formed on the base refer to events that are many years ahead.

Place is indicated by the parts of the cup in which the leaves settle. Those nearest the handle tell of events that affect the home; the leaves on the sides suggest distance according to their proximity to the handle, and the ones on the base show the place of birth, nationality and hidden nature of the client.

Letters of the alphabet represent the initials of people concerned in the reading; the nearer they are to the handle, the closer their relationship to the client.

Clear symbols are lucky, with the exception of those that represent illness or death.

Faint symbols tend to be unlucky, suggesting a weak character or lack of purpose.

In occult lore the bowl of the cup corresponds to the dome of the sky, and the leaves to the stars, and there is therefore said to be a connection between tea-leaf reading and astrology. There are also correspondences between the cup, the sky and the palm of the hand, and tea-leaf reading is linked with palmistry as well as with the stars. Other correspondences, such as the link between the leaves and the moles on the body and the bumps on the head, have also been observed.

BASIL IVAN RAKOCZI

Third Eye

The third eye of esoteric speculation is the invisible eye of spiritual perception and second sight, said to be used by psychics and sensitives to see beyond the limited material realm, and observe things hidden to ordinary sight. Closed in most people, it is supposed to be located around the middle of the forehead, just above the junction of the eyebrows. The third eye is believed to be either connected with the pineal gland or identical with it. Far in the distant past, the theory goes, human beings had a third eye on top of their heads that enabled them to see into spiritual realms, it gradually atrophied and sank into the convolutions of the brain, and so human spiritual perception was dimmed.

The pineal, which takes its name from the fact that it is shaped like a pinecone, is a tiny gland the size of a pea, attached to the midbrain. It is in fact sensitive to light, which causes it to release the hormone melatonin into

According to yoga practitioners, the third eye can be awakened through meditation and imagination.

the bloodstream, and through its link with the pituitary it is connected with the early development of sexuality. The pineal is farther back in the head than the brow, where the esoteric third eye is located, but occultists say that it moves forward on an invisible stalk to its position in the forehead.

Hindu tradition links the third eye with the *sahasrara* or crown chakra, the highest of the energy centers in the human body, and identifies it as the doorway through which the human being can experience the spiritual cosmos. According to yoga practitioners, the third eye can be awakened through meditation and imagination, and in the West, too, the pineal has long been connected with the powers of imagination and the soul. In the fourth century BC the Greek anatomist Herophilus (335 BC–280 BC) believed that the pineal gland regulates the flow of thought and René Descartes (1596–1650) in the seventeenth century described it as 'the seat of imagination,' which acts as the channel through which the soul or the mind influences the body.

Visions

The word vision is used in the religious sphere to mean what elsewhere is called an apparition. The percipient of an apparition has the experience of 'seeing' (in some sense or other) something that is not present in the same way as ordinary physical objects are. Sir Francis Galton (1822–1911), in his research into human faculties, encountered a perfect example of an apparition. A lady novelist assured him that she once saw the principal character of one of her novels come through the door and glide toward her. As the character was fictional there was no possibility that the apparition corresponded to any external cause. The experience thus originated within the lady's mind and can be described as *endogenic* (caused from within).

Apparitions are sometimes loosely called hallucinations (from Latin *hallucinatio*—I dream) bearing the implication that they are endogenic. This is because apparitions commonly result from drugs, fever, exhaustion, or mental illness. The present writer reserves the term 'hallucination' for endogenic hallucinations, and to use the word apparition or vision for an appearance whose cause may be internal or external.

Are there in fact any apparitions that are *exogenic* (with an external cause)? Religious visions are difficult to interpret but psychical research provides good evidence of exogenic apparitions. Occasionally, at a time

Annunciation, illustration for *The Life of Christ*, (c. 1886–96) by James Tissot (1836-1902), showing the announcement by the angel Gabriel to the Virgin Mary that she would conceive and become the mother of Jesus, the Son of God, marking his incarnation.

of death or crisis, the likeness of the person concerned appears in recognizable form to a friend or relative, perhaps on the other side of the world. The apparitions are sometimes clearly unreal, being transparent or appearing in a 'pool of light' or in a 'picture frame,' but quite often they are natural enough to be mistaken for the actual person. Theories differ as to how these crisis apparitions come about. Some writers claim that the person whose apparition is seen has an 'astral body' that is a duplicate of his physical body (including clothes) and is 'projected' to the vicinity of the percipient. A preferred explanation would be by telepathy or 'thought-transference;' a violent 'thought wave' impinges

on some level of the percipient's mind and is translated into a picture of the person in crisis.

More than a century ago the Society for Psychical Research carried out a census of apparitions and obtained 17,000 replies to its questionnaire. It appeared that about one person in sixteen sees an apparition once in the course of a lifetime. More than one-third are of persons living or dead and known to the percipient. It was found also that about one in thirty of all apparitions are of a religious, exalted, or highly poetic nature.

A large proportion of apparitions are *hypnagogic* hallucinations (from Greek *hypnos*—sleep) and occur on the borderline between sleeping and waking, being

very akin to dreams. Like dreams, these apparitions are mainly endogenic but some may, like crisis apparitions, have an external cause, because there is evidence of telepathic or clairvoyant effects both in dreams and in the hypnagogic state.

All the same, many interesting visionary experiences cannot be reliably distinguished from dreams. They contain revived memories, but in new combinations. If the Jungian and Freudian psychologies are true, hallucinations may also contain symbolic representations of unconscious urges, aspirations, or anxieties. This is true of sane people and especially true of the hallucinations of the insane.

Emotion certainly is productive of visions. Jung (1875–1961) speaks of a spontaneous vision experienced as a child while in a choking fit. He saw above him a glowing blue circle about the size of the full moon. Within it there moved golden figures that he took to be angels. Once, when my own father, a seacaptain, was trying to extricate his vessel from a whirlpool and debating whether to change course, my mother's apparition appeared before him on the ship's bridge and told him, with emphasis, 'You will get out if you change course!' —as in fact he did.

A Wavering Rose

Many hallucinations are extremely vivid and lifelike so that, as with some crisis apparitions, the percipient may think he is actually seeing in the ordinary way. However, with many visions, particularly in the religious sphere, it is hard to decide from the visionary's words exactly in what sense the vision was 'seen.' Roman Catholic theorists such as St. Thomas Aquinas (1226–74) recognized three types of vision: the intellectual vision, the imaginative vision, and the corporeal vision. The theory of the corporeal vision was akin to the modern astral body explanation of crisis apparitions. If one had a vision of Jesus, it might be a corporeal vision; one was actually seeing either the resurrection body of the Christ or alternatively a kind of wraith fashioned by the angels. On the other hand, it might be that the percipient received only an imaginative vision—a purely mental image, though a vivid one and induced by the action of God. St. Thomas, like all reputable theologians, reserved the possibility of a vision being an endogenic hallucination not divinely caused.

Goethe could mentally visualize a rose.

Some people have a remarkable power of mental visualization, so that what they 'see in the mind's eye' can be as vivid as things actually seen. Such exceptionally clear imagery is described as *eidetic* (from Greek *eidos*—form), and is sometimes aided by looking at a plain or dark background. When Goethe (1749–1832) shut his eyes and thought of a rose he would clearly see a rosette for as long as he wished, though it wavered a little and moved its petals.

Galton came across a few visionaries who said that they received their visions in two entirely distinct ways. Thus one informant could experience eidetic images at conscious command, but these were vague and shadowy in comparison with his spontaneous visions, which occurred unexpectedly and quite outside his mental control. These visions were of landscapes more strange and beautiful than any he had ever seen in the ordinary way. Such visions that arise, as it were, of their own motion can be called autonomous, but they are not necessarily exogenic. The visions of people with a poetic or literary bent, like their dreams, have an intellectual and idyllic content. In 1944 Jung, who was recovering after a heart attack, would awake at midnight and spend an hour or so in 'an utterly transformed state' as if 'in ecstasy,' as he watched unfolding before him various mythical occurrences such as the wedding of the Cabalistic beings Malkhuth and Tifereth in the 'garden of pomegranates.'

Ecstasy is a peculiar state that is sometimes entered spontaneously or in the course of prayer or meditation on sublime themes. During it the ecstatic person consciously experiences any or all of a variety of thoughts and feelings. Visions are common but there can be also a sense of bliss or of union with the deity or a benign cosmic power. Contact with the surroundings is not always completely lost. Jung could eat his supper and comment to the night nurse on his visions.

One of the most remarkable visionaries of all time, Emanuel Swedenborg (1688–1772), spoke of three distinct kinds of 'spiritual sight' (apart from dreams). There was vision 'with the eyes closed, which is as vivid as with the eyes open.' At other times, when wide awake and walking in the city streets, Swedenborg would be 'in vision, seeing groves, rivers, palaces, and men.' He described his third type of experience as differing entirely from

> *Swedenborg believed that he had some kind of direct sight of actual spirits and divine beings in these latter visions that, he said, came to him only when in ecstasy or 'trance.'*

'the common imagination of men' and as a state 'when those things which are in heaven, such as spirits and other objects, are represented.' Swedenborg believed that he had some kind of direct sight of actual spirits and divine beings in these latter visions that, he said, came to him only when in ecstasy or 'trance.'

The English poet and painter William Blake (1757–1827) was erroneously regarded by some as mad because of his visions, which he described in poems and epics. Chastised by his mother for seeing the prophet Ezekiel in the garden, at the age of eight he saw 'a tree filled with angels; bright angelic wings bespangled every bough like stars.' It is possible that children experience eidetic imagery and autonomous visions more commonly than adults realize. In Blake's case his visionary faculty expanded to cosmic proportions in adulthood. Once, by the seashore, everything in the world appeared as 'men seen

afar.' Eventually all objects fused and combined into 'One Man, the Christ' on whose bosom Blake reposed. When asked about the reality of his visions, he replied that he saw them 'in imagination' and, pointing to his forehead, said that he saw them 'in here.' The visions reported by prophets and saints were, he believed, merely poetic.

Numerous visions of divinity have been described by their recipients as ineffable and incapable of expression in words. The German mystic John Tauler (1300–61) said: 'Sometimes the grace is so manifest that it is impossible to doubt that God has actually shown Himself,' but '. . . no [distinct] idea of what has been seen is retained. We cannot understand what it was. Only we know with certainty that we cannot analyze it.' Tauler's comment suggests not only ineffability but, with visions as with dreams, also a tendency to forget them. We may suppose also that some visions, like dreams, are subject to the process of 'secondary elaboration' by which they are modified in the recollection. This is to be suspected in the case of such rhapsodical visionaries as Venerable Marina of Escobar (1554–1633) who found herself before the heavenly Jerusalem, which was encircled by an exceedingly vast river. When interrogated by her confessor, Marina declared that her clearness of perception was not much inferior to St. Paul's.

Moving Statues

Other mystics have described their experiences in rather different terms. Blessed Angela of Foligno (1248–1309) said: 'When the most high God comes into the rational soul . . . and she [the soul] seethe Him within her, without any bodily form . . . the eyes of the soul behold a fullness, spiritual not bodily.' Such visions seem to be essentially cases of seeing with 'the mind's eye.' However, St. Ignatius Loyola (1491–1556), founder of the Jesuits, whose description of his visions can be relied on, perceived 'the Divine Being, not obscurely but in a vivid and highly luminous brightness.'

Loyola distinguished between visions of this compelling sort and 'intellectual perceptions' (that is, mental imagery) that he also had, particularly when gazing into running water. This recalls the German mystic Jacob Boehme (1575–1624), who once saw a vision in a shining pewter dish.

The factors that seem to be operative—suggestibility, expectancy, and narrowing of attention onto a single object—are perhaps adequate to explain some of the famous cases in which numerous observers have seen statues move or weep. In 1919 at Limpias near Santander in Spain, a girl of twelve said that during the sermon she had seen the figure of Christ on the altar of the parish church perspire visibly and move its eyes. Before long the number of daily pilgrims rose to 4,000. The majority saw nothing, but some saw tears in the Saviour's eyes, others blood on the brow, or the head turning. Significantly, most of these prodigies occurred only after the percipients had stared for long hours at the altar.

The Accuracy of Visions

Literary problems arise with the very extensive writings in which a long series of mystical ladies have reported their revelations received during ecstasies. St. Bridget (1302–73), patron saint of Sweden, said that our Lord remarked to her that she retouched her visions through not having properly understood them; but he approved her secretaries for adding 'colour and ornamentation.' St. Bridget often saw heaven, Earth and hell simultaneously, as did St. Lidwine

of Schiedam (1330–1433) every night for twenty-eight years. The vision of hell had been, of course, a common literary theme ever since Plato (427 BC–347 BC) wrote the *Phaedo*. Visionaries, one suspects, are somewhat at the mercy of what they have read.

St. Hildegard (1098–1179), Abbess of Rupertsberg in the Rhineland, received her scientific knowledge from a 'divine light' experienced in ecstasy since the age of four. Her numerous treatises are, unfortunately, replete with just those factual errors prevalent in the twelfth century. Confidence in her treatment of the sapphire or the lodestone evaporates on encountering her scientific explanation of the griffin and the unicorn. St. Frances of Rome (1384–1440) failed in astronomy. When she visited the celestial regions in her visions she distinctly saw the sky as a hollow sphere of blue crystal, an admissible idea in the fifteenth century, but tending to be outmoded even in Spain when Blessed Maria of Agreda repeated the same error in her *Mystical City of God*. Maria, a woman of intellect and good sense, actually doubted the accuracy of her visions, until her faith became absolute after a visit to the throne of God. The Eternal Father produced a richly decorated book that the Blessed Virgin certified to be her own true history. Maria was gratified to find the text in perfect agreement with her own *Life of the Virgin*. However, the biographical details appear to have been revealed in two earlier books, a *Nativity of the Blessed Virgin* and the *Raptures of Blessed Amadeus*.

The greatest of the mystical doctors of the Church, St. Francis de Sales (1567–1622) and St. John of the Cross (1542–1591) were profoundly suspicious of the accuracy of visions. St. John used to quote with some relish the posthumous appearance of St. Teresa of Avila (1515–82) to a Carmelite nun. The great founders

and mystics warned the visionary that the vast majority of visions were untrustworthy. Whether the saint actually returned from paradise is uncertain, but her advice was in character. In his

Mater Dolorosa and the nativity according to the vision of St. Bridget (1503)

old age, Loyola doubted the validity of his own youthful visions.

The wisdom of the Church and the teaching of its greatest intellects and holiest saints has made it cir-cumspect. In the seventeenth century it denounced more than a score of false visionaries. When it specifically approves an apparition or revelation, it does so in terms of a formula laid down by the learned Pope Benedict XIV (1675–1758). Even approved revelations are accorded only the probability of being true, and have at most the credibility 'of human faith according to the rules of prudence,' and any Catholic is at liberty to reject or criticize. Discretion is certainly justified, because in Western Europe between 1930 and 1950 the Church investigated thirty series of apparitions of the Virgin Mary alone, and 300 cases of individual apparitions to children. Only three apparitions have been recognized in the present century: Fatima, Beauraing, and Banneux, though the Church sometimes authorizes shrines without officially endorsing the visions that have led to their foundation.

It is clear that visionaries often make gross errors in matters of ascertainable fact. And in questions where the truth is not verifiable they are apt to conflict with the Church, or with scripture or with one another. Are they ever right? It is easy to satirize the poor visionaries. But occasionally, it must be admitted, they gather information by other than normal means. Among the reams of unverifiable material that Catherine Emmerich (1774–1824) dictated concerning the life of Jesus are many accurate topographical details concerning the Holy Land, including place names. In view of the limited knowledge of Palestine available in Europe in her day, it is hard to see how she could have acquired this information by normal means.

The Vision of the Blessed Gabriele, by Crivelli

But what of the apparitions of Jesus, or the Eternal Father or the Holy Virgin? Do they represent communications from God or from Mary? From theology we know that the visionary cannot be receiving a direct view of God in the same sense that he sees Mr. Jones who lives down the road, because God is unlimited and immaterial. The visionary is therefore either seeing a wraith fashioned by

the angels or is experiencing a mental image. In the first case the agency would be supernatural, but there is no real evidence that any visions are 'corporeal ones' in the sense of Aquinas. In the second case the image may be

> *And many scholars have wondered if mystical experience is not just this, a comforting illusion that the mind, in spiritual or other travail, spins for itself.*

purely endogenic. But this cannot be logically proved to be so.

We would be helped in this enquiry if we really knew what value to put on mystic experience in general. The mystic feels a sense of certainty as to the 'truth' of his experiences and a feeling of union with the ultimate power in the universe. These are certainly weights to be thrown into the scales of judgment, but it is difficult to know just what weight to give them. St. Teresa, describing some of her feelings of spiritual comfort and assurance while in ecstasy, compared the soul to the silkworm in the cocoon it has spun for itself. And many scholars have wondered if mystical experience is not just this, a comforting illusion that the mind, in spiritual or other travail, spins for itself.

A Matter of Fashion

It cannot be denied that there are 'fashions' in visions. In the Middle Ages visionaries saw saints and martyrs and, in certain limited circles, apparitions of the child Jesus were extremely frequent. Later, visions of the suffering and wounded Jesus or of his Sacred Heart were favoured. In recent times the Virgin Mary has almost monopolized the field. Since Lourdes there have been definite series of apparitions occurring at dates announced in ad-

vance by the Virgin to her visionaries. On a skeptical view, this conformity of visions to fashion points rather to their being the products of auto-suggestion in harmony with the prevailing climate of religious devotion. However it needs to be said that this argument is something of a two-edged sword if we accept the possibility that a mental impulse, actuated from on high, may be elaborated into a vision from such materials as are available in the mental storehouse of the recipient. Religious psychology is no less replete with subtleties than ordinary psychology, and the present writer would consider it foolish to hasten to a final conclusion concerning the presence or absence of the supernatural in religious visions.

A. R. G. OWEN

FURTHER READING: H. Evans. Visions, Apparitions, Alien Visitors. *(London, UK: Aquarian Press, 1984); A. Huxley.* The Doors of Perception. *(New York, NY: Harper & Row, 1970); C. C. Martindale.* The Message of Fatima. *(London, UK: Burns & Oates, 1950); R. C. Zaehner.* Mysticism: Sacred and Profane. *(New York, NY: Oxford University Press, 1980).*

Virgo

This is one of the 'mutable' signs in traditional astrology (the others being Gemini, Sagittarius, and Pisces), so termed because the sun is 'in' them at times of the year when one season is changing into another. In Virgo's case the dates are August 23 to September 22, when summer gives way to autumn, and the effect on you, if Virgo

Opposite page:
Depiction of Virgo from Palazzo Schifanoia, Ferrara, Italy

is important in your birth chart, is to give you a strong impulse to be of service to others, as a parallel to the way in which the old season is making way for the new to further the progress of the year. Astrologers also say that you will be changeable and adaptable, but this is modified by the fact that Virgo is associated with the element of earth, which in terms of personality analysis is translated into 'keeping one's feet on the ground.'

Those born under the sign of the Virgin do not, of course, necessarily have defective love lives as a result, but they are expected to be quiet and undemonstrative in affairs of the heart. They may be genuinely affectionate but not fully involved with their partners, and in general they tend to keep themselves to themselves and to shrink away from very close relationships with other people. Unassuming and retiring, they are modest, prudent, and possessed of considerable cool charm. Strong Virgo influence is said to produce a personality that is spinsterish in the bad sense.

The influence of Mercury, the sign's ruling planet, brings intelligence, excellent communicative abilities, possibly a knack for languages. The Virgo person is likely to be logical and tidy minded, suspicious of abstract ideas and emotional attitudes, fond of exactitude, perhaps pedantic.

Sensible, reliable, busy, cautious, careful with money, the Virgo person's preference for practical concerns is not a mark of materialism but is harnessed to his genuine and idealistic bent for service. Natives of Virgo are said to make good doctors, teachers, accountants, and secretaries.

H. G. Wells

Herbert George Wells (1866–1946) broke his leg at the age of seven. It turned out to be a significant event. The consequent enforced rest introduced him to the world of books, a world to which he was to make an enduring and original contribution.

His parents had met while his father was a gardener and his mother was working as a lady's maid at Uppark, a country house in the south of England. They bought a retail business that never thrived and which almost brought the family to ruin. The result was that when he was thirteen, his parents effectively separated, his mother returning to Uppark as house-

> _Much of his writing was prophetic in content and his science fiction novels were to set a standard that later writers would seek to emulate._

keeper, a position she was to hold until the age of seventy. Wells started work in a draper's shop, and eventually began an apprenticeship. His academic ability and creative energy was already in evidence but the chance that he would have any opportunity to continue his education seemed extremely remote at this point. Against the odds, he eventually graduated in 1890 with a Bachelor of Science degree from London University, thanks to his determination and academic ability. One of his lecturers was the great biologist, Thomas Huxley (1825–95), grandfather of Aldous Huxley (1894–1963).

Wells had remained a voracious reader, and early on became interested in the idea of socialism that was then gaining ground. To his own harsh

experience of the social and cultural inequalities was added, amongst others, the theories of Plato (427 BC–347 BC), Thomas Paine (1737–1809), and the US political economist, Henry George (1839–97). He became committed to a vision of a different world. The combination of a scientific education, intellectual curiosity, a powerful imagination, and the ability to write well and convincingly, ensured that by the time he was twenty-seven, he was well positioned to become a professional writer, having been forced to abandon an embryonic teaching career due to ill health. His output was huge, including nonfiction as well as fiction, articles and reviews encompassing science, satire, political theory, romance, social comment, and fantasy. Much of his writing was prophetic in content and his science fiction novels were to set a standard that later writers would seek to emulate.

As early as 1888 while still a student, Wells had written a futuristic short story on the subject of time travel, _The Chronic Argonauts_, which appeared in _The Science School Journal_. This was a precursor to his novel _The Time Machine_, which achieved instant popularity on its publication in 1895. Wells followed up this success over the next six years with four more works of science fiction—_The Island of Doctor Moreau, The Invisible Man, The War of the Worlds,_ and _The First Men in the Moon._

At this time he was also busy on a nonfiction book cumbrously titled _Anticipations of the Reaction of Mechanical and Scientific Progress Upon Human Life and Thought_ published in 1901. The compass was huge including the mechanization of war and the role of aerial combat (although he was unable to envisage a future for the submarine), changing sexual mores, the development of motor transport creating large suburban cities as well as global politics. In 1913, he published a war-gaming book—*Little Wars*—but more significantly that year wrote a novel, *The World Set Free* dealing with nuclear warfare. He lived long enough to see the effect of the atomic bombs on Hiroshima and Nagasaki.

FURTHER READING: Michael Sherborne. H. G. Wells: Another Kind of Life. *(London, UK: Peter Owen, 2010).*

Zodiac

In astrology, a circle in the sky through which the sun, moon, and planets appear to move; divided into twelve 'signs,' each allotted 30 degrees; a planet's position in the zodiac is believed to affect the way in which it influences people and events on Earth; the signs of the traditional 'tropical' zodiac are not identical with the actual constellations in the sky, the 'sidereal' zodiac.

The zodiac showing the twelve signs: capricorn, aquarius, pisces, aries, taurus, gemini, cancer, leo, virgo, libra, scorpio, and sagittarius

Glossary

Altruism   Selfless, concerned only for others.

Aura   An energy field formed by the spiritual and emotional level of a person.

Bigotry   Intolerance.

Boggle   To confuse or astonish.

Cabala   Jewish mystical tradition.

Cogent   Clear, sensible.

Conjunction   Two or more events occurring together in time or space.

Duality   Instance of contrast between two separate concepts or aspects.

Eminent   Respected, well known.

Equinox   The date at which the Earth's equator passes the center of the sun.

Erratic   Without pattern or predictability.

Iambic   Describing a genre of verse of a iambus metrical foot, an unstressed syllable followed by a stressed one.

Inductive   Related to inference.

Mantle   A shawl or sleeveless cover.

Meander   To wander, to move aimlessly.

Mesmerism   Hypnotism, involving causing one to become unaware of their surroundings.

Mitigate   To lessen, specifically something painful or offensive.

Natal   Dealing with birth.

Occult   Mystical or supernatural.

Ostensible   Appearing to be true.

Papyrus   An ancient scroll made from water reeds used for painting and writing.

Prognosticate   To predict or foretell.

Prostrate   To lie stretched out, usually in submission, to be helpless.

Sciatica   Pain cased by compression of a spinal nerve.

Shrewd   Discerning, having good powers of judgement.

Sidereal   Dealing with the stars, specifically constellations.

Solstice   The date at which the earth's equator is either at it's highest or lowest relative to the sun.

Stolid   Dependable, sensible, showing little emotion.

Superlative   The best, surpassing all others.

Theosophy   Philosophy based upon knowing God through spiritual ecstasy, founded by Helena Blavatsky.

Trance   A half conscious state.

Unbidden   Appearing without invitation or conscious effort.

Index

Author List

Contributors to *Man, Myth, and Magic: Prophets and Prophecy: Predicting the Future*

Geoffrey Ashe is the author of *King Arthur's Avalon; From Caesar to Arthur; Land to the West; The Land and the Book; Gandhi: a Study in Revolution; Camelot and the Vision of Albion*, and several other titles.

Hans Biedermann is the author of a German language encyclopedia of magic.

John Blofeld is the translator of Chinese and Tibetan Buddhist texts. He is also author of *The Book of Change*.

S. G. F. Brandon (the late) was formerly Professor of Comparative Religion, Manchester. His numerous books include *Man and his Destiny in the Great Religions; Creation Legends of the Ancient Near East; History, Time and Deity; The Judgment of the Dead; The Trial of Jesus of Nazareth;* edited *Dictionary of Comparative Religion*. He is special consultant to *Man, Myth, and Magic*.

C. D. Broad was formerly Knightsbridge Professor of Moral Philosophy, Cambridge; former President of the Society for Psychical Research; author of *Five Types of Ethical Theory; Psychical Research, Religion and Philosophy; and Lectures on Psychical Research.*

Richard Cavendish is the editor of *Man, Myth, and Magic;* author of *The Black Arts*.

Raymond De Becker is the author of *The Meaning of Dreams*.

Alan Gauld is a Lecturer in Psychology, Nottingham; member of the Council of the Society for Psychical Research; author of *The Founders of Psychical Research.*

Rupert Gleadow is the author of *The Origin of the Zodia and Your character in the Zodiac*.

Christine Hartley is the author of *The Western Mystery Tradition*.

Douglas Hill is the author of *Magic and Superstition; Return From the Dead; The Supernatural* (with Pat Williams); *The Opening of the Canadian West; Regency London*.

Ellic Howe is a specialist in the prehistory of German National Socialism; author of *Urania's Children; the Strange World of the Astrologers*.

Elizabeth Loving has worked in publishing for many years, and is a historian with a special interest in landscape change and development, and environmental psychology.

Francis King *(Amida; Japan; Shinto)*: novelist, and expert on Japan.

A. R. G. Owen is a Fellow of Trinity College, Cambridge; Director, New Horizons Research Foundation, Toronto; author of *Can We Explain the Poltergeist?; Hypnosis and Healing; Science and the Spook*.

H. W. Parke is Vice-Provost and Professor of Ancient History, Trinity College, Dublin; Author of *Greek Mercenary Soldiers; Delphic Oracle; Oracles of Zeus; Greek Oracles*.

E. D. Phillips is Reader in Greek, the Queen's University of Belfast.

Kathleen Raine is a poet, and authority on William Blake; author of *Blake and Tradition*.

Basil Ivan Rakoczi is author of *The Painted Caravan; Fortune Telling*.

Stephen Skinner is a writer on esoteric subjects, whose books include *Feng Shui, The Oracle of Geomancy;* and (with Francis King) *Nostradamus* and *Techniques of High Magic*.